"Probing and persuasive, Kramer gets you thinking in new ways about the eternal interplay of autonomy and connection." —*People*

"Completely absorbing."
—*The New York Daily News*

"A pleasure to read."
—Robert Coles

"A fascinating . . . thoughtful, finely nuanced work. Kramer is that rare psychoanalytic theorist who is as comfortable invoking Tillie Olsen as Freud, and his composite case histories have the verisimilitude and insight that is the hallmark of the best—and truest—fiction."
—*Publishers Weekly*

"An illuminating look at the complexity of people and advice-giving in general."
—*The Rochester Democrat and Chronicle*

"Wonderfully . . . and vividly recounted."
—Molly Haskell, *The New York Observer*

"This book is concerned with answering more than just the title's basic question. It also delves into the intricate and compelling issue of psychotherapy and advice itself. . . . Written with a keen ear for narrative, this nonfiction title reads more like well-written fiction: smooth as silk . . . highly recommended."
—*Library Journal*

"Full of plenty of other insights garnered from literature and the social sciences . . . Kramer's book about how psychotherapy works has much substance. It is easy to learn a lot from it."
—*Booklist*

PENGUIN BOOKS

SHOULD YOU LEAVE?

Peter D. Kramer received his M.D. from Harvard. A clinical professor of psychiatry at Brown University, he has a private practice in Providence, Rhode Island. He is the author of *Moments of Engagement: Intimate Psychotherapy in a Technological Age* and the landmark bestseller *Listening to Prozac*. His writings have appeared in *The New York Times*, *The Washington Post*, and other national publications.

SHOULD YOU LEAVE?

PETER D. KRAMER

PENGUIN BOOKS

PENGUIN BOOKS
Published by the Penguin Group
Penguin Group (USA) Inc., 375 Hudson Street, New York, New York 10014, U.S.A.
Penguin Group (Canada), 10 Alcorn Avenue, Toronto,
Ontario, Canada M4V 3B2 (a division of Pearson Penguin Canada Inc.)
Penguin Books Ltd, 80 Strand, London WC2R 0RL, England
Penguin Ireland, 25 St Stephen's Green, Dublin 2, Ireland (a division of Penguin Books Ltd)
Penguin Group (Australia), 250 Camberwell Road, Camberwell,
Victoria 3124, Australia (a division of Pearson Australia Group Pty Ltd)
Penguin Books India Pvt Ltd, 11 Community Centre,
Panchsheel Park, New Delhi – 110 017, India
Penguin Group (NZ), cnr Airborne and Rosedale Roads,
Albany, Auckland, New Zealand (a division of Pearson New Zealand Ltd)
Penguin Books (South Africa) (Pty) Ltd, 24 Sturdee Avenue,
Rosebank, Johannesburg 2196, South Africa

Penguin Books Ltd, Registered Offices: 80 Strand, London WC2R 0RL, England

First published in the United States of America by Scribner,
an imprint of Simon & Schuster, Inc., 1997
Published in Penguin Books 1999

12 14 16 18 20 19 17 15 13 11

THE LIBRARY OF CONGRESS HAS CATALOGUED THE HARDCOVER AS FOLLOWS:
Kramer, Peter D.
Should you leave?/ Peter D. Kramer.
p. cm.
ISBN 0-684-81343-2 (hc.)
ISBN 0 14 02.7279 8 (pbk.)
Includes bibliographical references and index.
1. Marital psychotherapy. 2. Marital conflict. 3. Man-woman relationships.
RC488.5.K76 1997
616.89'156—dc21 97–19060

Printed in the United States of America
Set in Garamond
Designed by Brooke Zimmer

FOR SARAH, JACOB,
AND MATTHEW
AND, AS ALWAYS,
RACHEL

CONTENTS

Misgivings

Merit

Meeting

"Why do people expect to be happily married when they are not individually happy? You go on so in America about marital contentment. Every magazine has an article with Nine Keys to it, or Seven Steps, as though the quest had any more sense to it, or any more hope of fulfillment, than the search for El Dorado. In no other country is this juvenile ideal so naïvely held out—and with what failure! How do you expect mankind to be happy in pairs when it is so miserable separately?"

Peter De Vries, Reuben, Reuben

"You have come because you feel that I stand posted at some point outside your world, because you think that from my outpost there might be descried a third possibility beside the banal alternatives: I love him, I don't love him. . . . You have a decision for life in front of you, and you can't simply take refuge in convention."

Hermann Broch, The Sleepwalkers

MEETINGS

1

A Piece of Advice

ALL YOU want is a simple piece of advice.

There is a decision you must make—stay or leave. It is a decision in a matter of the heart. You do not want psychotherapy. You have had psychotherapy, enough and more than enough. Or you mistrust psychotherapy. It is not a question of wanting to change or grow or understand, but of needing to make a choice. Psychiatrists must be familiar with dilemmas of intimacy—have seen them many times, know how they turn out. Nowadays, there is professional help for everything. In this matter that concerns you, psychiatrists are experts. You want an expert opinion.

It is a hazy New England summer afternoon, and I am talking over glasses of iced tea, rivulets of condensation running down the glasses, with a senior psychiatrist, Lou Adler. We are sitting alone in my small urban backyard, sweating politely, and I ask Lou, whom I consider my mentor, should I or should I not write a book of advice? I have written a best-seller, and when a psychiatrist writes a best-seller, he is next urged to write a book of advice.

The question is provocative and, I fear, even hurtful. Lou, a maverick when first we met, has become rigid, a staunch defender of psycho-analysis. But even in the early years, Lou taught that we consistently underestimate the otherness of others. We do not know what is best for the stranger before us. That I, who value this legacy, should consider a book of advice may strike Lou as a betrayal.

I broach the idea in a cautious way, through raising technical concerns about books of advice. I am suspicious of the form—the chain of illustrative vignettes, too convenient to be fact, too predictable to be decent fiction. I have trouble imagining writing in the second person, the way advice books are written: You have this problem, you have that. I have more trouble yet deciding what it is I might know.

Still, for some time (here I begin making my case) I have been fascinated with the question of advice. Fifteen years ago, when I moved to this town, I was solicited for a charity auction to donate an item from my business. Those were still the days when the "better" therapists, the ones people went to if they were au courant, were largely silent and withholding. I assumed that among the participants in a charity auction there might be some who would have so had it with psychotherapy that they would bid on a special "item from my business": a piece of advice from a psychotherapist. There it was, when I arrived at the auction, a folded beige rectangle of tagboard, standing on its edges like a tent, offering a piece of advice—"This is not medical treatment for mental illness," the tagboard specified—in the silent auction, and it was contested by a number of bidders, though I never gave the advice.

The high bidder said her husband would contact me, it was about his relationship with their son. The husband is a colleague of sorts, a surgeon. I doubted he would phone; doctors don't call strange doctors for advice in family matters. It was unsettling to catch a glimpse of a family problem—to have the woman open the door a crack. The exercise lost whatever whimsy it might have had, and I was left wondering whether I could in fact have been of use. Can we help in any straight-forward way? The point is, I was already thinking about advice. And not long after, I had occasion to give advice in a quite serious context.

Comfortable now, sinking into the heat of the day, I begin to tell Lou about the time I was wakened on a summer night—the night of a day much like this, steamy and close—wakened by a phone call from a neighbor who said his wife had died suddenly, and could I answer a question. To my half-alert mind, the news seemed an element of a nightmare. I'm so sorry, I must have said, and, I'll be right over. This was the question: Should he bring their young children to the funeral?

I threw on clothes and set off around the block. I remember feeling perturbed, as we do in these moments, by the contrast between the orderliness, the optimism of the physical world we have constructed for ourselves—streets, houses, lawns—and the arbitrariness of so much else we live amidst.

When I arrived, the house was filled with neighbors and relatives. There is such a bustle about death: negotiations with the hospital and funeral home, plans for the religious service and the reception. At the center of the hubbub was the poor man, colorless and slack-skinned, in a state of shock and exhaustion. I did not know him well, but evidently he had reached past all the ready help that surrounded him to contact me, as an expert who might answer this one preoccupying question.

He took me aside and shook off my condolences. He was insistent, he needed to know: Should the children attend the funeral? I wanted to do the right and helpful thing. I said: Either will be wrong. It is not good or bad to go to the funeral. It is bad to have your mother die when you are young.

I knew the literature, the old accounts of children traumatized by funerals, the newer studies that find children do okay, should go if they want to. But I was moved to say what I said and nothing more. The man seemed grateful, and in later days he made it a point to thank me, not insistently but warmly, in a way that seemed to confirm that I had struck a right note.

As I walked home—my clothes were sticking to me, the city felt oppressive now and dirty—I tried to understand why I had replied in the way I did. Not to say however you choose will be fine, but to cast the uncertainty in the negative. I realized that to say you can't get it right makes the decision an ordinary act of parenting, binds it to what people are always saying, that you can't win when it comes to pleasing kids. And absolves the man in advance for any blame he might later receive from his children. Having assuaged unspoken guilt, I was able to say what mattered more: It is understandable that this decision should seem weighty; what has happened is more serious than the bustle about you suggests. He knew as much, and the acknowledgment calmed him. It occurred to me that we rarely respond in so helpful a way, perhaps precisely because we are trained, as psychotherapists, not to reply immediately and directly to the questions posed us.

And ever since, I tell Lou, I have been thinking about advice, which may be why I am willing to entertain this project.

"Few things so harrowing . . ." Lou mumbles, sotto voce.

I know the passage, have used it when teaching psychotherapy. Harry Stack Sullivan, perhaps the greatest American psychiatrist, warns against the expression of opinion: "There are few things that I think are so harrowing as the occasional psychiatrist who knows a great deal about right and wrong. . . ."

And then I catch the flicker of an ironic smile—perhaps recognition of the advice contained in the proscription against advising, perhaps understanding that we do not find our tasks so much as they find us. Lou asks whether I offer much advice to patients, and I am able to say that I do not. I hew mostly to the old conventions—staying out of people's way when possible, hoping to catalyze their own discovery of what they want and how to get it. But patients so often know our opinions anyway. Opinion has a way of bleeding through into the therapy. Lou used to teach about this process, how for all that a therapist may aim to be unobtrusive, he or she becomes known to the patient with as much intimacy and exactness as the patient is known to the therapist. Or rather, on both sides there is a tension between the precision with which the other is known and the invisibility and isolation that remain.

I tell Lou a story about a resident I'm supervising: In the course of psychotherapy with this resident, a patient asked whether she should leave her boyfriend. Not a terrible guy, the resident thought, though maybe an overcautious solution to the woman's problems. The resident declined to offer an opinion, asked the patient to say more about how she experienced the relationship. But toward the end of the session the patient pointed out that the resident had begun referring to the guy in the past tense.

That draws a smile from my mentor: "Ears to hear."

The reference, I know after many years of interpreting Lou's shorthand, is to Freud's Dora case. "He who has eyes to see and ears to hear becomes convinced that mortals can keep no secret. If their lips are silent, they gossip with their fingertips; betrayal forces its way through every pore." The mortals Freud was writing about were patients, but Lou has always applied the statement to therapists.

Lou continues: I suppose we always have advised. A matter for wistfulness, the tone of voice says. The iced tea pitcher is empty, the tree's shadow lengthened.

All you want is advice in a matter of the heart.

Here (I imagine) is how we come to meet. You approach a senior psychiatrist. By chance, this psychiatrist has just sat with me in my garden and drunk a special iced tea, with mint leaves and lemon halves floating in the pitcher and too much sugar, and has learned that I am interested in the topic of advice and may even write a book on the subject. You ask this psychiatrist for a referral to someone who will slice through the baloney and give you a simple answer—and soon my telephone rings and it is Lou, who tells me of your request.

I understand Lou's reasoning: The situation is as close as I am likely to come in psychiatry to the material of advice books—someone about whom I know nothing in advance wants my time for an hour or two, to assist in the making of a decision. I can guess which one: Stay or leave? To have invested so much effort in a relationship, to have invested so much imagination in dreams the relationship does not fulfill, and now to have to choose—this is the moment that pains us, confuses us.

Yes, Lou confirms: Stay or leave?

I ask, since Lou has not said, whether the person seeking help is a man or a woman; and Lou asks in reply whether I don't think it best to know as little as possible. Do I still set aside mornings for writing? Lou can arrange for the advisee to be at my office a week from Wednesday at ten.

Ah, I say. My "you." Lou has engaged to supply me with what I feared I would not find, a "second person." The referral says: Feel free to ignore my doubts. Write advice, if the topic seems compelling. Wouldn't sweet Lou just set this generous plan in motion. I am free to conjure you, to imagine you in different guises, to address you as I review one or another theory, to sense you looking over my shoulder as I write. There is advice in this thoughtful gesture. Lou is inviting me to approach my subject from the clinician's viewpoint—to look ahead to an encounter with a particular unknown seeker, you, who in a short while will present a dilemma in a matter of the heart.

2

Al Fresco

THE BELL RINGS, and rather than buzz you in I walk through the waiting room and open the outer door. You are someone I recognize, someone I know too much about already.

Iris, I say, not concealing my surprise.

You apologize, you know you haven't played cricket. But you do want a piece of advice, and when Lou gave you my name as a referral, you thought you might as well let the comedy play itself out. You assure me you're not looking for psychotherapy. I might have misgivings about a prolonged encounter. You want help with a predicament.

I am hesitant. During your divorce and after, I treated two people who know you well. To them, perhaps to many in our small city, you are an icon, and the story of your marriage is a moral fable, about the beastliness of men and the vulnerability of even strong women. I ran into you now and again in those days, when your marriage was unraveling. My daughter played on the same grade-school soccer team as your nephew. You accompanied him to games when his parents were otherwise occupied, and I remember admiring your spirit in what I knew to be a trying time.

You were a legend in your profession: in young middle age,

co-publisher of a phenomenally successful regional magazine. Part of what impressed me about you was your physical appearance. Large-boned and angular, you wore insistently close-cropped hair, flaunting a frank-faced, almost masculine look. The businessman who believed in you, who bankrolled you, who knew all along what you might accomplish, decided, once you had made it, to take on the daunting task of wooing you. He became your lover and finally your husband. Then came public humiliation—his affair with a younger woman, reedy, doting, pouty, your opposite. You put up with more than you should have, and when at last you protested, he pushed you aside and gave her not only your bed but your job—the magazine that was the product of your drive and your vision.

The story was worse than that. You had been distracted by family pressures. Your sister, mother of the nephew you supported on the soccer field, had fallen ill with lymphoma, and you had found yourself involved in her care, badgering doctors and administrators. And of course there were earlier losses and betrayals. The faithless do not fail to choose their victims with care.

When it was all over, sister buried, magazine turned banal, lawyers paid and coffers drained, you found yourself angry and isolated. There were small publishing projects and spurts of freelance writing. If it took you time to relocate your balance, that was a private matter. My patients, your friends, found you hard to help. You shrugged off attempts to sympathize, picked fights over small matters, retreated into isolation. Recently you have been firmly back on your feet: another successful magazine, a radio talk show. Riding in the car, I have heard your voice at noonday and been glad to do so.

And now you are at my office door. Listen, you insist. You understand my misgivings, have anticipated them. Here is your point. You will not tell your story to a stranger, do not want to argue with narrow-minded professionals the question of psychotherapy, which has disappointed in the past. You rely on your independence, the quality that sustained you when little else did. You are willing to talk to me—you present your demand as if it were a privilege—because of a small thing, the way I held myself on the sidelines of the soccer field, those few years ago. I seemed neither to crowd nor to dismiss you.

If I spoke my mind, I would call that posture happenstance. I was negotiating the dilemma of the therapist in a small community—wanting to have ordinary encounters be ordinary. But I hear what you are saying. This appearance at my threshold is your offer to the profession as a whole, take it or leave it. If you were a stranger, I would never accede to your blackmail. But I feel involved with you already, through my respect for the friendships you formed, through my respect for your posture at those same sidelines.

I propose a compromise. There is a university ballfield not far from my office. On sunny days, I have walked there with certain patients, some who seem inhibited in the consulting room, others too restless to sit still. Let's keep this informal. We will walk to the ballfield, sit in the bleachers, chat. Whether our meeting is professional or just neighborly will remain ambiguous.

This morning the field is in use for a summer camp. The sport is kickball, the action intermittent. Still, in the children's rumpus, the counselors' whistles, the public display of private developmental tasks, there is much that echoes the setting of our past encounters.

Today, you are slightly masked: hair, still short, hidden beneath a broad-brimmed summer hat, cheekbones softened by outsized sunglasses. But you begin on a confident note. Professional ups and downs have never worried you. Publishing is rocky for everyone. When set beside your sister's death and her family's pain, business problems feel trivial. Your concern is in a different sphere. You want a family of your own, and you have not done well with men. They are unreliable. Your stature, and what they call your fierceness, scares them off. Those few who are attracted to tough women don't give support when you need it, disdain your prolonged grieving for your sister, hate any sign of vulnerability—or are outright sadists. Cowards and sadists, all reminiscent of your ex.

Your frankness pleases me. Harry Stack Sullivan stressed the importance of knowing how we appear to others. You are unflinching. My only concern arises from your blanket statements about men—commonplaces, I know, but I wonder why you have had just this experience, unreliability.

Randall, you say, seemed the sole exception. You had commissioned a story on him. When it appeared, he called to thank you. Lunches followed, then dinners. By now you have more or less lived together for two years, bunking at one or another's house. Randall works with wayward youth. He is separated, en route to divorce. And childless—rare virtue in men his age.

I have heard of Randall, but we have not met. I begin to indicate as much. A cry from below distracts me. A boy has kicked a ball almost straight upward, impossibly high, creating one of those cartoonlike moments that breach the continuity of time. The ball drops, children squeal and scatter. You continue your account of the relationship with Randall. For me, the spell of your recitation has been broken. I become aware of an uncharacteristic attempt to win me over through reasonableness. I know that presentation. It hides and reveals the plea "Tell me I'm not crazy," a frequent concomitant of "Shall I leave?"

Randall courted you vigorously, tried to sweep you off your feet. He grew up in a difficult family in a neighborhood that chews up its children. He is a survivor. You like that he has not fled his background. He is a man with enough confidence to enjoy forthright women and enough awareness of his own wounds to allow for frailty. What you mean is— your laughter sounds natural enough—he has the mixed virtue of being full of himself. You like that he's in a helping profession. His work has flourished since he took up with you, perhaps because you have given him some backbone in business dealings. He is sweetly handsome. Best of all, he loves you alone. This is your point: He has given you the happiest two years of your life.

It would only make you self-conscious if I told you that I have been trained to mistrust claims of happiness. Too often they are bargaining chips, put forth to conceal evidence of a partner's cruelty in a relationship a person fears she cannot do without. And you can just be mistaken about happiness. Living in fog, you forget what sunshine feels like.

Without my protesting, you insist: You have been happy, he has been devoted. At least that was what you thought until things started sliding. The divorce did not progress—though what Randall said was true: The case was transferred to a judge notorious for her favoritism toward wives; perhaps it made financial sense to go slow.

Suddenly you remove the sunglasses, look me in the eye. You say you interviewed a sociologist once. She said: People will do anything rather than accept the truth about someone they love.

How strange. A crow has been cawing in the stand of trees beyond the field, and I find I have been straining to recall the T. S. Eliot lines about the children in the leaves and the bird saying go, go, go and human kind not being able to bear much reality. I shake my head as if to clear it. Did you really look at me and say what I think you said? I am pleased that we are in the out-of-doors. In the office, your self-interruption would have felt, well, psychotherapeutic—a "free association," to be interpreted and then scribbled into the notes. Here it is only what it is, a cry from the heart. And although you deny its impact by replacing your glasses and hurrying on, we are both aware of how honesty has broken through your recital.

There is, you are saying, the matter of Shatzi—a Bernese mountain dog, a terrible shedder, barker, chewer. Randall was keeping Shatzi for Liesl, a co-worker Randall has befriended for years. A prickly pear, he once called Liesl, barbed on the outside, tender within. You cringed even then, at the cliché. You met Liesl once. She seemed bitchy and neurotic in a way you know is attractive to certain men. Liesl moved to San Francisco to work on a prevention grant—AIDS in adolescents. She is living in group housing. Impossible to keep a pet, and yet she cannot bear to think of Shatzi in a stranger's home. This is a dog who went to obedience school for a week and returned to gnaw a corner off each Oriental rug in the house.

Yes? I ask. In complaining about a dog—what a familiar, homey dilemma—you are marking time, postponing the moment of shame.

Randall's condo board asked him to get rid of Shatzi, and you agreed to take her in, if he would come over to walk her. You say this quickly, as if in hopes that I will not hear it, and then, perhaps in response to a hint of annoyance on my part, you move to the climax.

Two weeks ago, when you went to download your e-mail, you received an extraordinary bundle, twenty or so messages, all forwarded from a single address, "bunny@univ.edu." You knew who Bunny was. A social worker who runs a clinic Randall consults at monthly in a nearby city. A touchy-feely woman, quite unattractive, you have always thought. But deferential, your opposite. You knew what would be in the e-mailbox. The modern equivalent of the stack of letters, tied in a ribbon, deposited on the wife's dressing table.

The letters were, you say with a measure of control, at once better and worse than you feared. He had not slept with Bunny, at least there was no evidence of that sort of liaison. But in his postings to Bunny, Randall kept referring to Prickly Pear. Why, you wondered, should Randall write Bunny about Liesl? And then you realized that Prickly Pear was not Liesl but you.

You cannot stay with this man, I think. The humiliation is too great, the cruelty too precise. Say what more you will, my job is done.

You talk about the e-mail, electron after electron of platonic betrayal. Tough and fragile, impossible and oversensitive: Everything Randall said to you about Liesl, he was writing to Bunny about you. And that Bunny must be a piece of work, trying to blow you out of the water by forwarding the notes. You understand Randall's m.o.: commit to one woman, then denigrate her to another. He must hate and fear you. Nor are you unaware of other possible implications of his having called Liesl by the same term of endearment he now applies to you.

In the e-mail, Randall revealed only a few of your intimate secrets, but they were more than enough to make you physically sick at the violation. When you felt able to stand, you left work and headed home to corral Shatzi into the car. Stopping only for a moment at a florist, you drove to Randall's condo. There you shoved your purchase, a small cactus, into the open lips of the disk drive on his PC. For good measure, you erased his hard drive and threw his modem in the oven and set it to self-clean. You packed your clothes and bathroom paraphernalia. Then you pulled a jar of gravy from the fridge. You spread the contents onto Randall's favorite rug and left Shatzi to do her worst.

As you drove home, you were overcome with the awareness that you love Randall as you have never loved another person, that you love even his attraction to vulnerable women and understand his need, given his own childhood losses and betrayals, to have an ace or two in the hole.

And you realized that everything you had just done to break off the relationship might turn out to be a step in a bizarre courtship, a way of fighting for him amidst all the prickly pear women, you and Liesl and Bunny and Shatzi and any earlier ones, presumably his mother among them, who represent the type in his imagination.

What a farce, to try to face this mess outside the safety of the office. The children's games below fail to charm. The singsong of teasing is followed by a chase, one boy in bright Umbros pursuing another, then adult shouting, the blowing of whistles, a general breakdown in discipline. The disorder on the field seems to mirror my vain attempt to marshal my thoughts.

You say you have attained some perspective. Randall has done the right things. Broken off contact with Bunny, resigned his post at her clinic. Phoned Liesl to tell her Shatzi is heading west. Called the lawyer and directed that the divorce be set in motion. Plied you with flowers. Resumed treatment with his therapist and invited you in for joint sessions. This perfect and complete response on his part has confronted you with the question: Even if everything goes just as you wish, can you stay?

You are, you know, in one of the classic bad arrangements between lovers. Randall is behaving like a naughty boy who sobs apologies and buries himself in the skirts of the mother he has injured. A cruel oscillation can continue forever, Randall needing your strength, hating you for it, committing infidelities, recoiling at the injury he has done you, squealing sorry, sorry, sorry all the way home. This is how one plays with prickly pears. Looking back, you see that even your tornadolike attack on his apartment was only an enactment of his fantasy, woman as avenger. How can you stay with a man who sees you this way?

And yet you are tempted to. That there is something flawed within Randall makes him seem more accessible, less puzzling, more complete. Here is what is strange: Now that his flaws are laid out, you feel peculiarly well matched with Randall. Before the e-mail, you did not quite understand why he had chosen you; you feared your achievements blinded him to your insecurity. After the fall, he seems more truly yours. You feel alive when you are with Randall. You also felt alive when you were with your husband, and look where that led. Still, feeling alive is a wonderful thing. Those years between men were frightful; alone, you were moody, erratic, lost.

Your friends tell you to drop Randall like a hot potato. (The solitary exception is a cynic who believes that Randall's level of defect is about average for men.) They see you as larger than this; do not understand why you would settle. They tell you he has demonstrated an absence of integrity. You know this word, "integrity"—have published any number of self-help articles built around it. Without integrity, there is no basis for trust. The moment the man shows he lacks integrity is the moment to leave.

But Randall has integrity, you say to your friends. You are saying it to me now, and for the first time in this justification of self and Randall, I hear open tones of pleading. Your case is this: You still have some capacity to judge character, and you find that integrity is precisely what Randall has. Is integrity something that shows in a man every moment and from many angles, like a strong chin? Can't a man who has integrity stumble? Did Lord Jim have integrity? Your friend's so amusing husband, the one who buys advertising space for tobacco companies, what gives him such a claim to integrity? And what happened to humor, intellect, vigor, common sense, empathy, warmth, and for God's sake sexual electricity—who named integrity king?

Hearing you go on in this vein, your friends worry. They are certain that you are repeating the mistake you made with your husband, only here with a man who has less to offer. To continue with Randall is to give him permission to hurt you. They insist: This is the moment to leave. In seeing Randall cut the ties with other women, in seeing him act crushed (as he has for weeks, moving you to comfort him), you have regained enough dignity to walk away. To stay is to invite pain. And yet you hesitate.

Partly you hesitate because you do so poorly when relationships end. No one knows how terrible the divorce was for you—worse, you are certain, than divorce is for other women, even though you managed to appear to march right through it. To this would be added now the despair of (for this is how you think of yourself) the older woman. If not

Randall, have you any future at all? Besides, you want to sustain this complex, intimate liaison that you have done so much to nurture. You wonder whether your friends know what relationships are—how each has its own life and character—if they can say let this one go. These are weak thoughts; you begrudge their hold on your mind. But they are not, you want me to know, why you lean toward staying on.

Because you do trust Randall, and admire him. Are you mad? Do these things ever work? You are so immersed in feeling that you cannot make a judgment. Can't someone give you a signal from the outside?

Dogs, nicknames, radio talk shows, vengeance, integrity, relationship—I see what comedy is playing itself out, the human comedy. The counselors have rounded up the campers for lunch, and we are alone. I am moved by the strength of your desire to hold on to past illusions, the wish, in the phrasing of the country song, that you didn't know now what you didn't know then. I do not entirely mistrust your defense of Randall. To say the obvious—that you must leave a man who is compulsive, dishonest, contemptuous, self-absorbed, and incapable of commitment—no longer seems to suffice.

I am struck full force by the question that hangs over this enterprise of advising: Have I anything to offer? Anything particular to my profession, to my experience in that profession? Your friends know what you must do: Leave now. Except for the one who embraces the other commonplace, that even reasonably decent men are hard to find. Can we improve on commonplaces? It seems unlikely. They contain the wisdom of the age.

My perverse uncertainty is grounded in the not-knowing that Lou taught me. I know too little about you, too little to answer the question you are asking, which is not whether most people should leave in these circumstances (they should) but rather whether you, you and Randall, form an exception.

Like your friends, I see the urgency of preventing further harm. I would move vigorously to protect you if it were not for my sense that your story coheres. I am taken with the odd detail that you feel more comfortable with Randall after the fall; to you, it is a relief to know that for all his kindness he is as crazy as you. You have, I take it, a sense that you are matched in some way, in terms of maturity (if only we knew what that is) or impulsivity or pride and pain. You respond to each other's movements, fulfilling one another's fantasies and nightmares, a circumstance that many people find worrisome but that I sometimes find promising. I like your argument, defensive though it is, about integrity; even after the betrayal, there remains in your ledger a balance of trust or entitlement in Randall's column. Those details I count for the good, unless they are a matter of self-deception, unless you are, and I doubt this, utterly possessed rather than self-possessed.

It is almost a matter of how the question is phrased. If you were to ask in an annoyed way, Should I stay with this guy, I would say no, absolutely not. But since you are indicating (this is how I hear you, despite your talk of the perfect moment to leave) that you have every intention of letting the relationship proceed, I feel unmotivated to throw myself in your path. You're making a bad bet, but I have seen worse bets succeed.

I say, "I like the baked modem."

You smile. Your nose is quite red. You hate the compromises life demands. You wish that other people, the self, relationships, were more transparent. You wish that romance were possible, that you did not have to apply skills from the world of work—threats, clear boundaries, open negotiation—to the world of love. You do, of course. I underline the fact. "To go ahead with it will require all your skills." This is all the blessing I can give.

Do you understand the skills I have in mind? Business skills, people management skills, scripting and editing skills, every skill you possess—there can be no more treating this menace-filled story like bland romance. You can risk continuing the relationship if you make that risk an occasion for your own maturation, for your attaining something you can bring with you if the relationship fails, as it likely will. Is there no more hope than that? If you can be single-minded about what you need, not by way of threat to Randall but as a matter of satisfying yourself; and if you can let him be who he is, without insisting he grow backbone—in that pulling back, that delicate combination of self-assertion and car-

ing and disengagement, there will be hope that you will grow and that
he will then grow to meet you. I am serious about liking your tantrum,
its momentary clarity.

Our talk appears to have ended. You have assumed the posture of a
publisher and radio hostess, look commanding even as you sidle down
the bleachers. Let me know how things progress, I suggest, suspecting
that you will not. You will struggle privately with your confusion about
when to cling fiercely and when to let go, when to choose connection
and when autonomy.

3

Finding You

O R PERHAPS YOU have little in common with Iris. Your story is simpler, quieter, less obviously desperate. You do not share Iris's career success, nor her self-destructive flamboyance. In imagining her, I have mistaken you completely.

In that case, and I suppose that case is likely, Iris says more about me than she does about you. After Lou rang off, I set to asking myself who you might be, and that led to daydreaming and, through all the mechanisms that guide our thoughts when they are otherwise unchanneled, to Iris at the door. To have conjured up someone who is commanding, rash, desperate, vulnerable, and, to make matters worse, an acquaintance of mine and a friend of my patients—someone to whom, it could be argued, I should not consult at all—this choice betrays unease on my part. Despite the psych jockeys on the radio, despite the widespread acceptance under managed care of therapies that entail little more than the quick proffering of an opinion, despite my own enduring curiosity about advice, I must find the prospect of advising slightly illicit.

My unease arises in part from my awareness that you will be hard to find. We have not met, and I know it would be difficult enough to locate you if we had. The message of traditional psychotherapy is that the self is subterranean, hidden even from itself and all but deliberately concealed from others. Precisely because human kind cannot bear reality, people distort their identity, deny their fears and longings. After years of acquaintance, a patient will surprise me, and that occurrence will not in itself be surprising.

It is a commonplace of our culture that appearances are deceiving. Unexpected aspects of self fascinate us: the suburban wife who was a 1960s terrorist, the suburban husband who is a spy, the clean-cut gridiron hero who beats his ex-wife. These extreme examples point to the more ordinary: men with second families, women whose children are not their husbands'. And these in turn represent in bold form the subtle secrets endemic to relationships, however trusting and intimate.

The epiphany in our literature is often the moment when the hero learns that he has utterly mistaken someone he loves. In the denouement of James Joyce's story "The Dead," Gabriel Conroy finds that his wife's thoughts are turned not to his success as a speaker but to the passion of an early romance that makes conventional marriage seem lifeless by comparison. Or it may be we, the readers, who find ourselves deceived. Think of Richard Cory, the subject of the Edwin Arlington Robinson poem that taught the lesson of impenetrable perspective to generations of schoolchildren—Richard Cory who glittered when he walked and one calm summer night went home and put a bullet through his head. This is a theme of our culture: Selves are individual and clandestine.

In this task of finding you, psychotherapy has all the advantages over a quick consultation. Therapist and patient locate one another through successive approximations. The therapist says something quite wrong, and the patient responds in a telling way; the therapist revises her understanding of the patient, while the patient, noting the therapist's mistake, revises his of her. Therapist and patient are like hidden submarines that seek each other through emitting sonar and by that very act reveal their own position.

We will not have time, and still I will want to bring to the table certain tools of psychotherapy. You want expertise, and in this matter of going beyond appearances to find you, the expertise I bring is the psychotherapeutic attitude. That attitude has been compared to the "negative capability" that Keats admired in Shakespeare, "when a man is capable of being in uncertainties, mysteries, doubts, without any irritable reaching after fact and reason." This comparison captures the openness to surprise, the tolerance of ambiguity, the aversion to forced conclusions that allow one person to find another. But "negative capability" is an incomplete characterization of how therapists attend; it misses qualities that inform good treatment and, I suspect, good playwriting as well.

. In describing the work of Harry Stack Sullivan, Leston Havens, a teacher of mine and colleague of Lou's, coined the phrase "fictive attitude." Fictive refers to the way a therapist, agnostically rather than cynically, mistrusts the claims, implicit and explicit, that people make about themselves. The fictive attitude begins in skepticism, in skepticism's original sense, without overtones of disdain. But fictive, meaning also inventive, goes on to acknowledge the need for the therapist to generate scenarios. To know you entails shedding assumptions—setting aside your edge, your wardrobe of excuses, your mask of rectitude, your embarrassing overfamiliar gestures, your shopworn anecdotes—precisely so as not to replicate the automatic mistakes that greet you elsewhere. And looking for a story, some other story that suits you better.

One way or another, I must come to know you. Otherwise I will be limited to something that is not quite advice—perhaps the transmission of values; because what passes for advice outside the individual encounter is often just the transmission of values.

This problem was impressed on me not long ago when a patient new to my practice, Fay, brought in an advice column clipped from the newspaper. In childhood, Fay had learned painful lessons about the gap between who people purport to be and who they are. This experience left her on the lookout for hints of hypocrisy in everyday life. And today she was exercised by Ann Landers.

The column was one of a sort Ann Landers prints occasionally, in which she lets her readers take her to task. Apparently an "Iowa wife" had written to ask what she should do about her husband's habit, after thirty years of marriage, of reading magazines or solving crossword puzzles at the dinner table when the couple eats out; and Ann Landers had advised the wife to read up on subjects of interest to the husband in order to engage him in table talk. In a follow-up column, the one Fay brought along, readers from around the country registered their protests.

The correspondents reminded Ann Landers that the days when women behaved "like Donna Reed clones . . . are long gone." A "14-year-old Girl in Pennsylvania" crystallized the objections: "You told the wife to read up on sports or business, whatever he was interested in, even though it might be boring to her. Doesn't that defeat the basic idea of being your own self?" In the face of these corrections, Ann Landers confessed that she is the one who didn't get it. She went further: Reading at the table is a hostile act, perhaps even grounds for divorce.

Fay's complaint was: Everyone is ignoring the Iowa wife. Doesn't Ann Landers see that all the poor woman wants is for her husband to pay attention to her at the dinner table? Ann Landers is taking advantage of the woman, using the woman's understandable worry, about how to bring round an inattentive husband, as a pretext for a lecture on assertiveness as a virtue.

I understood Fay to be asking me to see the world as she does, a place that demands too much of undemanding women, and to avoid pushing her to be the sort of woman that world honors. I wondered whether the neatly clipped column contained a complaint that, like the Iowa husband, I am inattentive—perhaps with the added message that Fay would be too polite to tell me so directly. Fay's indirect meaning aside, I could see her point about the clipping. In the way that small discrepancies sometimes illuminate the limits of scientific theories, Ann Landers's little error (telling the Iowa wife to read the sports page) and its correction illuminated the nature of advice columns. Their purpose is less to lend a hand in the individual circumstance than to spread news about modern standards.

In her original reply, Ann Landers had neglected the requirement that advice columns repeatedly signal the culture's adoption of Søren Kierkegaard's motto: "to be that self which one truly is." Readers then had the pleasure of chastising Ann Landers, reminding her of the rule that one should defend and expand one's individuality within intimate relationships. As the Donna Reed reference indicates, prior decades had different ideals—for wives, adjusting to or gently manipulating their husbands. A woman asks for advice: How should I get my husband to stop reading at the restaurant dinner table? What she gets is news: Today's woman focuses less on accommodation than on making space for herself. The first priority in a conflicted marriage is to protect one's own dignity.

So familiar are these bromides that it is only a critical reader, such as Fay, who will realize that the Iowa wife has not gotten what she asked for. Just how is the wife, being who she is (a maladept Donna Reed), to elicit attentive behavior from her husband? The reply—that she is not yet herself (a new, assertive "own" self quite different from Donna Reed)—answers a different question. To help the Iowa wife in the way that she asks to be helped, an advisor would need to know more about who she is, what matters to her, and how her marriage functions. It may appear that the nature of her request reveals all anyone would need to know about the wife's character—she is too accommodating. But the opposite belief, that she is not accommodating enough, is also plausible: It was implicit in Ann Landers's first piece of advice, that the woman should educate herself in her husband's areas of interest.

Even knowing the Iowa wife may not suffice. The correspondence raises a difficult issue: Should an advisor focus on the wife as she is now or as she might be if she "grew" in a certain direction? We may imagine two Iowa wives: the present self with outdated values and a potential self with values more likely to succeed in contemporary life. Which wife is the proper object of advice?

Columnists need not wrestle with this problem of identities. Ann Landers is not really counseling one Iowa wife; too little is known about this person. But a wise columnist can signal to her, and to a larger audience, a consensus about cultural ideals. Even Ann Landers's initial admonition to read the sports pages was intended less as advice than as news about norms. The mistake was not that Ann Landers's initial advice must fail in its goal—one can imagine a husband who responds to such efforts—but that the news was outdated.

An advisor cannot duck the issue of whom to address: you as you are now, with your current values, or some future, transformed you with other values, perhaps mine, or the culture's, or your current ones extrapolated in a certain direction. Stanley Cavell, a philosopher whose courses I attended as an undergraduate and whose work has been important to my psychiatric viewpoint, writes that "the achievement of human happiness requires not the perennial and fuller satisfaction of our needs as they stand but the examination and transformation of those needs." After locating this thought in Plato, Rousseau, Thoreau, and Freud, Cavell applies it to the Hollywood "comedy of remarriage," films like *The Philadelphia Story* that entail two people making, or rather remaking, the right choice in matters of the heart. Cavell is referring to a moral of both philosophy and popular culture. To the extent that this ancient and modern thought is right, advising necessarily requires a dual vision, of who you are and who you might become.

You may resist this demanding sort of wisdom. You do not want transformation. You want what will bring you happiness as you are now. This was Fay's hope, to be happy through change of circumstance or modest enhancement of social skills, not change in self. (It was this longing she attributed to the Iowa wife.) Perhaps, despite Cavell's conclusion, your or Fay's wish can be honored.

But should it be? Because as an advisor I am faced with the task of assessing what it is in you that your stated values represent. When Fay insists on her right to reject the demand, as she phrases it, that modern women act like 1950s men, I realize how difficult it will be for me to distinguish values from desperation. Perhaps Fay has been victimized in some fashion and has adopted the aggressor's dismissive opinion of her own capacities. To join Fay in her hope that she need not change may constitute a betrayal of some suppressed but essential aspect of her self. Fay believes that to turn assertive would be to gain the world and lose her soul, but is her apprehension accurate or self-deceiving? To locate Fay becomes crucial.

As regards rules, I realize, under Fay's gaze, that I have little hope of doing better than Ann Landers: The rules of the advice column are the culture's prevailing imperatives. But to admit that conventional advice is culture-bound is not to say that a person can flout it. When wives were more financially dependent on husbands, self-help columnists preached compliance; now that women need to hold jobs, columnists preach autonomy. Circumstances have changed. Once, acquiescence was a promising strategy; today, assertiveness is what will allow women to flourish. Even when advice is not quite advice, you can't ignore it, because no one else does. Today, if you act compliant or accept a tongue-lashing or cast a blind eye on gambling (or if you act domineering or engage in verbal abuse or gamble), you send a more extreme message to your partner than you would have fifteen years ago. If Fay chooses to remain different from the sort of woman Ann Landers's correspondents admire, there may be a social price to pay.

One reason that it is hard for a therapist to improve on commonly held rules is that they are already based on the tenets of psychotherapy. Advice columnists, novelists, and screenwriters are exposed to psychotherapy and incorporate its values and techniques into their work. If television is to be believed, law offices and police stations and hospital wards and private homes all function best if the conventions of psychotherapy are followed: Listen empathically, entertain diverse viewpoints, hold fast to your sense of self, reflect others' perspective back to them and let them wrestle with it, tell people what they are able to hear and then stretch them a little further, take emotional crises to be opportunities for growth, and so on. Characters advise one another continually: Walk away from abuse. Don't bet on actively reforming an alcoholic. Communicate. Leaven "livability" with novelty. Compromise on practical matters. Expect and accept imperfection.

Self-help books about relationships even coach spouses to act like therapists within the marriage, aiming for an optimal balance of distance and intimacy, understanding current roadblocks in terms of past trauma, and the like. Listen without blaming, don't respond to emotional complaints by suggesting concrete remedies, give space and let the other come to you—these rules, which appear in every book about relationships, would serve equally well in a beginning psychotherapy text.

No one is a stranger to these commonplaces. I often work with demoralized, isolated, awkward, socially inexperienced patients. Such people occasionally respond to antidepressant medication. When they do, they reveal remarkable interpersonal skills. If I ask such a patient how after years of social isolation she has so rapidly learned just how to handle an importunate lover, she will express annoyance: Everyone knows that. Her companions for years were late-night radio call-in shows, popular romantic novels, television dramas and comedies. What this company provides is precisely exposure to modern wisdom of all kinds, including the directive to move slowly with overurgent men.

■   ■   ■

The ordinary standards for social choice are reliable, grounded in the tenets of psychotherapy, and widely understood. Any advice that deviates from those commonplaces must arise from some adequately complex account of your identity and values; but you will be hard to find. As regards the prospect of advising, these preliminary thoughts would be discouraging—except that they may contain clues to your identity.

After all, if the rules are widely understood—if socially unpracticed patients know them—then surely you, you with a relationship substantial enough to be worth consulting over, surely you know the conventional wisdom. That assumption leads immediately to another: that, like Fay and Iris, you hope to be an exception. At least this is a likely reason that a person who knows the rules might seek advice. You have your case to make. The relationship seems abusive, but it is not. Or it is, but there is reason to believe it will change and therefore for you to stay. You have been telling yourself as much, and you hope a neutral observer will agree. The desired advice is: You need not swallow the bromides.

To this picture I might add that you have a healthy regard for perspective. Why else seek an expert opinion, when advice permeates the culture? You want to know how it looks from the outside, this troubled relationship of yours. Is your partner impossible, or do you bring out the worst in others? Are you too tolerant, or too demanding? You are painfully aware that you are trapped in your isolated viewpoint. If you could decide which view of the situation to accept, you would know just how to behave. You may wonder whether the way you evaluate people is flawed. You make the same mistake repeatedly. You are frustrated by an apparent limitation in your perception or your imagination.

This aspect of your developing image gives me hope. Even when I am unconfident about whether I bring special wisdom to our encounter,

I do imagine I can contribute my idiosyncratic perspective. That perspective is informed by theory—by ways in which psychotherapists have understood dilemmas of the heart. And if it is true that psychiatric theory has seeped out into everyday life, there might still be some use in teasing apart those assumptions, so that you and I have a better sense of the basis for the advice you are tempted to ignore.

■   ■   ■

You know the rules, hope to be excepted, crave perspective. In requesting advice and not psychotherapy, you may be signaling something else as well: You want me to face you in a frank and simple manner. I am sympathetic with your wish for immediacy and plain talk. It is my own. Part of what draws me to advice is the hope of addressing a person straight up: Here's how I see it. But can it be done?

During medical school, in conversations with Lou I raised the issue of direct address: Why don't therapists say what they mean? Lou responded first by suggesting I read a couple of pieces by an obscure psychoanalytic theorizer Hellmuth Kaiser. Kaiser was a German-born lay analyst who, before being invited to Topeka by Karl Menninger in 1949, had spent the prime of life, almost seventeen years, as a refugee in Mallorca, Switzerland, France, and Israel, supporting himself as a woodworker. Just before his death in 1962, Kaiser wrote two odd narratives in English that have the force of speech after long silence.

The odder is a brief play in which a peculiar therapy occurs. A woman, Mrs. Porfiri, is concerned because her psychoanalyst husband is depressed but refuses all help. She convinces another psychoanalyst, Dr. Terwin, to apply to her husband as a patient and treat him from within that role. Given the freedom to speak his mind, Dr. Terwin points out that the "therapeutic" stance keeps Dr. Porfiri distant from what patients say, "so that you cannot manage to take it in, not as you would take in an ordinary telephone message or the question of your neighbor when he asks you whether your electricity has been cut off too." Terwin is so difficult a patient that Porfiri snaps at him—in his annoyance, Porfiri says what he feels like saying rather than what he "should" say. Herein is a sort of cure. It has been Porfiri's distance from plain speaking that has kept him depressed.

Kaiser's beliefs are made explicit in the second odd narrative, a wandering mixture of diary notes and case histories, spanning the genres of autobiography, fiction, and professional monograph, the whole written in apparent imitation of Kierkegaard. A distressed psychiatrist in his late thirties finds that both he and his patients have noteworthy patterns of speech. They display "duplicity," a term that covers a range of confusing, self-protective language: expressions of self-doubt, sidetracking remarks, amendments, and apologies. But duplicity is also present when a person gives an organized, overly compelling account, one that coerces the listener and leaves no room for dialogue. Or when someone talks in quotes, as if not speaking to the listener but merely in front of him. Duplicitous speech contains important but undiscussed messages that are not part of the text.

Kaiser saw in defensive language an attempt to avoid experiencing oneself as an individual, to avoid Kierkegaard's existential dread. People are willing to submit to others or to dominate them, but never to face and state their own independent needs and desires. To speak intimately and clearly—not trying to please or bully the other, not trying to exaggerate one's degree of certainty or uncertainty—is to experience separateness, a frightening but crucial step on the road to mental health. From observations of his own and patients' speech, Kaiser developed an idiosyncratic version of psychoanalysis grounded in the analyst's attempting to speak in ordinary language while repeatedly questioning the patient's communicative duplicity.

This may be what you want instantly in a consultation, direct speech. But what is direct speech? Just to say what is on one's mind can create confusion or arouse false expectations. Ordinary speech, even an inquiry about loss of electrical power, tends to be highly inflected, because secondary messages are so important. Consider a sensitive moment in a psychotherapy. A paranoid patient begins to complain that neighbors are plotting against him; the therapist realizes that the man's delusions are spreading and that she herself may soon be included in them. To head the patient off, the therapist listens intently as the man unmasks the neighbors; then she exclaims, "The bastards!" This forceful joining has a number of effects. Most important to the therapist is that it blocks the patient's impulse to project the paranoid fantasy onto her.

And it is much more effective than the therapist's speaking her mind in uncalculated, straightforward fashion—more effective than her saying, "Oh, but you can trust me."

This forceful technique was the subject of a second bunch of off-prints Lou pressed on me, essays on "counterprojection" by Leston Havens, the interpreter of Sullivan who characterized the fictive attitude. Counterprojection requires an active imagining of the other's perspective and the fashioning of a tailored response. Much daily speech is counterprojective. As a friend threatens to become overly dependent, you find your voice becoming firmer so as to say that you are not especially maternal. You block your friend's projection onto you of motherly qualities. Your counterprojective stance helps your friend to locate you, so that the friendship is more fully with you and less with a fantasized person who shares a few of your traits. Often the most fully communicative speech contains messages that are not part of the text.

So one of my earliest lessons in the theory of psychotherapy related to the difficulties of plain speaking, in two senses: Direct speech is difficult to produce, and unless it takes projection into account, it may create difficulties for the conversation. Despite Kaiser's quest for singleness of meaning, speech often contains its most important message in the sub-text—I am not who you think I am. The problem of direct speech mirrors central problems of relationship: How much calculation is required? Must the other be accepted, or shaped? How best to reveal the self?

When you say you don't want psychotherapy, I take you to mean that you don't want passive encouragement to come to your own conclusions. Nor do you want "games." You want a direct answer. But it is hard even to address you without knowing you. If they are to have their intended effect, the simplest of comments must be tinged with elements of psychotherapy, like counterprojection. Human perspectives are so multiple that useful advice must indicate who I am and take into account who I see you to be.

* * *

Thinking of duplicity and applying the fictive attitude, it occurs to me to question whether you even want what you say you do, a piece of advice. You may want something quite other, for example, a fight. Often people who ask for advice are looking for someone to blow up at, say, out of frustration that the rules indicate they should leave when they dearly want to stay. Fighting allows people to avoid recognizing their isolation. Or perhaps you are like certain patients in psychotherapy who, when they ask for advice, want what is often called permission and might equally be called benediction, or even willpower.

A woman knows that she must leave a stagnant relationship with a man who has become dependent and demanding. But she will move on only if she can share the resultant guilt. She asks for advice when what she wants is absolution. The therapist may decline to give the advice. Or—this is the case that interests us—the therapist may do what is requested, second the patient's own conclusions, which are also the obvious conclusions dictated by common social norms. And then the woman feels strong enough to leave. That she is given advice seems less important than that she is given a loan of the therapist's strength.

Some theorists understand the matter in this way: The therapist becomes an inner function of the patient, the conscience, say, or the heart. The usual analogy is with a child who can skate only when a parent is on the ice right beside; the parent is the child's nerve or guts, or even the stiffness in the child's ankles. You may need what a child skater needs, additional self. We can all use additional self. (Outside therapy, people often enter relationships in order to get self and then complain that they have not gotten something else, say, romance; and to point out the distinction may help them to evaluate the relationship.) We borrow parts of people constantly. If self is what you require of me, the advising aspect of my job will be easy. You will tell me what you already know, and I will confirm your conclusions.

I don't imagine I can dismiss this sort of motive. Most requests for advice contain other hopes—of ventilating feelings, garnering support. What makes me moderate my skepticism is Lou's having referred you, to present an occasion for practical advice in a matter of the heart. I can assume that in Lou's opinion you have a reasonable supply of self, a self-sufficiency. And if you have a goodly supply of self, then the choice you are confronting must be a difficult one—a close call—or else you would have made a decision already.

I take it that you are in love, or have been, or think you might be in time. That's the sort of ailing relationship that is worth consulting over, one where love is in the offing. Love, not operatic passion. Those who are swept off their feet rarely ask questions. If you are in the grip of passion, it is at best passion hedged by serious doubt. The relationship seemed so right, but now you are not sure. Can this person be trusted, over the long term? You may have experienced love, but you are asking about compatibility.

And since you go to the trouble to seek an expert opinion, you must have a concern for relationships. You may prize domesticity or be drawn to it ambivalently. Intimacy matters to you, shared experiences, time together. Entropy seems a shame. You value the investment of emotion, the creative effort you have put into your relationship. The fact that a relationship has lasted and developed complexity gives it worth in your estimation.

But even among those who value relationships, there are people who do not fuss over them. If these people are unhappy, they call it quits. Or else they stay without fretting, since they would rather tolerate a stable, imperfect relationship than bother to make changes. Or they leave the whole affair in the hands of their partner, or of fate, since they believe that people have little control over their destinies.

That you do fret says something about you. You imagine that people should and can exercise control in affairs of the heart. It may go beyond that. You are a perfectionist, perhaps. You demand mastery over your social environment, or approach decisions with a degree of obsessionality. I don't mean that you suffer a mental illness—surely in that case you would have been referred for treatment rather than advice. But this wish to be an exception must come from somewhere.

Perhaps you hold yourself above the common herd, although it might equally be a matter of thinking ill of yourself. You suffer a hidden handicap of which you are keenly aware. You fear that you are inept at judging partners, so that when it is time for others to leave, you should stay, because you will do no better the next time. Or you are more vulnerable than other people, less able to bear transitions. Whether this means you should stay or go is uncertain, but you do know that conventional advice does not take your special needs into account. So that this matter of self-sufficiency is only relative—you are strong but with a troubling area of weakness—and we will need to think together about what constitutes a handicap in matters of the heart.

This process of mental construction leads to a detailed portrait. You are in a difficult relationship, one it feels painful to stick with or to leave. The decision is fraught because you value intimacy, believe people should be able to shape their private lives. You have substantial independent strengths, enough to request advice straightforwardly, not as a pretext for support or a good fight. You know the usual rules, but you feel different enough to ask whether they apply to your special predicament. You imagine there is something particular a psychiatrist can offer, perhaps fresh perspective. You have had it with the slow, self-directed process of psychotherapy; you want a plain and immediate response. You risk the wrenching feelings that come with the end of a long and imperfect relationship. Or the despair and apprehension that attend its continuation. What is at issue is your happiness, your most intimate relationship, your future—small considerations when viewed from a distance, but crucial to you.

It seems that you are, in large degree, knowable even before we meet. At the same time, even after an extended interview you might remain unknown in important ways. This is the advisor's dilemma: Like a partner in a troubled relationship, an advisor faces an other who is at once transparent and opaque.

4

Welcome to the Club

IT OCCURS TO me that I may have a quite concrete clue to your identity. The evening of the visit to my house, Lou was headed to a book party. Ten years back, Lou had dashed off a homiletic children's story about stepgrandparenting; the illustrator, Jonnie, was from our small city. And now Jonnie and her husband, Adam, were celebrating the publication of a new book for young readers, one in a series with artwork by her and text by him. As a former collaborator with Jonnie, Lou was invited. Because of her prominence in the local publishing world, Iris would have been on the guest list—that may be another reason I thought of her. It is easy to imagine Lou and Iris hitting it off, these two charismatic types. I can see Iris, sunglasses pushed back atop her head, wineglass in hand, filibustering the inscrutable professor of psychiatry.

But you might be anyone at that party. You are a neighbor on the modest street where Jonnie and Adam live, a graduate of our local art college, a librarian or bookseller or publicist, a parent of a child in Little League, a favorite teacher of Jonnie and Adam's kids, a friend of Jonnie's mother, the word processor who types Adam's manuscripts, a student who baby-sits for the family, the elementary school principal who invited Jonnie to spend a month as "artist-in-residence," a buddy from

Adam's bachelor days, a fellow volunteer at Habitat for Humanity, a member of the book club Jonnie attends sporadically, the minister of the Unitarian church, the contractor who rebuilt the side steps. You chanced to meet Lou, got into a conversation, made your case.

As it happens, I know Jonnie glancingly, because of Lou. Back when she was working on Lou's book, Jonnie's marriage began to fray, and she asked Lou who there was to speak with in town. Lou knew only me. My practice was full, but I agreed to see Jonnie to make a referral.

That word "glancingly" may have crept in for a reason. I had noticed Jonnie here and there. She was a shy woman with an aggressively homely face and a knockout figure, like a grotesque a child might make from a mix-the-body-parts flip book. I remember speculating how her looks played out socially. A target for rakes and mashers, I guessed. And—which is more dangerous, given the difficulty in assessing their motives and intentions—for insecure and sentimental men who want to tell themselves they are befriending a retiring, plain-looking girl when what drives them are aggressive urges they find it uncomfortable to acknowledge.

I had entertained these idle thoughts, and then Jonnie showed up in my office. She said that since adolescence she had felt an outsider in her social group, New England blue-bloods; there seemed to be something unacceptable about her. She found solace in her artwork, especially as her parents' marriage collapsed. Her social life had been troubled in more or less the way I had imagined, and she had married young, in part, it seemed, to escape men.

Adam was Jewish, an aspiring writer eight years Jonnie's senior, a stable and reassuring figure, if a bit gruff and moody. Plump, ungainly, and devoted, for her purposes he constituted a protector from the unkind and confusing forces of the social world. Jonnie had also chosen Adam—she was aware of this much—as her late father's precise opposite. Adam was honest and graceless, committed to a calling, and a social and professional failure.

It surprises nobody when these marriages, the ones that serve a discrete function or solve a problem particular to one stage of life, run a troubled course. Before the honeymoon is long passed, the couple need to begin to develop lasting and internal reasons for collaboration and intimacy. Whether Jonnie and Adam had moved far in that direction was unclear. Adam's writing—ambitious, literary—found no audience. With agents and editors he was overbearing, rigid, hard to work with, self-destructive. Jonnie had aimed lower with her drawing and done better. Soon she felt protective toward Adam, tender, but without ardor.

Jonnie was torn, uncertain whether to see Adam as the world did, talented but impossible, or as she had seen him first, admirable in his steadfast adherence to internal standards. When she judged matters in a favorable light, it seemed that his obtuseness complemented her own fragility, so that each spouse shielded the other. But people do drift apart. Another figure had appeared on the scene, an old schoolmate of Jonnie's, her peer in age and social class, a man sobered by a failed marriage and willing (so it sounded to me) to settle for Jonnie. She felt torn between these men, torn between possible lives. She moved back in with her mother—to get some distance, Jonnie said, a frying-pan-to-fire move. She developed stomach pains, concentrated poorly in her work, obsessed over which way to turn.

The key to approaching a case like this is finding purchase. The detail that caught my attention was the apparent precipitant for the marital crisis, a trivial disappointment. Jonnie's mother had given the couple an unusual third anniversary present: an offer to pay for their membership in the beach club to which Jonnie's family belonged when Jonnie was a child. Jonnie enjoyed the trial season, she was so much better accepted now than she had been years before. But when the couple came up for membership, they were blackballed.

The problem was clearly Adam. Why could he not extend himself that little bit, for his wife's happiness? Actually, Adam seemed to have tried, but the efforts only highlighted his social clumsiness. Adam resented Jonnie's criticism. The club had once been notoriously anti-Semitic. Despite the handful of Jewish members Jonnie could point to, Adam believed it still was. He felt himself the victim of a put-up job set in motion by his mother-in-law. As Jonnie fumed, Adam became bristling, pompous, unreasonable.

This sort of fight sounds workable, the tug-of-war between mother and husband, only, in this case, with the husband declining to tug. I listed for Jonnie the concerns she had raised about the marriage, and then I recommended a couple counselor, as well as an individual therapist, in case that was what Jonnie preferred. She took down the names dutifully but looked dissatisfied. She felt cheated, having spilled her guts, to get a referral and not an answer. Couldn't I say how things seemed to me? She gathered, from the expression on my face when she told me about the swim club, that I had an opinion.

"Why pick on me?" is Harry Stack Sullivan's question. "When patients want my advice, I am usually given to some sort of feeble witticism such as, 'Why pick on me? You can ask anybody, anywhere for advice and get it. Now why in the world waste your time with a psychiatrist by asking for advice?'"

But perhaps there were reasons to pick on me. A look had flickered across my face; Jonnie had Freud's "eyes to see." As long as we were not going to do therapy together, why should I hesitate to express an opinion?

Jonnie was right, I had opinions.

About the club, for instance. For reasons of his own, a patient of mine, an acerbic man prone to exhaustive analyses of social hypocrisy, had spent a chunk of a session critiquing this very club and its membership pattern. He had concluded that in the local anthropology a Protestant with a Jewish wife was acceptable, men of substance being permitted to bedizen themselves with what exotic accoutrements they pleased, but the reverse was not. (The psychotherapist's view of a small city is strange—overlapping data filtered through decided feelings, a world as seen by those who are not happy in it.) I found my acerbic patient's analysis convincing, if not in its detail then in some general way. My belief was that high honors from charm school would not have opened the club's door for Adam and also that the club was a dangerous place for the innocent.

At the same time, I wondered why Jonnie was more comfortable there now than in prior years, more acceptable even when burdened by her unwelcome husband. Perhaps she was displaying a new level of self-assurance. It did seem that Adam was willing to change; by Jonnie's own account, Adam had stepped out of character to accept the gift of the club membership. Adam had taken a risk (at least it could be construed this way) in order to let Jonnie pursue a small dream. And say what you might about his social skills, Adam proved himself content to stick with Jonnie even when she sided against him in a matter that must have been hurtful—an insult to his identity. In brief, both Jonnie and Adam seemed to be growing in confidence and flexibility. Hints of growth, and of tolerance of another's efforts at growth, dispose therapists to think well of a marriage.

The other view, that Jonnie had already outgrown Adam, seemed less likely. She was still completing the tasks of adolescence, uncertain whether to accept her mother's values or resist them. The schoolmate seemed only to be the other pole of the ambivalence—saying yes to mother rather than no. If a second marriage is to do better than the first, it is usually because those sorts of issues have been put to rest.

Adam's new failings did not worry me. Men like Adam flounder when a wife withdraws her enthusiasm. This problem is inherent in the business of sorting out crises: People show themselves badly when their intimate relationships are threatened, and it becomes hard to assess their enduring traits. I assume that generally a woman marries a man at her own level of maturity. Since Jonnie depicted herself as sturdy, I doubted that over the long term Adam would be as impossible as he appeared now.

Jonnie and Adam, in their response to a modest disappointment, reminded me of couples who suffer serious misfortunes—the handicapping of a child or a child's death. Profound loss, though it can sometimes pull partners together, more often causes each to understand compromising truths about the other. The revelations sorrow brings are indisputable, but facts have such different valences in happier times. Granted, Adam is overbearing on the best of days, but when things are going well, insufferability has its allure. If a person in Jonnie's position has the strength to bear this sort of analysis—but who does, in times of grief?—the failings of the other can be fruitfully reframed as a crisis of the self. For instance, can Jonnie bear to be well and truly rid of her mother's values?

All in all, I thought that Jonnie was at an ordinary stage in the progress of a marriage, the important moment when the dust has settled and the simple initial decisions about bank accounts and work schedules and meals have been made, the moment when the marriage is real and ready to begin. At that very juncture, Jonnie's mother tossed in an apple of discord—to show Jonnie that she was more acceptable than she once had been, to let Jonnie see that she could after all have the life she was meant to have but that Adam could never be part of it. I thought these messages were true and not terrible ones for a mother to want to deliver—prodigal daughter come home—and part of what Jonnie needed to face if she was to continue her marriage through choice and not routine. I considered this a moment of potential remarriage. Any marriage worthy of the name entails repeated remarriage, active choices to stay on in the face of new perspectives on self and spouse. Cavell goes further, claiming that "only those can genuinely marry who are already married."

In brief, I had scads of opinions—was aware, as Jonnie spoke, of opinions I had held before she walked through the door. I might have been less conscious of these formed views if I were intent on doing psychotherapy; the negative capability of the therapist can be so thorough that quite straightforward matters sound (usefully) confusing. But facing Jonnie, I seemed to know certain truths from the well-formed world we live in, the world filled with chance observations, gossip, personal experience, and prejudice—the many skewed contributors to ordinary wisdom.

I took note, even then, of this undemanding woman's insistence on an answer. Why *was* she picking on me? Especially as I was a Jew and a man and an aspiring writer and, like most outsiders, a person who resents class snobbery and privilege. Why ask advice of a man who so resembles your husband? Did Jonnie want to be reprimanded for her disloyalty to Adam? Or to be excused from her dalliance with classmate and mother, to be sent back to the marriage, where she belonged?

I suspected as much, that Jonnie wished to be told what she already believed. How to perform even that simple service? To encourage Jonnie directly would make me only another Jew, man, writer, outsider—a person whose opinion is all too predictable. If I said, "Stay, by all means," I would have been heard as indicating something about myself and not the dilemma. To speak usefully I would need to begin by countering Jonnie's projection, even if partly accurate, that I was simply Adam in a white coat. Nor was that task onerous, since I did not know whether Adam would make a good husband, did not know whether the marriage could or ought to continue.

In the event, I told the story back to Jonnie as I had heard it. I said that I thought the swim club fiasco was what had most disrupted the marriage. It cast Adam in an unflattering light, and it made Jonnie realize that she felt separated from the world of her childhood. Despite her mixed feelings about that childhood, the disconnection was painful. She blamed Adam for his inability to end that pain. Her mother had shown Jonnie that there was a way back. Especially with Jonnie's schoolmate on the scene, that path was appealing. Adam was hard to live with, and a reasonable person might choose to leave him, however hard he was trying—and it sounded as though, once she began to withdraw, he had given up. I guessed that perhaps Jonnie was considering having children. How she would pass on her heritage to her children was a question that might cause her anxiety, and she needed to decide whether she wanted to face that negotiation with Adam.

In my brief reflection of her own account, I assumed Jonnie would hear something like the whole of what I thought. By giving her full permission to leave (but in this unacceptable fashion—inviting her to choose a path laid out by her mother), I was suggesting she might stay. That is, she might stay and remain aware of the truth laid bare by the swim club fiasco, that in marrying Adam she had made a difficult choice, to forsake her roots, a choice she might want to mitigate in some fashion. What had given Jonnie's adult life meaning was the ability to reject her parents' style and values. If she wanted to move forward, to make her rebellion assume less importance, she could begin the process without leaving her husband. The point was not to satisfy her mother by taking one action or another. Much of the change that was called for was internal, which was why psychotherapy might make sense. Jonnie might still leave the marriage later, on different terms.

* * *

My involvement with Jonnie stopped right there. My impression is that she never took up the recommendation for therapy. She stayed with her husband. He has joined her on a number of book projects, though I hear that he is still at work on the Great American Novel and still cantankerous. The couple have two children, an unrevealing number. Both are in private school, which, given the pay scale of the children's book business, is probably a sign of grandma in action.

Is this a good outcome? Did Jonnie miss something on the road not taken? Passion, security, family ties, a sense of rightness of fit, money and social status, a good man? I suppose if I learned that she went on to experience either abuse and deep unhappiness or inspiration and deep contentment I might have a conviction about whether her staying was a mistake. Often even access to a great deal of information would leave that sort of question unanswerable, as it is unanswerable to many people about their own relationships. Nor can I say whether my brief meeting with Jonnie had any effect. Perhaps my small intervention interrupted a progressive distortion in Jonnie's view of her circumstances—that is the argument for advice. But most marital crises do not lead to divorce. Jonnie and Adam had hit a pothole in a road that they were, in all likelihood, competent to navigate on their own.

■ ■ ■

I fear you may find there is a quality to Jonnie and Adam's dilemma, call it insubstantiality, that makes it, in its different way, as distant from your own story as was Iris's. The stimulus for Jonnie's worry is minor, rejection by a club in which membership is its own punishment. Still, for Jonnie the episode raised questions of identity—who she was, how far she had strayed from her origins, whether the problem was out there (the wrong partner) or in here (a partner unlucky enough to have stepped into the crossfire of an internal conflict). These are questions likely to arise in any predicament of the heart; once they do, they have their own substance.

It is almost characteristic of couple treatment that insubstantial insults, injuries, and disagreements should be the subject matter. Often a sore point in the relationship will be inflamed by disagreement over the importance of a disappointment; the argument is over whether the disappointment is trivial. If so, the therapeutic stance may entail an oscillation between empathic and external viewpoints, taking an event alternately as overwhelming and manageable, outrageous and expectable. Perhaps your own request, to be understood as an exception, calls for precisely this sort of oscillation, between seeing matters as you do and as society might.

If, as I am imagining you to do, you consider Jonnie's crisis insubstantial when compared to yours, you may mean something different: Her circumstances are too simple. At the time of the consultation, she was childless, healthy, young, talented, and comfortable financially. But simplicity is what I like about Jonnie's story. I have mentioned Stanley Cavell's assertion that happiness requires the transformation of needs. Cavell goes on to say that this maxim "applies only in contexts in which there is satisfaction enough, in which something like luxury and leisure, something beyond the bare necessities, is an issue." It seems to me most fruitful to think about advice in the context of free choice: Are you suited to the partner you are with? I mean, independent of considerations that might keep you with someone to whom you are unsuited. Jonnie's dilemma was substantial in just this sense, that her decision depended only on the quality of the relationship. Were the partners likely to remain compatible? Could the marriage remain fulfilling to both? However complicated your circumstances, we will want to address the sorts of questions Jonnie's dilemma raises.

And you may after all have something in common with Jonnie. I have envisaged you as a guest at Jonnie's book party. Even if you met Lou elsewhere, I suspect that you are in what Thoreau called "moderate circumstances," neither the "degraded poor" nor (though this is possible) the "degraded rich," and that the dilemma you face has at least the lightness conferred by options, by the hopefulness of the American second chance. We are a society whose members are, in theory, privileged—endowed with rights in a nation dedicated to liberty and the pursuit of happiness. We love to mull over questions of aptness of fit in matters of the heart. To Europe and to the nineteenth century, questions of choice take on the cast of tragedy, as in: Should Anna stay with Karenin or throw her lot in with Vronsky? Even in the midst of a depression or a world war, modern Americans are more likely to wonder whether the Katharine Hepburn character should go through with the wedding to her fiancé, run off with the Jimmy Stewart character, or remarry the Cary Grant one. Or perhaps it is better to say that for us choice has these many facets, that it is wrenching, fateful, quotidian, revealing, defining, humbling, selfish, arbitrary, domestic, romantic, and comic.

You may find Jonnie's dilemma less substantial than yours in a third sense, that the answer to her question is obvious: Jonnie should try harder with Adam. Tiffs early in marriage need to be worked through, not fled.

And I would agree, it was obvious to me that Jonnie should return to Adam. The reason I responded to Jonnie's demand for advice was that I had a sense of clarity about her circumstances, felt I understood more than was reasonably possible based on our brief conversation. But that impression is often deceptive. I think of the Iowa housewife—too accommodating, unless she is too unaccommodating.

As a therapist, I lean in the direction of reconciliation. I lean that way in part because of my experience that simple interventions sometimes suffice to hold together couples who seem on the verge of separation, and that those repaired relationships proceed ordinarily well. And because second marriages do not seem gloriously better than first marriages; or, if they do, it is often because the second marriage benefits from efforts or compromises that might as readily have been applied to the first. But this line of thought says only that Jonnie can stay. Should she? Why not let matters be worked out in a second marriage? That Jonnie should persevere is obvious largely because I share a value I have attributed to you, preference for continuity over entropy.

The obvious is a function of values, and of beliefs about how the social world works. Obviously, Jonnie should try harder with Adam. But to someone who believes that interfaith marriages are anathema, or just likely to bring unhappiness, contrary advice is obvious. Or to someone who considers a shy young woman's choice of an older man to be a marker of overdependency and of selling the self short; or who believes that mother knows best; or who has a different take on the workings of the swim club, the malleability of asocial men, the role of variety and exploration in women's lives, the function of first marriages—there is no end to the topics that lend themselves to decided opinion.

So when you say (in my imagination) that Jonnie's dilemma is insubstantial because the right course is obvious, you may mean only that you and I share certain values and beliefs, including some we might do well to examine. Seen from any single perspective, the solution to most couple dilemmas is obvious. In this sense, your own question—should you leave?—concerns the nature of the obvious. Is it reliable? Is it escapable? Which aspect of the obvious applies?

5

Obvious Pitfalls

THE PROBLEM OF the obvious has bedeviled psychotherapy for a century, and it must bedevil my hope of advising you. To begin at the beginning: Freud insisted that the socially obvious must be ignored in favor of a special approach to reality. The psychoanalyst attends to what the rest of the world overlooks, the hints—in character or in slips of the tongue—that inadvertently reveal a primitive inner culture rooted in murder, castration, and incest. Freud developed a professional view that was distinctive from the popular account of the obvious, at least until that professional view disseminated. There is great debate about Freud today, whether he practiced and wrote in good faith, whether he understood women, memories, family life. But there is no doubt that he changed social perception. Today, many of the hidden postures Freud pointed to—ambivalence, covert hostility, inauthenticity—are themselves part of the obvious. And the question arises, can we now rely on what is apparent to us?

Freud believed that the attitude necessary for understanding the other precludes advising. He proudly compared psychoanalysis to surgery. Like the operating suite, the analyst's office must remain free of contamination—the analytic encounter must be untainted by so much as suggestion. The analyst derives data from a neutral elucidation of the patient's hidden thought. As for what psychoanalysis offers as a treatment, results flow from changes in patients' mental structure, not their daily circumstances. Freud's impossible standard was in part in the service of a campaign for scientific respectability. Psychoanalysis was to be considered a medical procedure, and care had to be taken to circumscribe the practitioner's role.

Freud could be unpleasant over the issue of advice. In an essay on "wild" psychoanalysis published in 1910, Freud mocks a young nerve-specialist who has chosen to offer a patient direction in an intimate matter. The consultation involves a divorcée "in the second half of her forties, fairly well preserved [who] had obviously not yet finished with her womanhood." She complains of anxiety, and the young doctor determines, correctly in Freud's view, that the symptom is related to sexual matters. Where the colleague errs is in telling the divorcée that to recover her health she must "return to her husband, or take a lover, or obtain satisfaction from herself." Freud holds that the woman's troubles are due to repressed sexual conflict, which she must come to understand in detail and in time, as it emerges from her unconscious. That is, happiness entails the examination and transformation of needs. If the solution were simply a matter of action, the woman would have taken it already. Here Freud applies the lash: "Or does the physician think that a woman of over forty is unaware that one can take a lover, or does he over-estimate his influence so much as to think that she could never decide upon such a step without medical approval?"

To be sure, Freud's scorn comes from an odd angle. He objects that the professional advice is overobvious and ineffectual—that it will lead nowhere. The more usual concern is that advice from a therapist will lead patients astray; that is, it will differ from the commonsensical and it will bear too much weight, coming from a doctor.

Freud's own errors were of this more active sort. He did advise, quite promiscuously at times. Perhaps this behavior is the dark side of the proscription against advising, the occasional eruption of the wish to be a wise man whose opinions are absolute. I wonder whether this other strain in Freud, his attraction to the guru role, has not been almost more influential than Freud's dicta in making advice taboo in psychiatry.

I am thinking of a case in which Freud gave vigorous advice on the very issue you and I will consider, whether to end a relationship. In the course of a psychoanalysis in 1921, Freud determined that the promising American psychiatrist Horace Frink suffered from "latent homosexuality." Freud considered latent homosexuality a dangerous condition, poorly responsive to conventional treatment. It was Freud's opinion that only a divorce from Frink's dull wife, Doris, followed by a new marriage to one of Frink's former patients, Angelika Bijur, an heiress and the wife of a millionaire, would hold Frink on the healthy side of the sexual divide.

Freud came to Frink's case fresh from a successful campaign of advice. For years, another promising psychoanalyst, Sándor Ferenczi, had dithered over a romantic dilemma. He could not decide whether to marry a family friend and former patient eight years his senior, Frau Gizella Pálos, or Pálos's daughter Elma, a former patient of both Ferenczi's and Freud's. Freud favored the mother as less neurotic—never mind that Ferenczi, also obsessed with latent homosexuality, was a virtuoso of neurosis, and that Pálos (like Bijur) was still married during most of the debate. Freud repeatedly pushed Ferenczi to propose. Finally Freud himself made the proposal for Ferenczi to Pálos. ("I have taken on this mission of trust because I, too, know of no other and better solution for both of you.") The couple married in 1919, Ferenczi remaining ambivalent.

Like Ferenczi, Frink moved only after a vigorous application of "medical approval" by Freud. According to Mrs. Bijur's later account, Freud warned her that if she "threw over Dr. F. now, he would never again try to come back to normality." Whenever Frink or Bijur evinced doubts, Freud urged them on. Frink became depressed and psychotic over the prospect of his own divorce. (He found Angelika looked "queer, like a man, like a pig.") Freud concealed his protégé's state from the future bride. In 1922 Bijur and Frink married. As his psychosis progressed, Frink became openly hostile toward his new wife. They divorced in 1924, after Frink had committed himself to the care of another leading psychiatrist, Adolf Meyer, at the Phipps Clinic at Johns Hopkins. Meyer called Freud's behavior "nauseating."

Here Freud appears the destructive meddler, blighting marriages and childhoods (the case was publicized in the 1980s by Helen Kraft Frink, a daughter of Frink and his first wife) and utterly mistaking his patient's needs. Frink almost certainly suffered from manic-depressive illness, and Freud found precisely the wrong cure for it, namely separating Frink from his supportive first wife. Particularly disturbing is the possibility that Freud was motivated by money. Freud sponsored Frink to be head of the fledgling New York Psychoanalytic Institute and then expressed hope, perhaps in jest, that upon marrying the heiress Frink would make a generous contribution.

Freud's disastrous advice was apparently widely known among psychoanalysts in the 1920s. I have wondered whether it influenced Harry Stack Sullivan—whether the Frink case helps account for Sullivan's outspoken opposition to advice. Sullivan was current in psychoanalytic politics, and in the early 1920s he practiced in the Baltimore area, where he came under the influence of Meyer.

When I first read about the Frink case, I thought, Here it is, the guild's dirty secret that explains the taboo against advising. The case is nauseating enough if one ascribes the whole business to venality. But in some ways the queasiness is worse if one assumes that money was only one factor among many and that Freud was moved equally by faulty common sense. By the 1920s, for Freud the obvious included formed beliefs—about latent homosexuality, about the role of sexual fulfillment—that made the right move for Frink appear self-evident. These beliefs justified vigorous intervention. How could Freud bear to let a promising, vulnerable colleague destroy his mental health in a marriage devoid, as Freud saw it, of "sexual gratification and tender love," when a perfect alternative was at hand? Perhaps quite conventional considerations played a role. Freud understood how the world works: Marriage to an heiress relieves life of certain pressures. And how pleasant that psychoanalysis might benefit as well, from Frink's leadership and his newfound wealth.

At first blush, the Frink case appears idiosyncratic. Freud's opinions are so extreme, his self-interest is so evident, his manner so insistent, the potential for calamity so great. But these factors are likely to be present at some level in any instance when distinctive advice—advice to make a bold move, cut against the grain, behave like an exception—is given by someone who hopes to have an effect. I am thinking now of my consultation with Jonnie. My intention was to hear her plain. I wanted to understand her needs from her viewpoint but (how often is this possible?) with a clarity that escaped her. In the event, I wonder whether I was ever able to let go of my own perspective, that of a man who has little use for private clubs, intrusive elders, or promising old flames. Perhaps I (as Jew, writer, outsider) empathized as much with Adam as with Jonnie, gave Adam great credit for sticking with Jonnie under the circumstances. And then there is the issue of how I responded to Jonnie's demands. She may have wanted a routine response, one she could dismiss out of hand. I tried to make our encounter disturbing. Self-interest, insistence, risk—these are inherent in advising.

Here is what else I thought when I first encountered the Frink case: It is not so different from Freud's successful work.

Back when I was studying with Lou, I was intensely curious about how the old masters worked their spells. Reading Freud (when Freud was still considered all but faultless), I wondered, Is the tour de force just as it appears, or am I being distracted by a magician's misdirection? And I came to think that some of Freud's success was due to his attention to the obvious, and to his ability to nudge patients toward practical solutions.

■　　■　　■

I developed my impression of Freud's practical side, and more generally of the role of the practical in psychotherapy, in long talks with Lou in the middle 1970s. Those were years when psychoanalysis was at its flood tide. Theory-building in psychotherapy was a locus of intense creativity, as poetry or film or neurochemistry might be in other eras.

Lou was a student of that excitement, a young expert on "modern" psychotherapy, which included the work of anyone active since the Second World War. Seeing Lou today—Lou the administrator, chair of too many committees, officer of too many professional societies—it is sometimes hard to recall the youthful iconoclast. Lou was passionate. Theorists who had a respect for the external drew Lou's attention— those whose interests extended past inner mental conflict to the practical and the mundane; and theorists who had a special affinity for method, how it's done. Monographs on Harry Stack Sullivan and Karen Horney studded Lou's bibliography, along with others on great mid-century figures, now relegated to obscurity, like Hellmuth Kaiser and Murray Bowen and Henry Dicks.

It wasn't Lou's theoretical papers that first caught my attention. Like other mid-century specialists—I am thinking of the physicist Leo Szilard, whose *The Voice of the Dolphins* was popular in the 1960s, and the psychiatrist Allen Wheelis, who was known for parables like "The Illusionless Man and the Visionary Maid"—Lou was given to writing moral or satiric fables. These were homely tales, often set in the uneasy mid-century world of the commuting husband and the housewife. At their heart would be a paradox concerning psychoanalysis, something to make the reader question accepted truths. (In the early 1980s, Lou's fiction was collected in a slim volume, *Pieces of Resistance*, but by then the popularity of the genre had waned.) As an aspiring writer, I read every story of Lou's I could get my hands on. I progressed to the monographs and succumbed to the allure of theory. Hoping to become an adept at the mystery, I courted Lou, culminating the campaign with a written request for supervision in an independent study on the modest topic, "How People Change."

In response came a summons to Lou's office, just off a ward in the small state hospital that the medical school used for training. I remember my first glorious view of it: grimy windows, exposed pipes, yellowed linoleum tile floor, standard-issue oak desk piled high with library books and manuscript pages. And behind the desk was Lou, conservatively attired, formal, distant, and, beneath that facade, perhaps a little flirtatious. Lou waved the audacious request before me and then, without speaking or inviting me to, signed at the bottom. "Meet me at the south entrance," Lou said, handing over the paper. "Tuesday at three. Be dressed for a walk." Our interview was over.

You have to understand the psychiatry department of those days to know how extraordinary this exchange was. Routinely, students were treated like analytic patients. To gain the least privilege, one had to admit to many levels of motivation, consider unconscious resistances, confess secrets of family life. Lou was willing to discuss substantive issues without demanding or offering any revelation of self. In the hallway, I laughed out loud. I was in for the intellectual equivalent of the zipless fuck.

Lou favored the out-of-doors. The chance to escape the hospital offered partial compensation for the extra teaching load I represented. So we walked the fens in all seasons, along a trolley bed, beside a trickling urban stream, below the old private schools and Victorian homes, nineteenth-century *rus in urbe* at the edge of the contemporary medical complex. We discussed the materials and methods of psychotherapy— formed the foundation for my perspective, the one I will try to apply to your predicament. Though Freud was not on Lou's bibliography, we started there. In those days, Freud's thought was the standard against which all else was measured.

Lou began our exercise with the earliest psychoanalytic cases, Freud's studies in hysteria. We avoided the gravely ill patients and instead gave our attention to "Miss Lucy R.," a patient who, though symptomatic, was, in Freud's judgment, "a person of sound heredity" with a mild disturbance and few symptoms. Freud intended for the vignette to illustrate the meaningfulness of hysterical symptoms. Lou and I put the case report to our own uses, to look at the question of transformation.

■   ■   ■

"Miss Lucy R." is compact and perfect, a cameo of the early analytic method. The year is 1892. Lucy, a thirty-year-old English governess, is beset with a series of symptoms—depression, a loss of the sense of smell, and then the perception of odd odors, of burnt pudding and cigar smoke. Freud traces the odors to memories of confrontations with the father of Lucy's wards, a stern widower. At the climax, Freud demands that Lucy face the undeniable: "I believe that you are really in love with your employer, the Director, though perhaps without being aware of it yourself, and that you have a secret hope of taking [his late wife's] place in actual fact."

At the end of her nine-week psychoanalysis, Lucy returns to Freud transfigured, "smiling and carrying her head high," even though she understands that she has no prospects with the Director. Her sense of smell is somewhat improved. Four months later, Lucy still seems chipper. A remarkable cure, but how?

Freud makes much of his technique, of the progressive connection of symptoms (the smell of burnt pudding) to moments when the Director showed himself to be ominously judgmental. Freud demonstrates to Lucy that at some level she knows the Director is not a man likely to tolerate a governess's romantic fantasies. But in my strolls with Lou, I began to ask whether the magic lay in the method at all. Blunt and confrontational with his patient, Freud is clumsy by subsequent psychoanalytic standards, even his own.

I came to believe that Freud succeeds because of his practical knowledge. Governesses do tend to fall in love with their employers, however ridiculous the social differences. ("I am only a poor girl and he is such a rich man of good family.") Freud's job is to make Lucy fully aware of what she mostly knows already, that she must rein in her imagination before she loses her credentials for the only respectable work open to a young woman of her social standing, and before she compromises her marriageability.

Anyone who sees the social circumstances as Freud does might find a way to help Lucy. To understand the impulses of poor governesses just about cracks the case—never mind burnt pudding and cigars. The only magic is in Freud's clarity of vision about social circumstances and his ability to get Lucy to accept his perspective. Freud's wisdom is not even especially deep. The danger of romance between governess and employer was a Victorian commonplace—it dominates certain Sherlock Holmes tales; *Jane Eyre*'s plot turns on it; and household manuals of the time discuss ways to avert this complication. Psychoanalytic interpretations of olfactory symptoms may or may not have been necessary in the treatment of Lucy. What surely mattered was Freud's ability to hold fast to everyday knowledge in the confusing circumstance of the clinical moment.

With Frink and with Lucy, Freud was emphatic in his application of odd theories. Indeed, Freud's hypothesis about Lucy, that her neurologic symptoms are due to inadmissible romantic longings, may have been more novel in its day than was the notion, three decades later, that Frink's symptoms are the consequence of latent homosexuality. The greatest difference between the Frink matter and "Miss Lucy R." is not that in one instance Freud relies on advice and in the other on psycho-analysis—Freud's confrontation with Lucy has the force of a decided recommendation—but that in one instance Freud is wrong about what needs to happen and in the other he is right.

I see now that, in starting my education with "Miss Lucy R.," Lou was engaging in a counterprojective maneuver—blocking my tendency to attribute magical powers to psychoanalysts. There I was, the parasitic student, hoping to suck out of my mentor the "real stuff" that beginners learning therapy suspect is being withheld. By exposing the common-sense foundation of Freud's work, Lou was saying, No, wisdom is ordi-nary; it is the capacity to discern the obvious through a screen of obfuscation. Lucy says she is suffering, in all sorts of particular ways; Freud's skill consists in his ability to continue to attend to the obvious, that governesses suffer from unrequited love.

Later, when we studied Harry Stack Sullivan, I said to Lou that "Miss Lucy R." was really a Sullivan case. I meant my comment in this way: Freud generally depicts his hysterical patients as resistant. When they do not know something inconvenient, they refuse to know it, and they use great deviousness to avoid coming to know it. Freud coined terms of art, repression and suppression, to describe this determined not-knowing. But Lucy's obtuseness is just at the surface; she can accept clar-ification with grace.

Working in Maryland during the Second World War, Sullivan did not see much suppression and repression. He saw a milder and more ubiquitous form of not-knowing, which he called selective inatten-tion—the topic of Lou's best-known professional monograph. Sullivan found that people simply ignore realities that, if attended to, would threaten their sense of security. Those realities are not forgotten (as in repression), nor are the defenses against them especially elaborate. But the defenses are of a certain consistent type: People create an atmosphere in which others around them will also ignore the inconvenient reality.

Sullivan gives as an example a patient who repeatedly tells the same sort of embarrassing story about himself, but each time as if it were new—a revelation. The patient lays out the key facts in such a way that their salience is obscured. It is only after "two or three hundred" such epiphanies that the therapist thinks to say what is important, namely that the embarrassing thoughts and behaviors are not unusual but constant and utterly typical elements in the patient's makeup. When Sullivan manages to keep his eye on the ball, the patient exclaims, "My God, yes! Why, I've told you so many times! How in the world could I have overlooked it!" Whereas in the case of Freudian repression, "you practically have to arrange for the universe to fall on a person before recall can be effected," the patient who attends selectively can readily absorb the more complete account of his life.

The notion of selective inattention gives hope for advice. Perhaps Freud was wrong, and the anxious divorcée, the patient of the young nerve-specialist, could after all have benefited from encouragement to take one or another concrete action, if what stopped her was selective inattention to her own needs. And turning directly to you: Wouldn't it be convenient for both of us if your problem turns out to be a matter of selective inattention, so that without any special wisdom I might be able, using the listening posture of one sort of psychotherapy, to discern a snippet of reality that you have overlooked?

On the other hand, it is not clear that practical wisdom always arises from this practice of attentive listening. More may be needed. Sullivan, like Freud when he was exercising good judgment, just seemed to know things. Practicality was Sullivan's distinguishing virtue. He was a rural pragmatist in a discipline of urban theorizers. This posture makes his opposition to advising particularly confusing.

Reading further into Sullivan undid Lou's counterprojective work—rearoused my envy of and longing for a special sort of wisdom. Sullivan's seemed to arise organically from who he was, a thoughtful

American from the heartland, an observant man in a demanding environment. He was born in a depressed town in upstate New York in 1892, the year Lucy consulted Freud. Sullivan's forebears included priests and judges, but more often farmers and farmhands. Early in adult life, Sullivan was hospitalized at least once for what he considered a schizophrenic break, and he worried constantly over his sanity and his sexual proclivities. He became a great student of schizophrenia, then a broad category that included most mental illness of any seriousness.

Sullivan strove to be a doctrinaire Freudian, but the intensity of his desire to reach patients, whatever their diagnosis, made him eclectic as a clinician. He had no use for generalities. He wanted to know everything about the individual before him. That stance drew widespread admiration. By the 1940s, this odd, irritable, and intensely private man had, through force of intellect and personality, created the imago of a certain sort of doctor, the American psychiatrist.

Sullivan's work is less frequently read than it once was. His influence is seen in a posture, at once forceful and formal, assumed by psychiatrists who may know nothing of his cases or theories. Perhaps the problem is that Sullivan was not much of a writer. The one book he wrote as a book is the most minor of his published contributions. He is remembered through transcriptions of his lectures, most collected posthumously, and through the influence of his teaching.

Lou introduced me to a mimeographed transcript of a 1940s case seminar with Sullivan, five Sunday-morning discussions of the care of a twenty-five-year-old man with serious mental illness. The transcript has since been published in book form, with comments by the surviving participants. What fascinated me when I first had the text in hand was the level of detail Sullivan demands in the evaluation of a patient. A resident reports the results of a six-week workup, a dozen pages of dense typescript in the published version. As the presentation ends, Sullivan asks, regarding the patient, "What is he like?"

The resident replies, and Sullivan elaborates the question: "I am trying to figure out what he would be like if he were not a patient. Trying to arrive at the obvious assets and liabilities."

Again the resident replies, and Sullivan cuts in, one imagines with annoyance, "What I would like to know about anybody is largely missing." Sullivan intends to evaluate the disturbed young man's capacity for human relatedness and for success in daily life. But how Sullivan expects to arrive at this assessment is peculiar. As a boy, the patient had a Czechoslovak nurse. Sullivan says, "I can't help but wonder whether she was Czech or Slovak, or something else." The young man is accomplished in tennis, but has he played team sports? Just what was his wartime service in the Navy? The experience on combat vessels is different from that on transport ships; destroyers offer more glory and more social space than destroyer escorts. A discussion ensues about the rigors of life on shipboard.

To Sullivan, people are hard to know from the inside. What they tell us about feeling must be taken fictively. But the social details do not lie. Czech nurses generally provide different experiences than do Slovaks— to Sullivan these specifics are apparently usable. He requires concrete information. He is unashamed to reach irritably after fact and reason.

The young man feels sexually inadequate, because he considers his penis small and because his sexual successes have involved the use of alcohol. Sullivan is disgusted that the resident has not brought the young man up to speed: "Statistically half the human race is sexually inadequate in feeling that their penis is not large as some other penis that they know of. . . ." And again: "That makes him a regular member of the human race. Don't you think that most well people who decide to have a heterosexual experience and know anything about alcohol find it a great help? If he thinks it is sexual inadequacy, he is uninformed."

Here is something like Freud's scorn for the young specialist who said the self-evident to the anxious divorcée, except that the imperatives are reversed. Sullivan is concerned that the patient does not understand the obvious or has lost touch with it through selective inattention. Perhaps the young man obsesses over sexual inadequacy in order to avoid attending to difficulties in other areas. Sullivan instructs his trainees to look past a patient's catastrophic thoughts and demand that the patient bring more humdrum concerns into the discussion. Social norms are the proper material of the treatment.

Sullivan seems to reclaim for psychiatrists the right to insist on the obvious. A deeply disturbed young man denies that a failed love affair was of any importance. Sullivan recommends swift interruption of the patient's protestation: "Nonsense, you were happy with her." Sullivan wants to capture the young man's attention and restore to him the right to treasure the successful moments in the liaison, however disappointing its ending.

And Sullivan is willing to resort to vigorous advice when a patient, however healthy, is, in Sullivan's view, bent on a disastrous course of action. Sullivan says he will first ask, " 'Why, how did you ever decide upon that?'—and then listen. If the irrational nature of the impulse is quite clear and quite certain disaster lies ahead, it has been my policy to say 'No!' in quite an emphatic fashion as a way of interrupting the person. I then follow this up by saying, 'Merciful God! Let us consider what will follow that!' " Sullivan then outlines for the patient the probable course of events and asks whether the patient has reason to doubt the scenario.

Sullivan stands, it has always seemed to me, on the threshold of a psychotherapy that would include advice as an acceptable intervention. He demands that therapists be fluent with the social markers of the culture—Czech or Slovak, tennis or baseball, transport vessel or combat vessel. He finds moments where it pays to call a spade a bloody shovel. But for the most part, Sullivan does not cross the threshold, because he is so aware of the foolhardiness of psychiatrists (like Freud) with opinions.

Together, the Frink and Lucy cases, along with Sullivan's lectures, raise a question I have discussed with Lou off and on for years, one I formulate as "May we use what we know?" I mean what the therapist knows independent of the patient's report. Most therapies are driven by patients' accounts of feelings and memories—a therapist might ask the patient how things went with the Czechoslovak nurse and then accept that answer as the raw material of the treatment. In conventional (non-Sullivanian) therapy, the therapist need not hold an independent opinion. In helping people to change, what counts is a reliable method—eliciting free association, assuming an empathic posture, giving patients space to explore. The therapy demands technique, more than wisdom.

This stance supports the needs of the profession. Results are replicable; the art can be taught and learned. In this country, many of the leading psychiatrists of the middle decades of the century were immigrants, and it was convenient for them that psychoanalysis was culture-free; one did not need a special sensitivity to American social norms to treat American patients. To be fair, the great students of societal influences on psychological development, like Karen Horney, Erich Fromm, and Erik Erikson, were also immigrants. But the main thrust of psychotherapeutic theory and training has been to minimize the role of the therapist's concrete and local knowledge.

Sullivan cut counter to the grain. He wanted his trainees to have the greatest possible store of wisdom about social norms and likely outcomes, and to put that awareness to use. The role of alcohol in romance, the pleasures in failed love affairs, the ubiquity of sexual self-doubt, the special problems of life on destroyer escorts, that sort of common knowledge is the Sullivanian therapist's stock-in-trade.

Many theorists today make out psychoanalysis as a sort of ethereal method in which a painstakingly unopinionated listener catalyzes change merely by making room for a troubled other. Adam Phillips, a psychoanalyst-philosopher, concludes a book on the analyst-as-expert: "If psychoanalysis does not also facilitate the patients' capacity to know themselves, it becomes merely another way of setting limits to the self; and the analyst becomes merely another expert on human possibility, something no one could ever be, despite the posturing of our favourite authorities." The first half of this thought, about the value of self-exploration, is easy to agree with. But must we accept the dichotomy implicit in the second half? Is it really facilitating self-knowledge *versus* offering expertise?

Awareness of the limits of knowledge is an element in expertise. Despite those limitations, people commonly require and expect all sorts of expertise regarding human possibility. How likely is a relapse in my depression? More specifically: How likely is it that I can remain in this abusive marriage without suffering a relapse in my depression? The answers are not always right, but in any field experts deal in probabilities and commit errors. Freud postured as an authority, as did some of his mid-century followers. Even those who tried to posture as non-experts, like Sullivan declining to advise, relied in their work on estimates of human probabilities. I wonder whether there is any useful therapy that does not entail an awareness of norms, a keen eye for social likelihoods, and fond glances, at least, in the direction of practical wisdom.

With his emphasis on how the social world operates, it was perhaps inevitable that Sullivan should communicate his opinions in the course of psychoanalysis. And that is the impression given by one of Sullivan's prominent carriage-trade patients, Dorothy Schiff. A wealthy Long Island homemaker with Republican family ties, Schiff approached Sullivan for help with anxiety attacks arising after the birth of her third child in 1934. According to Schiff's account, Sullivan was stiff, formal, wraithlike, distant, unemotional—an automaton who gave the appearance of not listening. But opinion seeped through around the edges.

Schiff came quickly to understand that Sullivan did not approve of her lifestyle, that he was indifferent to the worries of the indolent rich. She became fascinated with Sullivan's "socialistic ideas." While in treatment, Schiff enrolled in the New School University in Exile, where she studied the Progressive movement. She began to change her political orientation and soon became a confidante of Franklin Roosevelt. Sullivan then helped Schiff, a shy woman, deal with her anxieties over speaking in public and may even—this is less clear—have worked with her on the text of her first major speech, concerning her ideological conversion. (Schiff quit the analysis when she learned Sullivan had not bothered to listen to the talk on the radio.) Schiff went on to edit and publish the *New York Post* and lead a gratifying life dedicated to liberal causes. So Sullivan demonstrated in practice what he denied in his lectures, that there is room for a psychiatrist with an opinion.

My early exposure to Sullivan's work gave me a healthy respect for everyday detail. And those walks along the fens taught me that the most theory-driven therapeutic method, like Freud's, is never far, in its raw material, from this question of social probabilities. Nor is practicality divorceable from theory. Sullivan's students have speculated that his inquiries about naval life, in the 1940s case seminar, related to the thought that the young man's anxiety may have been catalyzed by the homosexual drives sometimes made evident in the tight quarters of a destroyer escort. Sullivan's posture and Freud's are not so distant as might at first appear. The difference between prudence and folly is less belief than judgment—what we do with theory.

Freud's involvement with Frink should stand as sufficient warning against psychiatric advice. Even Sullivan's successful work with Dorothy Schiff seems to flout a certain standard. And yet, despite its foolhardiness, advice, and the practical expertise that supports it, seems an ordinary element in psychotherapy, just as advising is an ordinary part of daily conversation. The "obvious" may turn out to be folly—latent homosexuality is the example here—but it is hard to imagine any good faith attempt at helping that ignores the obvious.

6

Guy Talk

Y OU ARE A thoughtful and considerate young man and, for those
very reasons, a hazard to women. They are attracted to what looks
like stability. But despite your seriousness or even because of it—you
tend to obsess about whether a given woman is right for you—the only
thing that is reliable about you in relationships is the pattern of your
leaving, certainty giving way to doubt, anxiety, and an apologetic bolt
for the exit. You dislike this tendency in yourself, disliked it so much as
you approached thirty that you underwent a brief psychotherapy to
understand and change your pattern of behavior. Actually, you were
twenty-six when you began treatment. Your sense of the passage of time,
its oppressiveness, is such that for most of your twenties you felt you
were approaching thirty.

Your first relationship after therapy lasted six months. The next
lasted a year. Now you really are almost thirty, and you find—to your
surprise, to everyone's surprise—that you have spent two years with the
same woman.

The wrong woman, an inner voice has always told you. Lena has the
ambiguous beauty of a Modigliani. She is sleek and quiet, a Siamese cat
of a woman who seems to have moved into your life without particular

invitation. Shaggy, bespectacled, tentative in your gestures, you are more of an Ed Koren cartoon. On good days, you find Lena intensely desirable—far above you. You wonder whether you have stayed with Lena for this reason alone, a thought that rankles. You are a highly moral man and dislike the implication that you might "take advantage" of a woman. At the same time, you fear that Lena intends to take advantage of you—that what attracts her is your academic success or, since your success is not so very marked, your promise.

Mostly what is wrong with Lena is that she is not intellectual, though she is smart. At work, she rose from technician to lab director to middle manager. She has mastered complex information systems (you could not succinctly say what an information system is) through in-service training and an innate feel for the material. In your social dealings, Lena's intelligence shows itself selectively. Sometimes after a movie you will sit with friends, all of you animated in your opinions, while Lena, that elongated face propped on an elongated hand, those elongated legs tucked beneath her chair, sits quietly by. Then, when the last guest has left, she will ask a question that slips the keystone from the span of argument you spent the evening constructing, and you will wonder whether she is mocking you or expressing naive curiosity.

Alone with her, you find yourself at loose ends. You carp at her for her passivity and her complaisance. You dislike the person you have become at home, derisive, pedantic, tyrannical. She brings out the worst in you. Periodically, you make efforts to pull back and treat her as she should be treated, with consideration and respect. Briefly, things go well. But no sooner does Lena begin to show herself than something arises that makes you feel contempt. She wants to shop for overstuffed furniture, when you value an ascetic look and hate wasting time on life's petty comforts. She annoys you, she bores you.

Now Lena has been offered a promotion that entails relocation to a nearby city. You have no intention of asking her to forgo the change; you are clear-sighted enough for that. The only question is whether you will move with her. The switch would require a small step backward in your own career, one you might be willing to make anyway to expand your range of experience. Your relations with friends would be disrupted. Implicitly you would be making a stronger commitment to Lena.

Your own inclination is to use the move as a pretext for letting the relationship slide. You feel the pressure of age; you want to be with the right woman, the one you will marry. But your friends are alarmed on your behalf. They like how you are doing with Lena, see the two of you as compatible. It is time for you to fish or cut bait. Hence, your appeal to Lou and now this quick consultation.

You have a problem common to people who are haughty and finicky, which is that your presentation of self makes it difficult for others to keep in mind how deeply you suffer. Even for those who appreciate your discomfort, it is hard to know how to approach you—how to slip through the Scylla and Charybdis of a man who is at once thin-skinned and contemptuous. I do not know just how I will negotiate these dangers. But having heard this little bit about you, I do have an opinion, and a sense of what I might say if I could speak my mind directly.

Look, you know the old joke about serving cocoa to the picky child: How would you like it, too hot or too cold? Women are going to be bitchy or they're going to be simpy. For you, I mean. (My great-grandmother would have said, *Auf dem Esel ins Theater,* a stubbornly untranslatable clucking over men which means something like, you might have to decide which entertainment you prefer, the donkey ride or Lincoln Center.) I am saying: There is no special problem with Lena.

We know why your friends are alarmed. It's because they are your friends, and they think you're lucky to know Lena. Yes, she has limitations. She is insecure. Fine. Her unease is the emotional equivalent of your prissiness. That is to say, you and Lena are well matched in terms of your social handicaps. You know as much, and that knowledge is part of why you want to bolt. She represents your worth not as an accoutrement (the "trophy wife") but as a reflection—in the sense that people tend to partner with people at a similar emotional level. That's all right. People do like Lena, imperfect though she is. They like you, imperfect though you are. Worse things could be said about you than that you are Lena's peer.

Lena has limitations, and to stay with her entails tacit acknowledgment of your own limitations, and perhaps the limitations of relationships. And then it might be better to stay, since coming to grips with this truth, that you and relationships have limitations, is an important form of personal development. Acceptance of limitations is the transformation characteristic of comedies of remarriage and much romantic literature. Think of Dickens, for example—David Copperfield moving from the charm of his child-wife, Dora, to the sobriety of his sisterly guide, Agnes. Or of Shakespeare, where Beatrice and Benedick learn to forgive the flaws of the opposite sex: woolly beard, sunburnt face, dull wit, sharp tongue, and every form of food for disdain. Or of any fiction in which sense triumphs over sensibility—or the reverse, comic lover finding comic lover, matched in their foolish flaws. The form of romantic comedy is contented homecoming to imperfection.

If you leave Lena, will you find greater satisfaction? You might choose someone better educated in the areas that matter to you. Doubtless you can find a woman louder and more confrontational than Lena. These are matters of taste, and there's no arguing about them. But Lena has her strong points, and given your own quirks and shortcomings, I wonder whether you are likely to end up with someone more complete as a person than Lena is.

So, stay or go? Some men leave just for the sake of change. Didn't Kierkegaard propose the "rotation method" as a way of dealing with tedium? But you value continuity—you entered psychotherapy out of concern over your tendency to cut and run. And you know that in the end Kierkegaard recommended a different sort of rotation, not wandering but rather tending to one field and rotating the crop, which is oneself. The answer is not moving on but staying and altering perspective; limit yourself, Kierkegaard recommends, and become fertile in invention. So that Kierkegaard's sympathies might be with the part of you that wants to stretch your tolerance for extended intimacy, the part that wants to expand the possibilities of the relationship.

I lean that way, too. Because you're a leaver. If you were loyal and sentimental, quick to attach and slow to say good-bye, I might say bug out, by all means. In that case, leaving would represent facing your fears. But for you the challenge is to cleave to Lena. You have said as much in proudly relating the progression in your relationships: half a year, then one, now two. Implicit in that pride is recognition that coexisting is partly a learned skill. Most relationships are practice. That's why, in a culture that allows dating, people have many more relationships than they have marriages. Not (or not only) because they're finding the right person; because they're learning how to do it.

You have a point when you imply that for you any relationship that lasts longer than the previous ones can be counted a success. For you, the trick is learning how to stick with a woman without falling into contempt for her. In your self-presentation you have been generous—brave—in revealing your contempt. As a vice, contempt has a certain appeal. Contempt covers a lot of sins. To start with, your fear of women. Deep down you are afraid that if Lena starts to become less submissive she'll turn dominant. For all your protestation, I see you doing things that might undermine Lena's sense of self-worth. Not because you wouldn't desire a more confident Lena; because you doubt a more confident Lena would desire you.

I am implying that the matching between you and Lena goes beyond the broad level of maturity to the specific flaw. You, too, are insecure. In practice, Lena's continuing insecurity is amplified by your own: By fussing over the relationship, and thereby upsetting Lena, you hold her back. You complain about Lena's self-doubt, but her self-doubt may be what has made the relationship tolerable for you. We might even wonder whether your urgency in leaving Lena does not arise from fear that she is gaining in confidence and independence. After all, Lena is able to contemplate accepting a promotion that moves her from you. You are considering a preemptive move: "You're not leaving me, I'm leaving you."

There is a moment in relations between men and women that is to John Updike what the haystack was to Claude Monet, the endlessly fascinating subject. A man considers condescending to befriend a woman—to go out of his way, as a gentleman, to help her, because she is injured or socially marginalized and because it might feel good to comfort her in this way, from the top down. Just as he overcomes his ambivalence and reaches out to succor her, the man discovers that the woman is quite comfortable socially, beloved by everyone, and he is the hopeless supplicant. We see a fifth-grader thus deflated in "The Alligators," one of Updike's early stories; a man in his fifties reaches much the same posture in "The Journey to the Dead," one of Updike's most recent. It is a lucky Updike hero who does not find himself thus surprised. As I listen to your presentation, all I think of is Updike. Perhaps your question is: Dare I strive to hold on to Lena?

Here's my advice. Stay with her. Move with her. I can't be clearer.

But try the rotation method. Stay with Lena and you be different. Perhaps you are running scared, filling space with words to maintain your sense of self or your standing before others. Try being quiet. You be Lena. Be unobtrusive. Go further, be openly self-doubting. But not in a noisy way. Be sleek. Fail to take up space. When you wonder what Lena thinks, try really to wonder, as she wonders about your aesthetic opinions. I recommend this posture not because it is always preferable but because it is strange to you, a posture you fear. You fear disappearing. You will discover how brave Lena has been all this while: brave enough to disappear. Of course, you have been brave enough to appear in a bright and unflattering light; but you might find you enjoy taking on a different sort of challenge. Perhaps the relationship will prove exhilarating after all.

Likely you will protest that you have already tried holding your tongue, tried viewing Lena uncritically, tried letting Lena know she is free to be herself.

Now I can give you a piece of self-help in which I have complete confidence: No, you haven't. Here is my rule: Think how much you must change. More than you think.

Often I will have in treatment a college undergraduate who is socially overurgent. A young man will enter a relationship with a young woman, and immediately he will begin to telephone her incessantly. I will say, you can't phone her every five minutes. I may suggest he rent *Broadcast News* and take a good look at the scene where the Albert Brooks character wishes that insecurity and desperation made us more attractive. And the young man will return to my office with a smile on his face. He is doing it. He has halved his overurgency. Now he is calling her every ten minutes. And I will say no, we are working with logarithms, like decibels or the Richter scale, where you need a tenfold decrement in energy to register a unit's worth of change. Worse than that—a phone call a day is too frequent. The issue is not what it feels like to you; it's what it feels like to her. How much do you have to change before she perceives a difference?

As he experiences how hard it is to keep his hand off the receiver, the young man will be forced to confront his motivation. Why can't he forgo telephoning? He discovers how strongly he is tempted to humiliate himself before women. How his wish to express his incompetency vies with, even exceeds, his wish to be loved. He wants to be loved as an incompetent. Or the issue may be his impulse to flout convention, to prove that he is an exception; he would rather do it his way than succeed. He may call social etiquette hypocritical; and then he may be led to ask himself what stands behind his intolerance of hypocrisy. As a teaching tool, the exercise in forbearance is stronger than any interpretation about his hostility to mother and sisters, his fear that no one will ever love him enough, his jealous conviction that women always take more than they give. These or other passions become evident as he sits uneasily beside the phone and later, if his forbearance bears fruit, as he squirms through the early stages of romance with a young woman.

When you say you have already tried deferring to Lena, you are like the undergraduate who phones every ten minutes and expects his fortunes to improve. In practice, brief attempts at changed behavior represent unchanged behavior. Your oscillation between attitudes, now encouraging Lena, now scorning her, serves only to further undermine her confidence. If you are to be quiet and accepting, it must be for enough time, and with enough curiosity about her views and respect for her taste, for her to feel the difference and for you to plumb your discomfort.

You will have other objections: It doesn't feel like you; it's the wrong moment; you could have used the relationship for this sort of exercise in the past, but now, when Lena is moving, is the least painful time to jump.

This from you, who scorn letters that end at the bottom of a page? The time to end is when you are ready to end. This relationship is alive. What is precious about Lena's impending move is that it allows you to see where you are. But I am pushing too hard. Let's keep it simple. Here is a piece of advice: Stay, and consider staying to be an opportunity for growth, through allowing Lena to grow.

We will never have this conversation. No one will ever have this conversation with you. Because you are too fragile, because we are all too fragile, because bludgeoning rarely constitutes helping. You are too tender for anyone even to think these thoughts in your presence.

But if I heard your story and you asked my opinion, I might say, in a serious manner to reflect your own, I think I would listen to your friends: Stay. If I sensed any ripple of self-awareness, any playfulness in you at all, I might add: You know, I have one more suggestion. Let Lena choose the furnishings for the new apartment. See how it feels to give over control, enjoy her taste, tolerate comfort. And if I cocked my head at the right angle, and let my gaze intercept yours at the right moment, there is a chance that you would know precisely what I meant, and I would have done my job.

MATCHES

7

Biancas

Not likely that I will get it right so easily with a man who is at once superior and brittle. He will detect the edge in my unspoken response and be put off. How to face such a man is a matter of art—neither to respond in kind to his contempt nor to empathize too openly with his shameful sense of vulnerability. But however difficult to put across, the advice I favor is, I believe, obvious or conventional: Lena's beau—call him Guy—ought to stay and struggle to grow. We are a culture that sets great stock in growth. Guy's story has the same moral as Jonnie's: If your urge to cut and run arises from immaturity, it makes sense to stay and confront your fears and disappointments.

Especially if you and your partner are well matched emotionally. In assessing the viability of relationships, this question of matching is as influential as any. My impression is that Guy and Lena are in some vague sense at the same level of maturity and may even be struggling with the same issue, insecurity. That opinion gives me confidence; if Lena is not the only possible choice for Guy, she is at least a reasonable one. The same consideration comes to bear in my thinking about Iris and Randall: Any sympathy I might have with Iris's wish to stay depends on my agreement with her feeling that Randall's failings correspond to unfinished parts of her own makeup. Perhaps part of what holds you in your relationship is an apprehension that moving on would be just so much churning of mates, that your partner's shortcomings reflect your own. On the contrary, you may believe that you were well matched when the relationship started, but now you have grown, while your partner seems if anything more rigid and less generous.

In our daily speech, the idea of matching is embedded in the concept of growth. When we say, "she has outgrown him," what we mean, implicitly, is that people ought not to stay together, or just often do not stay together, if they are at different levels of something—of whatever it is that grows when one person is said to outgrow another. Whereas when partners are at the same level (as they might be when we say, "she only imagines she has outgrown him"), they ought to think twice about moving on. These rules about matching and growth are among the most important in our assessing relationships, and no doubt they have many sources. But one source, from within psychotherapy, I know to be especially influential in my own thinking.

Let me tell you an unpleasant fairy tale that in one version or another is told or played out in the training of every psychotherapist. The characters are more troubled than Iris or Jonnie or Guy, certainly more troubled than you, so you may wonder why they have a place in my anticipating your dilemma. But psychiatry begins in pathology; when psychiatrists consider small problems, it is by reference to big ones. The tale concerns a typical beginner's mistake.

Into the basement boxcar office of a neophyte psychiatry resident comes a young woman, Bianca. Poised and insightful, Bianca enters treatment readily. Only one thing seems odd about Bianca—her pairing with the Brute, her boyfriend of many years. As Bianca's tale unfolds, the neophyte therapist develops a horrifying impression of the Brute. He is overbearing and irrational. Perhaps his flaws are concrete: not overt violence, but alcoholism or sociopathy. There is corroborating evidence. Bianca produces his police records, or the mental health center receptionist reports that a man claiming to be Bianca's boyfriend has made loud and sarcastic remarks in the waiting area, or the Brute accompanies Bianca to a session and acts the perfect bum.

A few weeks into treatment, Bianca asks whether she ought not leave the Brute. In some manner that can later be pointed to as the cause of the breakup, the resident indicates that Bianca should give the matter serious thought. The advice—to leave the boyfriend—may be indirect. The resident may simply begin inquiring about Bianca's bad taste in men.

Given implicit permission, Bianca leaves her boyfriend. And then isn't there hell to pay. Suddenly, Bianca expects the therapist to satisfy a host of urgent needs in her life. Now this most stable and long-suffering of patients looks dependent, histrionic, suicidal, intrusive, impulsive, violent, sharp-tongued, alcoholic, and demanding. Gentle Bianca into wildcat Kate, no taming likely. If the resident is a man, Bianca may allege past promises of romantic devotion, and she may not be entirely wrong. (Indeed, too often she is entirely right.) If the resident is female, Bianca will style her a bad mother, jealous and competitive and purposely misleading. The tale is a variant of Beauty and the Beast: Under the skin, Bianca is the Brute.

Bianca is one reason psychotherapists shy away from giving advice. Help-seeking may conceal rage; anything helpers say can and will be used against them. Fear of Bianca makes therapists retreat into the silent, hidden posture of classical psychoanalysis. The Bianca story teaches therapists to mistrust those who turn to them. Wilfred Bion, a pioneering group therapist, was known for a remark, variously quoted, to this effect: "Why are you so angry at me? You must think I've tried to do something to help you."

But mistrust or simple irony takes the Bianca story too narrowly. From the point of view of its principals, the fairy tale appears quite different. Here is Bianca, for the moment uncharacteristically stable but feeling an edge of desperation; and along comes this resident who seems to promise her a level of caring she has only dreamed of. But when Bianca lets go her hold on the Brute and swings, like a trapeze artist, toward the resident, there is no one to catch her. Seduced and abandoned—no wonder Bianca reverts to her customary angry state. From the vantage of the Brute, whose real name is Hank, something odd is occurring. Hank loses a girlfriend, but he gains self. How he was with

Bianca—that was not Hank. He never wanted to treat a woman that way.

The constant lesson is, we just do not know who is sitting across from us. What the resident lacks in the encounter with Bianca is the fictive attitude, the ability to look past Bianca's presentation and generate a set of stories that cast her in a different light. But which stories? That is the beauty of this fairy tale: It contains the answer to its own riddle. One way to imagine you, fictively, is to look to the company you keep. The resident asks, of Bianca's ties to Hank, whatever does she see in him? The answer is, she sees herself. More precisely, she sees someone at her own level of maturity.

But how does she? This issue of maturity is slippery. Think of your own circumstances. Your lover is impatient, you are self-contained. Your lover is self-critical, you are smug. Where your lover is painstaking, you are quick to judgment. Your lover complains that you never admit to being wrong, you complain that your lover never commits to a plan. You disdain your lover's paralyzing sensitivity; your lover wishes you would show psychological insight. These traits reflect not only temperament but also values. Your lover admires subtlety; you, boldness. Or the roles may be just the reverse. In either event, how, in the face of contradictory ideals, do we measure maturity?

And how do we factor in the interpersonal context that so shapes presentation of self? This was the resident's problem; Bianca looks entirely different outside the relationship with Hank. Facing you, I will need a sense of how you might look free of the relationship you are in, not to mention a sense of how you look outside my consulting room, since some people organize themselves, and others regress, under the doctor's gaze.

Many therapists have tried to understand Bianca and what makes her tick, from the inside. That effort gives rise to whole schools of theory and to an extensive and unpleasant vocabulary: borderline, splitting, acting out, rescue fantasy, bad hysteric, as-if personality, countertransference, projective identification. But the theorist who had most to say about why Bianca and Hank are together, about their emotional matching, was a pioneer of family therapy, Murray Bowen.

Bowen was curious about a series of issues concerning maturity—which parts of a person's functioning change under stress and which remain steady, how a person's resilience is reflected in the behavior of those around him, how a person evaluates a potential partner. Bowen thought he might be able to capture, in an integrated way, the level of people's adaptive capacities—their resistance to emotional illness, their openness to opportunity, their ability to develop and maintain a continuity in their values and beliefs. He conceptualized a single measure meant to be for emotional maturity what Charles Spearman's g-factor is meant to be for intelligence, a number that indicates where a person ranks on the scale of human potential. Bowen called his measure "differentiation of self."

The measure is breathtakingly simple: It is the ability to remain oneself in the face of group influences, especially the intense influence of family life. Here is a practical test of differentiation of self: When you return to your parents' home—from college, a trip, years of living apart—for how many minutes can you remain yourself, neither reverting to the childhood self who fits into so many fixed, repetitive, unproductive family scenarios nor shutting out your relatives emotionally? Or if you are the parent, how long do you remain yourself in your child's presence?

People at the low end of the differentiation scale are those who lose self—lose identity, values, convictions, perspective—under the pressure of group life. (The prime example in Bowen's time was the schizophrenic, who was thought to absorb and enact the anxiety of the entire family.) In relationships, poorly differentiated people merge with one another, sharing strengths and weaknesses in confusing ways: The more submissive partner lends self to the more demanding, creating one apparently strong, high-functioning partner and one apparently weak partner. These strong and weak personae are, in Bowen's terminology, pseudo-self. Fused couples—and we are all this way to some degree—are like two on a seesaw; one partner is up and one is down, but the aggregate level of self for the couple is constant. Basic self—the entity rated on the differentiation of self scale, the self you can take with you and invest in a new relationship—remains the same for each individual. Bowen's contention was that differentiation of basic self is fundamental to human identity; it pervades styles of thinking, feeling, and social functioning. Level of self is so important, and we are so adept at detecting each other's level of self, that we invariably choose as partners, in marriage or other long-standing intimate relationships, people at our precise level of differentiation. An amalgam of traits like maturity, autonomy, and integrity, differentiation is Bowen's answer to the question of "what grew" when we say one person has outgrown another.

Bowen's vision makes Bianca's story transparent. What Bianca presents in the resident's office is pseudo-self, a level of functioning based on her status in the relationship with Hank. Hank's apparently low differentiation of self should serve as a warning to the resident—proceed with caution. This is not to say that Bianca must stay with Hank. But if Bianca is to leave, the resident must be prepared to deal with a patient who looks less well differentiated, which in this case is to say less autonomous, than the woman who once lit up the little office.

I read Bowen with Lou. Later, in residency, that exposure to Bowen kept me out of certain sorts of trouble—the Bianca sort.

I recall a man, Asa, who came to my office contemplating divorce. To all appearances, Asa was a peaceable husband complaining about a bellicose wife. Nikki ran roughshod over people. Standing up to Nikki, Asa said, would require traits utterly foreign to him. To follow the path of loyalty to self would be to walk away and let Nikki be "right" in solitude. Only, having shown such bad judgment—during the courtship he had seen Nikki as merely forthright—Asa mistrusted himself. Should he leave?

I cannot overstate Asa's reasonableness. He addressed me with undemanding directness. He acknowledged ambivalence, spoke of the shortcomings he brought to the marriage, expressed acceptance of the imperfectibility of relationships and of the compromises that partnership demands. He picked up subtle cues regarding my feelings. I found myself admiring his social skills. At the same time, I recognized him. He was Bianca.

I don't mean I imagined that Asa would slash his wrists on my doorstep once he left Nikki. Nothing about him was disorganized or impulsive. But the fictions I entertained were shaped by an expectation that I would find in Asa an equivalent of the failings he described in Nikki. How could such an observant man have chosen so poorly? Perhaps the premise of that mystery was false: When Asa chose Nikki, and she him, it was with precision.

If Asa and Nikki had comparable levels of self-differentiation, I would find in Nikki strengths absent in Asa's description of her. Perhaps Nikki was attuned and responsive to Asa's signals. As for Nikki's combativeness, I wondered whether it might not arise from Asa's using his skill in psychological matters to undermine her authority. Similarly, I held myself open to discovering a part of Asa that corresponded to his wife's tendency to ride roughshod over people. There are many ways to ignore others' ideas, many ways to attack a person's confidence. I came to believe that Asa's measured behavior served to undermine Nikki. For reasons of her own, and Asa knew these reasons, Nikki was uncomfortable with passive and polite men. The less Asa resisted, the more unease Nikki felt.

The marriage had deteriorated after Nikki suffered rejection by colleagues. She expected Asa would join her in her outrage. Uncomfortable with anger, Asa held back. Nikki became more belligerent. She seemed to want an emotional response, of any sort, but Asa remained reflective and rational. Asa and I discussed why, with his skill at setting others at ease, he behaved in precisely the way that would alienate Nikki. She needed what Asa withheld—outrage, or even a good fight that would let her know he cared. And so forth. We were on familiar ground now, the ground of marital conflict. Wife asserts herself, appalls husband, perceives husband's disapproval, and, feeling shamed, flaunts her aggressive qualities, wondering whether he will love her anyway.

There are many ways to arrive at this view of the marriage; I had begun by listening for signs that Asa was less gracious in the face of challenge—less differentiated—than he appeared. When Nikki acts tough, Asa tightens up. This automatic, counterproductive response signals a limitation in Asa's ability to maintain self in a social setting.

In our work, Asa and Nikki's came to seem an ordinarily viable marriage, one whose survival depended, as much as anything, on Asa's willingness to appear less affable. The problem was that Asa had defined any such change as a loss of integrity. I remember a turning point in that brief therapy. Something of my belief about matching must have seeped into the conversation. I have said Asa was a perceptive man. He asked, with irritation: If Nikki were hit by a Mack truck and suffered brain damage, would I still find grounds for likening his condition to hers?

He was right, of course. Being hit by a truck would be *force majeure*, a consideration that overwhelms the principle of matched differentiation of self. There must be a thousand reasons why couples end up ill-matched. I wondered, did I seem to be saying otherwise? I smiled, and Asa began to laugh aloud, at the hostile fantasy he had blurted out. He was able to see that the aggression he scorned in Nikki was his as well, and that it was less terrible than he had feared. At the same moment that Asa found the voice to debunk my ideas, he found a readiness to reexamine the question of integrity and to rethink his role in the trouble at home.

I was grateful to Murray Bowen, grateful for this rule of thumb for making sense of the person before me. During my residency, I looked into the possibility of spending time in Bowen's shop, at Georgetown University. The arrangement never panned out, but Bowen did interview me. When I spoke with him, I was disappointed. Bowen seemed unfocused or preoccupied.

Bowen's work concerns the structure of families. In the course of our interview, he asked me to describe my own "family of origin." I did, not omitting a certain beloved great-aunt. It was this aunt who first served me the iced tea with mint and lemon and too much sugar that I drank with Lou in the garden. My aunt, a German-Jewish immigrant and an outspoken proponent of civil rights, had got the iced tea recipe from a cleaning lady and thought it just the thing to serve to American children. I remember her pouring it proudly from a brimming pitcher into ice-filled Tom Collins glasses with a frosted pattern of lemons on the outside. I adored this aunt, though others in the family did not. She seemed gracious, farsighted, and constant in her affections. To me, the tea had the flavor of her generosity.

I mentioned this aunt in passing to Murray Bowen, and he perked up. "You will find trouble there," he said, offering an opinion though I had neither asked for nor expected one. He continued: Psychiatrists are primed to understand families in terms of conflict. Idealized relationships are too often left unexamined.

I saw the aunt a few days later, at a family gathering. For the first time, I noticed that she laughed at me. She made a great fuss about my socks showing below my slacks—I lived in jeans and chinos, and by the time they were washed enough to be comfortable my pants tended to be unfashionably short. My aunt tittered over this failing with my grandmother and others. The form of my aunt's humor was in part a product of her years, the dread second childhood. But the content was familiar. If she was good with children when they were young and dependent, she had other, less supportive qualities that my devotion to her had caused me to overlook. She was undermining when a child showed any propensity to be too big for his britches.

A flood of memories confirmed Bowen's prediction that I would find trouble. This aunt was as demanding in her genteel way as my more openly argumentative relations. I had trained in seminars in which residents analyze their families, and I had given thought to family matters in my own psychoanalysis. But until Bowen made his incidental remark, it had never occurred to me to think of my great-aunt as anything but kindly.

The brief comment worked its corrosive and useful magic. My aunt's detractors rose in my esteem. I began to feel less fixed in my alliances within the family, more capable of appreciating diverse views of familiar grievances. This freedom was accompanied by a subtle self-reassessment: Certain of my own failings came to seem less grave. I noticed a new ease in my relationship with my fellow residents, as if I had been relieved of a burden of which I had been only faintly aware— the need to hold myself in a slightly superior position, like the aunt. I retained a warm sentiment for this aunt, a strong impression of her generosity and, yes, tolerance. But I felt liberated from her good opinion, which in retrospect came with strings attached, including requirements that one feel clumsy in the face of her gracefulness.

*   *   *

I kept Lou abreast of my various epiphanies in residency. *"Ex ungue leonem"* was Lou's comment on Bowen's emerging from his distraction to finger the great-aunt. By the claw is the lion known. My aunt's iced tea became a symbol for us of a tendency I had at the time, and may have still, to idealize certain figures—an *aide mémoire* for the truth that those we admire are fallible and that clear vision requires more than one perspective.

8
Homecoming

LIKE HARRY STACK SULLIVAN, Murray Bowen combined the power to perturb with a quick awareness of how things go. Bowen had only to say, Look to the kindly aunt, and soon I found myself more comfortable with my peers. It is this sort of gentle nudge—the incidental comment that says more than months of psychotherapy—that piqued my interest in advice. Bowen was a devoted theorist, a man who would say that wisdom owes everything to theory, and vice versa. I expect aspects of Bowen's theory will color any advice I am likely to give about leaving.

You may want the perfect lover, or at least someone who is "above" you. One cultural ideal is to marry up, Cinderella to the Prince, or Aladdin to the Princess. (Of course, this marrying up must also, in the storytelling tradition, turn out to be a marriage of equals, and the ability of the higher-ranking partner to recognize equality in a social inferior is a mark of differentiation.) Your current partner's weaknesses bother you, and never mind your own shortcomings. But from the outside, I can hardly base my advice on the premise that, flawed as you are, you should hold out for the perfect partner. From the outside, it seems that if you are immature, and your partner is only equally immature, then perhaps you are about where you should be or where you are likely to be in any other relationship. Your partner's imperfections may carry a certain appeal or reassurance, as Randall's did for Iris; even if they do not, the wise course may be to stay and strive for differentiation and see what happens.

The moral of the typical stories of our culture is that true marriage requires, as a precondition, the achievement of some hidden potential—call it adulthood—that can emerge in the course of negotiating the relationship. We have dramas of marriage and remarriage, couples meeting first as dependent, proud, selfish, unformed pseudo-adults and then, after an adventure, rejoining as differentiated selves. Shakespeare's comedies often have this form. Stanley Cavell would trace the story to our earliest literature—when are Adam and Eve, and their marriage, complete?

The notion of growing within a relationship constitutes a strong line in our cultural wisdom. In psychotherapy, this is Bowen's line. But Freudian psychoanalysis is "single-minded," which is why a typical fear expressed by spouses of patients in psychoanalysis is that insight will lead to throwing over the traces. Discovering that the marriage is founded on neurotic attachments, the patient will demand a divorce. (That sort of discovery is the basis for Freud's advice to Frink.) In contrast, Bowen subscribed to individualism in context. He wanted autonomy—but only within a family.

Psychotherapeutic theory is often veiled autobiography, and in Bowen's case the veil is thin. Like Sullivan, Bowen came from the heartland. He was born in 1913 to a large, cohesive family in Waverly, a town in rural Tennessee. Their roots in the frontier antedated the American Revolution. Relatives ran the funeral home, furniture store, and ambulance service and went on to hold positions in local government. Bowen's father was an imposing figure, a carefully groomed man who knew every adult in the county by name, a man who spoke little, but then with trenchant humor.

Bowen was the oldest of five, the subject of grand parental expectations. Days on the family ambulance service led him to think of a career in surgery—he fiddled with an early artificial heart—but he began as a country doctor, and wartime experience drew him to psychiatry. Demobilized at thirty-three, he joined the staff at the Menninger Clinic in Topeka, Kansas.

At Menninger's, the great task was applying psychoanalytic principles to work with the gravely mentally ill. Bowen saw mixed results: Patients who recovered on the ward deteriorated upon discharge home. Hoping to understand these relapses, Bowen spent nights and weekends on his own research, studying whole families where a member had schizophrenia. Perhaps because of his stiffness (Bowen was often socially uncomfortable and had a tendency to pontificate), perhaps because his research broke with the analytic focus on the individual mind, he found himself an outsider on the staff.

Bowen experienced the atmosphere at Menninger's as constraining. He noticed that when he left the Clinic for a time, he thought more clearly and was better in touch with his values and beliefs. Returning to Menninger's, Bowen lost self. The same thing happened when he traveled home. As he approached Waverly, he felt less adult, less individual. However much he tried to retain his objectivity, the family would succeed in entangling him in old emotional issues.

Bowen understood his experience to parallel that of his patients. The idea of a continuous spectrum of health was prevalent at the Clinic. Karl Menninger held that schizophrenia and neurosis differ not in kind, as pneumonia does from asthma, but in degree, according to relative liability to anxiety. To this notion of a spectrum of health, Bowen added a second concept, perhaps borrowed from a colleague at Menninger's, Hellmuth Kaiser—the German-born theorist who analyzed duplicitous speech. Kaiser spoke of "universal psychopathology," a sort of everyman's neurosis whose basis is a retreat from autonomy into "fusion." Fusion entails a person's submerging his autonomy in a pseudo-relationship, in which both his own and the other person's individuality are denied. Kaiser defined a meaningful relationship as being formed "on the basis of equality or symmetry, keeping [one's] own personality intact and respecting the other personality's boundaries."

Bowen fiddled with these concepts the way he fiddled with the artificial heart. He was interested in altering a typical sequence: Bowen, as a doctor, would begin working with a healthy family member, say the father of a schizophrenic child. Somehow, other family members would intervene to interrupt the collaboration. The father's progress would lead to family turmoil, which would cause the father to retreat to a position of togetherness. The family stymied change or individuality. This sequence reminded Bowen of pressures in Waverly and at Menninger's, implicit demands that each member remain a vague or limited self. Too often, he found himself sacrificing his beliefs to what he called the "peace-agree mode" of the group. Bowen considered it shameful as a psychiatrist to be so unobjective, so subject to influence.

Observing his own family, Bowen noticed patterns—emotional triangles—that had more stability than any individual or pairing. When Bowen (known in the family as "Bo") supported his mother (nicknamed "Buh") on an issue, she turned that support into opposition to one of his brothers. In particular, Murray and his brother "June" (for Junior) were often at odds. If Bo was, briefly, freer of Buh, he was more enmeshed with June; if Bo reconciled with June, a crisis would emerge with Buh. Through these stable triangles, the extended family maintained equilibrium, both despite and because of the efforts of individuals.

By now Bowen had left Menninger's, first for the National Institute of Mental Health (where he admitted a schizophrenic daughter and her mother to the ward, and then added grandparents, and finally put up whole families as inpatients) and then to Georgetown. Married with four children, Bowen was concerned that the subtle irrationality of his "family of origin" was being transmitted into his "nuclear family" through an automatic replication of systems. After twelve years of frustration, he decided to make a concentrated push, to do whatever was necessary for one person—himself—to achieve a greater degree of differentiation. The struggle was also an exercise in a new sort of psychotherapy. Bowen intended to alter the way therapists think about change and, more broadly, to alter human beings' sense of how they fit into their environment and how they can challenge circumstance.

What followed was either one of the grandest or one of the most self-indulgent moments in modern psychotherapy. It was a moment Bowen would later compare to Freud's first interpreting dreams, a moment Bowen saw as a hallmark in the history of the family. On Saturday, February 10, 1967, Bowen and his wife, LeRoy, flew to Waverly. Bowen was in his middle fifties, an established psychiatric researcher; his parents were in their late seventies, showing signs of various ailments. He was headed home to achieve a goal—to maintain objectivity amidst emotional tumult while continuing to relate to those around him.

To that end, he had roiled his peace-agree family. Three months prior, his mother, Buh, had called with sad news. The brother of June's wife had died suddenly, unexpectedly, young. June's wife was distraught. Bowen believed in family shock waves; his fear was that one of his parents might die next. As it happened, within two weeks of the unexpected loss, the more vulnerable of his sisters went into one of her upsets. Two weeks after that, June was immobilized with symptoms of a herniated intervertebral disc. But to Bowen's relief, for the most part the family transmuted the loss into open conflict. The hot issue was the family business. June made an offer to become majority stockholder. Buh demurred. It was in this complex context that Bowen planned his moves.

Determined to frustrate "helpful" allies, Bowen wrote contradictory letters to members of every family triangle. The intent was to preclude cohesion. Those who were likely to take his side he took special pains to alienate. The crucial letter was a long one to June. Bowen passed lightly over the issue of stock ownership and turned to the family's old emotional conflicts. He settled on a narrative strategy, to relate gossip he claimed to have heard but disbelieved. The master stroke was a reference to an old, offensive story about June's immediate family. Bo said he had heard that June and his wife were worried over this story; Bo had been warned never to mention it, for fear of upsetting them. But since people were saying things . . .

The letter concluded with a series of "reversals," exhorting June to do what he was already doing: be responsible, throw himself into the business—"limber up his back and give it the good old college try." Bo wrote that June needn't bother to see him when he arrived. He signed the letter "Your Meddlesome Brother." When June exploded, Bo wrote him and their mother more contradictory and even deceptive letters, pretending not to understand what the upset was about. He signed one "Your Anxious Brother" and the other "Your Strategic Son."

The weekend in Waverly climaxed when Bowen, his wife, and his parents visited one of Bowen's sisters for Sunday dinner. After dessert, June arrived, brandishing a letter he said Bo had written when drunk. Bo agreed that booze was cheap in Washington and offered to get June a good price. When June threatened to sue for libel, Bo agreed that June should prosecute whoever planted the rumor. June changed tactics, trotting out negative stories about Bo, who cheerfully acknowledged there were even better ones. Buh offered herself up as a victim: "I hope I do not die and leave a divided family." June accused Bo of being in league with Buh. Bo applauded June's intuition and admitted he and their mother were in on a plot. Buh exploded and denied everything. June's wife ended the meeting saying the family members should do less talking about, and more talking to, each other. Bowen was exhilarated. "The end of that Sunday afternoon was one of the most satisfying periods of my entire life. I had actively participated in the most intense family emotion possible and I had . . . gone through the entire visit without being 'triangled' or without being fused into the family emotional system." Those two hours of autonomy amidst his relations were Bowen's victory, the proof of his theory, the hallmark in the history of the family.

In the aftermath, Buh wrote, "With all its ups and downs, your last trip home was the greatest ever." Bo's fragile sister claimed she had woken up, was capable of caring for herself, wondered what had held her back in the past. June's wife spoke intimately with Bo, as she never had before. In time, Bo's father traveled with him to see lost members of the family. June was chatting with Bo now; June said Poppa seemed ten years younger.

Bowen's success solidified his beliefs that differentiation of self is a good in itself, and that the only effective family intervention is a selfish one; to reenter the family of origin and strive for autonomy. This selfish striving, like the striving of entrepreneurs under Adam Smith's version of capitalism, has beneficial effects on the whole system. The family grows to meet the level of differentiation of the upwardly mobile member.

Bowen had ancillary beliefs: that all members of a family tend to be at the same level of differentiation (though there can be a modest spread, like the one Bowen discerned between himself and his vulnerable sister); and that people tend to date, mate, and marry people at their own level. Members of a couple may trade off ostensible levels of competency, but inequality is only apparent; matching is real. And Bowen's triumph in Tennessee suggested an answer to the paralysis implicit in "matching." The solution is not to leave the other nor to strive to change the other. The solution is to grow.

Bowen's next task was to promulgate his ideas while simultaneously differentiating himself from the family of family therapists. The occasion was the Family Research Conference in Philadelphia, organized by one of the founders of the family therapy movement, Ivan Boszormenyi-Nagy. Bowen approached his colleagues as he had approached June and Buh, with secrecy and mild deception. Before the conference, he circulated a preview of his talk, a dense updating of his views on differentiation. The monograph all but parodied his style—methodical, boring, excessive in its reach.

When he rose to the podium, Bowen set the technical manuscript aside and spoke from quite a different document that described his family of origin, its history, its members, and its recurrent triangles. Then he spun his yarn: the preparations for the trip home, the two hours of differentiation in the sitting room of his sister's house on that February afternoon, and the aftermath. When Bowen finished, colleague after colleague rose to praise him—these were the field's leaders. The audience understood that Bowen had replicated with them the extraordinary interaction with his immediate relations: He had generated a strong emotional response while remaining true to himself.

9

Allegiance

THE BOWEN STORY speaks to the degree of self-exertion and cunning required to win even a small measure of autonomy. It stands for the premise that change in the self takes place only in the context of a real relationship, with the substantial anxiety relationships elicit and the substantial inertia they possess. For Bowen, the locus of psychic life is the family as it is here and now, not the family reconstructed from childhood memories evoked on the psychoanalyst's couch. An adult who can administer a complex academic department is only as free as he is dealing with old family grievances in the shadow of a funeral parlor. One's identity is never far from one's role at home—meddlesome brother, strategic son. Individuation is a lifelong process; it is not shameful to seek it in middle age, nor to acknowledge that even elderly parents exercise psychological power.

These premises are useful. All the same, Bowen's pride in his achievement may seem suspect. What's the big deal? A socially awkward man manages in his middle fifties to spend a couple of comfortable hours with his family. And has he really succeeded? Bowen reports satisfaction at not being infantilized by his mother, not being drawn into the group affect of the family, not rising to his brother's bait. But that breakthrough is the sort one can fool oneself over. Perhaps Bowen appears self-congratulatory in a way that belies his claim to have discarded the role of the ambitious eldest child, Poppa's imitator and Buh's darling.

Even if Bowen is transformed—at what price and in what fashion? Blocking his brother with counterprojective remarks, Bowen inserts his technical skill as a therapist into the privacy of the family. Bowen has the advantage over June and Buh; he knows that the conflict is artificial. Does the accomplishment lie in his securing an interval of autonomy, however contrived the circumstance? Must one eternally create family crises whose consequences are predictable—or does differentiation, once attained, show itself even when a person is caught off guard? How does the momentary experiencing of the state relate to the trait of maturity?

I had these questions from the moment Lou introduced me to Bowen's work, but at the same time, I felt an affinity to Bowen, one that only grew as my training progressed. In residency, I felt hemmed in, as Bowen did in Topeka, by hierarchy. I was aware of how poorly, despite years of psychoanalysis, I maintained my sense of self in group settings and in intimate relationships. And I was drawn to a therapy that justified efforts at individuation while valuing a strong sense of family. Bowen's roots were different from my own—his relations had been here forever, mine had just arrived—but we both had highly stable, involving families; his saga spoke to me directly.

I was also drawn to Bowen's playfulness. Bowen sallies forth as the trickster, with both family and peers. Like Picasso with old bicycle parts, Bowen makes art, in this case the art of psychotherapy, by fiddling with material others overlook. Successful, thoughtful people can do poorly at "home," whether the home is with parents or in a close-knit work group; families are stable and resilient; substantial perturbation is required to catalyze minor change. These humble truths become the material for catalyzing transformation.

Even when I was most dismissive of Bowen's efforts, I found myself moved by this concerted work on family matters by a person for whom intimacy was difficult. And I admired Bowen for the open idiosyncrasy of his perspective. Bowen's self-treatment is that of a man who stands in awe of a demanding father and engages in admiring struggles with a meddlesome mother. It is the therapy of a man who sustains a profound sense of home but who appreciates space and distance.

As a first-generation American, perhaps what most drew me to Bowen is that his vision is thoroughly American. Americans look up to people who keep their bearings in emotionally charged situations, quiet leaders who can bring a runaway group up short by speaking a word of common sense. Especially after the Second World War, after seeing the mass mentality at work in Nazi Germany or at home in the McCarthy era, Americans came to value autonomy in the face of group emotion. Bowen locates a peculiarly American hero. Think of Henry Fonda resisting mob sentiment in *The Oxbow Incident* or *Twelve Angry Men.*

Bowen is also a comic American yarnspinner. Like Mark Twain in Hadleyburg or on the Mississippi, where Hemingway says modern American literature begins, Bowen appeals to a sense of the naughty. He worked in the era when every psychiatry department chairman was a psychoanalyst and when psychoanalysis was at its most rigid. Bowen's trip home, and his public celebration of it, mock the silent and passive analytic posture.

Bowen plays off the central imagery of psychoanalysis, starting with the triangle. Think of the Oedipal triangle: sexualized child, desired mother, forbidding father. Or the triangular structure of mind: id, ego, superego. Or the psychoanalytic instrument of cure—the three-sided interpretation that links the current problem to unconscious conflict to the reproduction of that conflict within the therapeutic relationship: present to past to transference. Bowen lifts this image, triangle, from the analytic context and puts it to new use. To Bowen, the relationships that matter are current ones among family members (Bo, Buh, June). The past that matters is family tradition. The transference that matters is the distortion that sets in when a family member tries to grow. This sense of playful frugality, of fiddling and reusing material, of giving European concepts fresh meaning, permeates Bowen's work and gives it a saving levity.

There is a Bowen-style therapy, and it consists of something like advice. The therapist acts as a coach, training people to do what Bowen did, return to the family and experience differentiation of self. If a husband complains of marital trouble, the therapist will ask about the man's family of origin; then the therapist will work with the husband, formulating strategies for disrupting alliances, anticipating relatives' responses, and emerging whole. As the husband grows in differentiation—as he learns how to retain autonomy and identity while remaining in emotional contact with his family—he will find that he increasingly welcomes his wife's individuality. She will be freed (and motivated, even gently pressured, through awareness of his increase in basic self) to grow with him.

Perhaps every psychotherapy reflects its founder's circumstances. Freud's many contributions—infantile sexuality, the Oedipus Complex, repression as a source of symptoms, compulsive character arising from rigid toilet-training—are in their own way autobiography, or a portrait of the mid-nineteenth-century Austrian or Jewish-Austrian family. Therapy is a palimpsest, it hides and reveals its history.

There are now a number of characteristically American psychotherapies based on the work of men I call heartland psychotherapists. To the names Murray Bowen and Harry Stack Sullivan, I would add Carl Rogers, who in the 1960s and 1970s was known as the "Psychologist of America." Rogers spent his late childhood on a working farm and claimed to have derived his notion of the scientific method from a feed manual. Rogers was most in touch with the part of human psychology that Freud ignored, people's native tendency toward self-awareness and their responsiveness to empathy. Much of what is optimistic in today's self-help derives from Rogers's thought. Rogers popularized the thesis, which he attributed to Kierkegaard, that personhood entails a process of "becoming." For Rogers, the measure of a couple's success is its ability, through mutual acceptance, to allow each member to become a "self-actualized" individual, fully in touch with his or her "human potential." Rogers's was a sunnier celebration of the ideal that Bowen recognized, autonomy in a person who remains engaged with those around him.

None of these native therapists—Sullivan, Bowen, Rogers—came from an especially intellectual family; for all, a professional career entailed cultural change. These men devised differing treatments that have in common a sense of the centrality of the dialectic between intimacy and autonomy, between the way that we are affected by one another and the way that we escape others' influence. And though they talk about balance, for the most part their concern is with impediments to individuation.

America is, after all, a nation founded in a regretful separation from a smothering mother country, on the premise that it is sometimes necessary, in the natural order of things, to sever the ties that bind. Our first great document declares our independence. Our second, meant to form a union, settles for a federation and is immediately tempered by a bill of rights to make certain that the constituted unity is not too pervasive or intrusive.

When I say that Murray Bowen is thoroughly American, I am saying that he, and the other heartland therapists, created treatments that are elaborations of Ralph Waldo Emerson's therapeutic advice a century earlier, in his essay "Self-Reliance": "Say to them, O father, O mother, O wife, O brother, O friend, I have lived with you after appearances hitherto. Henceforward, I am the truth's. . . . I appeal from your customs. I must be myself. I cannot break my self any longer for you, or you. If you can love me for what I am, we shall be the happier. If you cannot, I will still seek to deserve that you should. I will not hide my tastes or aversions. . . . It is alike your interest, and mine, and all men's, however long we have dwelt in lies, to live in truth." The person who follows Emerson's advice is Bowen's differentiated self, able to maintain values in all seasons and all company.

As a culture, we honor Emersonian ideals. The mature person is autonomous, able to live in a truth undistorted by the appeals of group emotion. It is this strain of American idealism that psychotherapy has championed, these values that dominate self-help and advice in all its popular forms.

10
Also Connect

istening to Prozac, my book about the effect of psychotherapeutic drugs on the contemporary sense of self, begins by considering marked responses to antidepressant medications. I came to that topic because of a particular relationship to the patients I described: I admired in them the very traits that caused their trouble in the world, their sensitivity, generosity, openness, vulnerability. When medication altered their temperament, as occasionally it appeared to do, my response was ambivalent. Yes, the men and women attained relief, but perhaps something precious was lost in the process. The issue was not only the means of transformation but also the result, the very growth in autonomy that is such an overriding social good.

Though not adept at tolerating isolation or demonstrating muscular self-esteem, some of these sensitive and generous men and women had their own genius, a genius for connection. Often they were romantic. They entertained impossible idealism. They threw themselves wholeheartedly into relationships. Routinely they gave more than we expect modern people to give. What medication offered them was autonomy, the ability to say no to others and attend to the self.

In treating such patients, I wonder whether a gain in autonomy is necessarily a gain in self-differentiation. "Good responders" to medica-tion do seem better able to negotiate the important arenas, love and work. But sitting across from them, sometimes I sense a loss—of intense specialness, perhaps of intensity altogether. One way of understanding the transformation is to say that what these good responders lose is pre-cisely the capacity to be different, that is, especially connected. They may need to mute their genius because some other trait—subtle masochism or bad judgment or impulsivity or a tendency toward depression—makes their exquisite ability to bond dangerous for them. But the loss is nonetheless apparent.

The beauties of connection raise questions about autonomy as an ideal. I have called Bowen's perspective Emersonian. In recent decades, Emerson has been faulted as inhumanly individualistic. The case in point is his essay "Experience," where Emerson considers the impact of a terrible loss.

Emerson's five-year-old firstborn son, Waldo, has died of scarlet fever. In his correspondence, Emerson once called Waldo a "piece of love and sunshine, well worth my watching from morning to night." In the immediate wake of the boy's death Emerson wrote, "I comprehend nothing of this fact but its bitterness." But now, in 1844, as he emerges from the acute phase of his bereavement, Emerson the essayist takes the stoic's stance: "In the death of my son, now more than two years ago, I seem to have lost a beautiful estate,—no more. I cannot get it nearer to me." Emerson compares the effect to that of a financial setback, which would cause inconvenience but leave him, personally, neither better nor worse off. "So it is with this calamity; it does not touch me; something which I fancied was a part of me, which could not be torn away without tearing me nor enlarged without enriching me, falls off from me and leaves no scar. It was caducous." Caducous refers to a loss that is natural to development—the falling away of a tadpole's gills. Taken at face value, Emerson's level of equanimity seems monstrous. Beloved children do not just fall away, traceless.

In life, Emerson was no ogre of autonomy. He continued to puzzle over the death, producing, in 1846, the elegiac poem "Threnody," for his "gracious," "wondrous," "hyacinthine" boy. In the course of Emerson's private emotion, the essay "Experience" seems to embody one stage of grieving, numbness. Before and after "Experience," Emerson is the painfully bereaved father. In much of his writing, Emerson frets over the loneliness of the human condition. Emotional isolation is less a goal than a difficult truth.

But as regards cultural values, the extreme posture of Emerson's "Experience" is not so easily explained away. The celebration of equanimity extends back to the real Stoics—and Cynics and Skeptics and Epicureans. The ancient Greeks valued *ataraxia,* freedom from mental perturbation, as a defense against the transience of attachments and, more broadly, as the highest level of emotional maturity. The Emersonian psychotherapists, and Murray Bowen in particular, bring *ataraxia* home—home to America and home to the bosom of the family.

Psychotherapists apply the ideal of autonomy every day. I think of a common contretemps. A man or woman, but let us say a woman, has been deserted. She is one of those people who bond so strongly that when her husband leaves he seems, in Emerson's words, to tear something away. Encountering her, we find she looks as she feels, depleted. She may have many depressive symptoms, and whether the state is to be labeled depression is a question of definition. In this diminished condition, she seeks help from a therapist. What will be the therapist's aim? To restore self. But also to make certain that this diminution does not recur, that the woman will in future be more capable of autonomy. Discussion will ensue of dependency needs, internal sources of worth, self-destructive tendencies. A similar process can occur without therapy, which is one reason that second marriages often are built around livability rather than high romance.

This choice to move from merger to boundedness reflects social realities—the relative ease of divorce, for example, and the necessity for flexibility within the two-career marriage. In a mobile society, intense bonding is frequently a precursor to terrible hurt. How much better if the falling away of a partner were caducous. But the choice also reflects values, a denigration of romantic attachment in favor of independence, a move toward pragmatism, although we might ask whether it is pragmatic to forgo so desired a human good as passion.

I have made the patient in this example a woman, not so much because these questions of merger and boundedness arise more often for women—men consult psychotherapists with the same concerns—as because this tension between autonomy and connection is the central issue in feminist psychiatry.

When we try to pin down what is disturbing about Bowen's perspective, one way to put the matter is to say that, as an ideal, differentiation is too "masculine." To point to the obvious, the therapists I have mentioned, the ones I studied with Lou, were men. Of course, the gender of the theorist is not the primary issue. One of Freud's favorite female colleagues was another Lou, Lou Andreas-Salomé, whose best-known contribution to theory was an orthodox treatise comparing fantasies about the vagina to fantasies about the anus. Karen Horney, whose work I read with my mentor, Lou, was as taken with Kierkegaard as any of her colleagues, and as focused on autonomy as a solution to impasses. In 1950, two years before her death, Horney wrote approvingly of *"that inner certainty with reference to others which is possessed by a person who is realistically aware of himself as himself and others as themselves, and who is not swayed in his estimate of them by all kinds of compulsive needs."* So that an ideal quite similar to differentiation of self enters American psychiatric thought through the writing of a German-born woman psychoanalyst.

Horney's career is of some interest. She is now taken as a protofeminist, but especially in her later writing, hers was feminism in an old key, in which the standards of a male-dominated culture are accepted. In the 1930s, Horney went to some pains to acquaint her readers with alternative values that might compete with autonomy; she wrote of societies in which the competitive spirit is considered indecent. By 1950, she had concluded that self-realization then and there in America would entail conformity to the American ideal of assertiveness. Her last book opens with the image of a compliant eight-year-old girl who "placed some of her toys in the street for a poorer child to find, without telling anyone about it" and went on to flounder throughout her youth. As with Sullivan, for Horney the question is not what we might wish to be true, but what is a hopeful direction for a person in this culture.

The foundations for modern feminist psychoanalysis were being laid in the 1970s, just as Lou and I were taking our walks along the fens. As did all new theories, the varieties of feminism fascinated Lou. In particular, Lou wanted me to read a series of monographs by a Boston-based colleague, Jean Baker Miller, that circulated in mimeograph form before appearing in 1976 as *Toward a New Psychology of Women*. Bronx-born, a Depression-era child, the daughter of a civil servant, Miller understood that autonomy is a delusion, that anyone who makes it does so with the help of the community. Early in life she suffered polio, treated aggressively with physical therapy, and she attributed her later success to encouragement she received from a series of caregivers and teachers.

Miller was mentored in college by the sociologist Helen Merrill Lynd. Lynd is best known for the pioneering study *Middletown*, co-authored with her husband, but her influence in psychiatry arises from a more philosophical work, *On Shame and the Search for Identity*. *On Shame* is a meditation on the way that definitions of maturity exert their influence on self-esteem. It appeared in 1958, at the beginning of the American romance with identity—just as Erik Erikson made his claim that the search for identity had become as important in his time as the study of sexuality in Freud's. Early in her book, Lynd writes what to me is one of the sliest and most devastating sentences in the psychotherapeutic literature:

> It is mature to handle money and work effectively, to adjust to reality, to take responsibility, to be decisive in action, to make vocational choices commensurate with one's ability, to be successful in what one undertakes, to use leisure productively, to have friends of both sexes, to have at the appropriate age heterosexual relations.

Listing criteria baldly, Lynd reveals their arbitrariness. "As rigid a code as that of any church or creed" is how Lynd puts it. In what sounds like an advance attack on Bowen and the idea of the family ego mass, Lynd writes, "It is not loss of oneself, an 'impoverishment,' but a way of finding more of oneself when one means most to others whom one has chosen. Nor must complete finding of oneself . . . precede finding oneself in and through other persons." Lynd's critique of unexamined conceptualizations of the good is expanded in the work of her student, Jean Baker Miller.

After medical school and residency, Miller joined a psychoanalytic institute that had broken off from Horney's on the grounds that Horney's own rump caucus had turned too conventional. What Miller discussed in that institute—what she observed in her practice—was a sociological truth, that society did not value women's special talents. Her typical patient was a woman who supported and tolerated the foibles of a professional husband, raised a large family, and became despondent and resentful for reasons she could not express. In Miller's view, the woman was not acknowledged for her special skill, at connection. And she gave without getting—the emotional ties in the family lacked mutuality.

Rather than Kierkegaard or Emerson, Martin Buber seems the philosopher whose ideas best relate to Miller's. Buber had lectured to American psychiatrists in 1957, and his influence was soon apparent in the work of a number of theorists, including Carl Rogers, Ivan Boszormenyi-Nagy, and Leston Havens. Buber's assertion was that people exist first and only in a field of relationships, what Buber called "the Between." He insisted, as Nagy puts it, that "the basic pronouns are not I, Thou, and It, but I-Thou and I-It." For Buber, autonomy is at best an incomplete account of personhood and at worst a destructive fiction based on unacknowledged reliance on relationships from which the "autonomous" person draws strength and to which he accords insufficient credit.

Miller had not read Buber, but she had sat across from her patients, and she gave voice to ideas very much like Buber's, ideas that despite Buber's following had not crystallized—not been stated with any force or consistency—in psychoanalysis. Like Lynd, Miller faulted psychiatry for recognizing only one model of maturation, namely, separation and individuation—growing away from, as opposed to growing toward. (This model, or ideal, may be not so much masculine as "modern." Lynd asks why Baudelaire is modern, when he is a contemporary of the early Victorians; her answer is his emphasis on the idiosyncratic individual perspective.) Miller was known at the time mainly for her tough advocacy on behalf of a woman's viewpoint, taking men to task for ignoring the legitimacy of women's anger. But what excited Lou about Miller's essays was that they constitute a critique of the Emersonian (and Greek, and Bowenian) ideal of *ataraxia*. Reading Miller, I had a sense that this humane ideal of over two millennia, the emotionally independent man, had become a burden for the culture and its members. Miller was demanding, among other things, a reassessment of differentiation.

To be sure, psychoanalysts before Miller paid attention to relationship. Harry Stack Sullivan, though he values growth toward autonomy, often holds the self to be an illusion, saying that it "makes no sense to think of ourselves as 'individual,' 'separate,' capable of anything like definitive description in isolation."

Murray Bowen writes about the "emotional cut-off" as an indicator of pseudo-independence and unresolved attachment; but Bowen's mistrust of the cut-off arises from the suspicion that excessive distancing signals hidden dependency. A teenager who abruptly pulls away from his parents is not truly autonomous; his rebellion is an homage to family ties. But devaluing cut-offs is not the same as admiring skill at connection. To Bowen, connections are just there—the family reaches out to grab its members. He ignores the idea that connectedness needs to be created, that Buh worked actively to provide it in his own family. The notion that one person might be quite merged with another and yet retain a valuable capacity for furthering the relationship is foreign to Bowen's theory, which sees fusion as avoidance of selfhood.

Even D. W. Winnicott, the British pediatrician-turned-analyst whose work inspired many mid-century innovations in theory, expresses a mixed respect for attachment. Winnicott is known for saying that there is no infant, only the infant-mother dyad. But he also talked about the "good-enough mother," a concept (however comforting for parents) that sets a low ceiling for affiliative skills. While these theorists acknowledge that every person lives in a social context, they find no way to value genius in reaching, understanding, or nurturing others—they lack a concept of "relational heroism."

Miller's point is that bonding is a special ability that can grow throughout the life cycle, an axis of maturity that needs to be taken into account alongside autonomy. To undervalue skills related to connectedness, Miller holds, is to mistake human ideals and capacities. Integration with others is as essential, as urgent, as profound, as admirable a human goal as individuation. Miller finds connectedness to be particularly important in women's development. For women, to feel connected (when there is genuine give-and-take) is to feel zest, vitality, validation, clarity, worth, empowerment. Sometimes Miller seems to allude to a biological need for attachment and mutuality that, if thwarted, results in ailments; other times she refers to a high talent for connectedness. The failure of the culture to acknowledge this genius results in asymmetry in intimate relationships. Women who seek connection are subjugated by men who seek domination. Men use threats of isolation to make women desperate.

Miller's contribution is primarily a shift in emphasis, but there are issues where emphasis is everything. A seeker returning home under Miller's model would behave quite differently than did Bowen. Far from plotting and scheming in isolation, she would try to negotiate "growth-enhancing mutually empathic connections" from within the heart of the family. Rather than a proudly autonomous self, she might create a negotiated self, one whose strength is most evident in the suppleness of her ties to the family—ties that she has revitalized and that, in return, sustain her.

In Miller's work, the traditional American figure and ground are reversed. Emerson's autonomy from Waldo is less valuable to her than the father's and son's continuing connection. She is less interested in Thoreau's trip to Walden (as recounted in America's one truly great self-help book) than in the family and friends who prepared him for it and supported him throughout. Thoreau claims to find himself by separating from society; Miller might say that if Thoreau put his efforts into his family, he would equally gain zest and clarity, and perhaps by more honest means. Miller represents a different strain in American transcendentalism, the dream of connectedness that gave rise to utopian collective communities, Fruitlands and Brook Farm.

* * *

When I read it in mimeograph form, *Toward a New Psychology of Women* evoked a warm response, because connection stood at the heart of my image of the family. As is the case for most people who are drawn to psychotherapy as a profession, I came from what theorists call an enmeshed extended family, one whose members share intense emotional bonds. When the family functioned well, it compensated for the limitations of one or another member.

The virtues of enmeshment were impressed on me in metaphor by my great-aunt, the brewer of iced tea, who, as I have implied, masked her toughness under a decided layer of sentiment. When I first told her of my wedding engagement—my fiancée and I were paying a duty call on relatives who summered in the Poconos—my aunt pointed to a pair of white pines planted close together. They had developed a cone of branches and needles around the two trunks, responding to the sun as a single tree; if you were to cut one down, the other would look unbalanced, bare on one side and rounded on the other. A couple, she said, should be like those trees.

My aunt's own marriage had been of this intertwined form. Her late husband was a mild and complaisant man whose success in business was attributable partly to his charm and partly to the direction his wife gave him at critical junctures. The two hid their undeveloped parts in the marriage and faced the world with their strengths. They were organically interdependent, not autonomous. And they functioned well, though each at times may have felt a bit stifled. Bowen expresses some of the longings of a member of an enmeshed family; Miller speaks to the hidden support that allows those longings to emerge.

An indicator of Miller's novelty is the couple therapy her theory has inspired. Rather than work for growth in each individual, the "relational" approach, as it is called, asks the partners to focus on the Between and its potential for change. At the core of the therapy is "relational awareness," often approached through exercises in which the partners generate metaphors to characterize the relationship as it is (fledgling, prison, leaky tub) and as it might be (soaring bird, flowering field, boat under sail). In terms of assessment—should you leave?—the operational question is whether the relationship has the potential to move toward greater connection and mutuality.

*   *   *

In *Toward a New Psychology of Women*, Miller anticipates a transformed culture in which "affiliation is valued as highly as, or more highly than, self-enhancement." She criticizes the ideal of autonomy, as containing an implicit demand that a person sacrifice attachments. She challenges the belief that emotional involvement entails the threat of being reduced to "some undifferentiated mass or state ruled by weakness. . . ." Sometimes it seems that Miller is creating a class of "exceptions"; she understands why a person might choose to stay and work on a gravely flawed relationship, and she understands why a person might choose to leave a seemingly effective relationship that does not offer the possibility of increasing mutuality.

But Miller does not entirely escape the values she critiques. When she speaks of the goals from which a woman is likely to be blocked by a male-dominated culture, Miller refers to empowerment, self-fulfillment, self-determination, becoming oneself, realizing authenticity, concentrating on her own development, resisting pressures to tailor her version of things to fit another's perspective, learning to see her own needs as distinctive, holding fast to those needs in the face of attempts by other family members to substitute theirs for hers, and so on. These phrases are modified to include connection as a social good; Miller's emphasis remains distinctive. But, as in Bowen's version, Miller's healthily developed person is vigorously self-possessed. And virtually all of Miller's case examples involve an already engaged woman moving toward greater awareness of and insistence on her independence—building on connectedness to achieve greater autonomy.

How to advise in a culture that does not value affiliation as highly as self-enhancement is problematic. Thinking of Iris, for example, prudent advice—the advice from which she hopes to be exempted—is not to exercise her proficiency at connection within the relationship with Randall but just to leave. My own inclination is to ask her to bring into the relationship the skills at autonomy that she displays in the business world. If she is to remain connected it must be through demonstrating her emotional independence and implicitly demanding that Randall react with corresponding growth. This choice provides protection. It allows Iris to stay with Randall while investing in her own increasingly differentiated self.

Miller's colleagues have struggled with this dilemma, that however much one admires connection, the safe response to a relational impasse is often something like self-improvement. One couple therapist has addressed the problem by proposing an alternative definition of differentiation: "By differentiation, I do not mean to suggest as a developmental goal the assertion of difference and separateness; rather I mean a dynamic process that encompasses increasing levels of complexity, structure, and articulation within the context of human bonds and attachments." That definition points in a useful direction: Like Helen Lynd, we might, we should, value skill at connection as an aspect of maturity, self-fulfillment, or growth. But, in practical terms, do we?

Even in recent years, Miller has said that men do not recognize a talent for affiliation when choosing a wife except, and this is to a minor degree, insofar as they feel admired or supported by the woman; and women still most often look for autonomy in a man. In other words, as regards matched differentiation of self, skills at connection count for little. Often the immediate problem for a "sensitive" woman is that she finds herself in a relationship with a man who has approximately her capacity for autonomy but who, lacking her special skills for attachment, is, in other's eyes—Miller's, mine—and eventually in her own, less mature. The same is true for sensitive men in relationships with insensitive women. An advisor or therapist or friend can help an "affiliative" person credit herself for her skills and efforts. But faced with a predicament, often the way out for the sensitive or affiliative partner is growth in autonomy, not because autonomy is inherently admirable, but because it works.

Even monkeys accord intermediate status to troop members who are adept at eliciting cooperation; as social primates, humans must always have placed some value on talents for crafting compromises, inspiring others, and the like. And perhaps the capacity for connection carries more social value in our culture than it did in the recent past. The change may be greatest when it comes to the society's assessment of men, the sensitive man having become a cultural icon, celebrated in story and film, and probably in the marital marketplace as well. But my impression, seeing people in couples, is that the capacity for inner certainty or self-possession remains the more critical factor in determining whether a pairing seems like a psychological "match." Indeed, with the culture's increased tolerance and need for career women, the centrality of autonomy as a value may have been consolidated, rather than eroded, in recent years.

■ ■ ■

Lou's collection, *Pieces of Resistance,* contains a disturbing story, written in the 1970s, that implicitly addresses Miller's challenge to the ideal of autonomy. The title is "You Will Be Fine Once You Meet Someone Else," a sentiment proffered by Lou's analyst after Lou's first marriage ended. The analyst was vindicated—Lou did well after hitting it off with Terry and heading into a second marriage. But evidently something about the sentence struck Lou as strange. Hence the short story, which concerns a supportive, sensitive wife named Connie whose husband has deserted her out of the blue. Distraught, Connie consults a senior therapist, a woman who makes the pronouncement in the title. Connie does meet another man and returns to report that she is, in effect, living happily ever after.

That is the whole of the story, except that Lou proceeds to retell it, each time introducing slightly different details, in the manner of Alain Robbe-Grillet. The story at first sounds plausible, almost contentless. With repetition, it becomes troubling. How unusual it seems for a psychotherapist, especially in the decade of self-actualization, to suspect this about a patient—that what she needs is not inner change but a second marriage—and to say it, and to be right. The comment is the sort any friend might make, but coming from a therapist, the words imply some special judgment, that Connie is not self-destructive, that Connie has merely run into bad luck. The statement is "performative"—it both declares and makes Connie well.

Just who is this therapist? At first, she sounds conventional and even sexist, grounding all of a woman's happiness in marriage. Then again, she sounds respectful and pragmatic—sometimes things do work out that way, and surely there are people healthy enough not to need therapy; to suggest to Connie, in her vulnerable state, that she requires a personality overhaul would be a form of fraud. From another angle, the therapist seems a feminist, willing to accord power to Connie's special affiliative skills, power that less attuned observers might overlook. The tension in the story is interpretive—between an account that Connie needs more self and an account that she has self aplenty and needs only opportunity to invest it.

In later retellings, it becomes less clear that Connie is a woman. Cues still point in that direction, but the matter remains clouded, and the reader is left to wonder what the same sequence might mean if Connie were a sensitive and distraught man. This withholding of a critical detail—gender!—from the reader creates an odd effect, perhaps suggestive of the condition of the therapist from whom aspects of even the most forthcoming patient will always remain hidden.

Then, as Connie is stripped of all markers of femininity, the story takes on overtones of gender politics. Abandoned, Connie (male, heterosexual) seeks counsel. The therapist says, you will be fine once you remarry. This sequence sounds as sexist as did, from one point of view, the therapist's advice to the presumptively female Connie and, strangely, for the same reason—it is demeaning to women. If we read in stereotypes, what we hear is the therapist saying to Connie (female): You will be fine when you find a man to dominate you and make choices for you. Or the therapist saying to Connie (male): You will be fine when you find a woman to serve you and inflate your ego. To "find" another might mean quite different things when said to people of different genders. In either case, the standard view has it that the search for other is a defensive distraction from the imperative to define self. In a culture with inequities in distribution of power, to recommend a new relationship as a solution to a social challenge is to buy in to those inequities. By the final retelling, which is just the original story stripped of what little detail it had, the simple sequence has become immensely unsettling.

What do we make of Connie's happy second marriage? A reader may doubt Connie's own account. What sort of Connie are we imagining? Perhaps Connie is deluded; perhaps the therapist should have insisted that Connie become more assertive. Alternatively, matters may be just as the therapist seems to characterize them: Connie has the resources to negotiate and nurture a satisfying partnership. A reader is likely to oscillate between being appalled at the therapist's simple advice and admiring it as arising from a clear-sightedness that bypasses convention—from a perspective that recognizes exceptions.

• • •

A former patient asks me for a consultation. He is considering remarriage to his ex-wife. He makes the case. The remarriage will be good for the children, good for the pocketbook. He and his wife have lowered their expectations and increased their determination to make things work. This time, they will be less focused on their careers, devote more energy to family life.

I have a strong wish to show the man the other side of the coin. His wife is sending signals that she intends to resume the marriage on her own terms, which is to say with her rigid character traits intact. For his part, he seems as vulnerable as ever; he is the male equivalent of the girl Horney wrote about, who placed her toys in the street. This man is a former group therapist who now makes a good living as a business consultant. I suspect that his success is due to the extra assets he brings to the work, his intuitive understanding of how seemingly incompatible people can get along and his optimistic energy for the task of reconciliation. As regards his own marriage, I wonder whether he does not see possibilities I am missing; at the same time, I want to confront him forcefully with my misgivings.

When I ask where my strong wish arises, I realize that it is a counterbalance to his strong wish. The man is hell-bent on remarriage. Don't you see, he says, my life would be impoverished if I did not have the opportunity to be generous. He will try to mean everything to his wife. What's in it for him? He cannot tolerate loneliness, nor can he tolerate failure. Repair of the failed marriage is his present goal. He feels creative, justified, well employed when he is working on a relationship. And he mates for life.

Well, he must learn to tolerate loneliness and failure and separation. If he had more autonomy, he would make a better choice. That is one possible response. Or I might respect his quest and his genius. This marriage will be his chef d'oeuvre: getting the impossible to work, and doing it without further capacity for autonomy; using the force of his desperation to make it happen. For him, a strong attachment is an imperative: He is less defined by who he is in isolation than by what he can make of a marriage. He has a destiny, a teleology that decades of psychotherapy and centuries of philosophy ignore. This is who he is, a man with this goal.

The man is consulting me. I should make some effort to confront his selective inattention—to bring to the fore reality that is hard to bear. I mean, tell him that the remarriage is risky, that the wife is sending signals that he ignores at his peril, that he is driven by compulsive perfectionism. Might I also say something about my appreciation for the beauty—I doubt I would say comic beauty—in his quest? Perhaps I will hedge by suggesting he resume psychotherapy. But as I have tried to indicate, psychotherapy is not independent of hunches about how things ought to go.

To me, one of the most impressive works of feminist psychology is a study of five Victorian marriages, *Parallel Lives*, by Phyllis Rose. Rose attributes to John Stuart Mill and his muse, Harriet Taylor, the chief prerequisite for marital happiness, a vision of the relationship that both partners hold in common. Mill and Taylor agreed that theirs was a marriage of equals. This shared story Rose takes to be "totally at variance with the facts," which were "that a woman of strong and uncomplicated will dominated a guilt-ridden man." Regarding his famous writing on political philosophy, Mill claimed that the greater intellectual contribution was made by Taylor. Rose shows Mill obeying Taylor's wishes in every detail of their private life. A typical disagreement ends with Mill's addressing Taylor in Victorian feminine (and un-Emersonian) fashion: "As your feeling is so directly contrary, mine is wrong and I give it up entirely." Taylor and Mill thought they had broken the mold when in fact they were entirely in the mold, except that the man was playing the stereotypical woman's part and vice versa. Rose writes, "A female autocrat merely replaced the male." In Rose's version, the age defines a range of roles but not who will inhabit them.

Jean Baker Miller reminds us that we as a culture are confused about the value of connectedness. I take Miller's work less as a political account of the lives of women, though certainly it is that, than as a first effort at correcting a long line of autonomy-centered philosophy and psychology. When you consult me, we will need to take this correction and this confusion into account, whether you are a man or a woman. Perhaps your difficulty in deciding—stay or go—arises from your ambivalence about the culture's universal recipe for improvement, namely growth in autonomy.

Autonomy is far from being a unique marker of social worth. Not everyone would choose the most autonomous person as the ideal mate. There are attractions in relaxation, unselfconsciousness, even dependency. The Emersonian ideal undervalues traits associated with bonding. These include the capacity to see and elicit the best in others, the capacity to understand and experience matters just as the other does, the capacity to lose self in a relationship, the capacity to gain zest through mutuality. Nor does it seem true, as many theorists claim, that those who are most autonomous have the greatest skill at connection; the two capacities are often quite separate.

What to make of people, like my ex-patient bent on remarriage, to whom the end of a relationship is devastating? Faced with their stories, I hear the siren song of autonomy—never again must they be so intertwined with a lover. Worse than unprotected sex is unprotected commitment. These mutilated selves must be safeguarded. Simultaneously I think, what a talent! To participate so generously in the life of another. If one cannot have both in fullest measure—independence of mind and capacity for joining—must autonomy always take precedence?

Still, when you arrive for your consultation, I may feel moved to nudge you in the direction of autonomy. Other choices seem risky. Even—or especially—Jean Baker Miller can be read as saying so. In this culture, to rely on a capacity for generosity, mutuality, and intimacy is dangerous, unless those talents are accompanied by highly independent judgment and the ability to walk away. For all that I value high romance and even everyday emotional union, I usually begin by seeing matters in Bowen's terms.

Might those terms be modified? In considering your predicament, I may want to begin by using the framework of "differentiation of self."

But the content of that framework has changed slightly. Connectedness is a plausible ideal. Refusal to move toward separation may be a declaration of idiosyncrasy, and therefore a sort of differentiation. In a world that prizes individuation, refusing radical autonomy can be a statement of autonomous values—that's what is compelling about gimlet-eyed Fay, outraged at Ann Landers.

This slightly rebalanced definition of differentiation is inherent in my advice to Guy at the moment when Lena is set to move—the advice that he stay with her, and struggle to grow, by taking on Lena's style and values, asserting himself less, disregarding certain of his own inclinations, exchanging action for passivity, accepting limitations, disappearing. That posture looks a lot like dedifferentiation; it is the polar opposite of what Emerson proclaims to his loved ones. And its success is measured very largely in terms of whether the relationship grows in connection and mutuality. True, someone might frame the same posture, the one I recommend to Guy, as differentiation; it entails letting Lena be herself, it entails Guy's shedding the partly false role assigned him in the partnership. Embedded in that sort of advice, however it is couched, is a concept of differentiation that includes respect for connectedness, and other traditionally feminine values as well.

●　　●　　●

Even mid-century family therapy included voices that favored reveling in merger over securing autonomy. One doubter about the primacy of differentiation was Bowen's colleague and rival, Carl Whitaker. When I was in the process of looking afresh at my civil libertarian great-aunt, I ran into Whitaker, whom I knew from a year I had spent on his turf in Wisconsin.

Whitaker was a big, comfortable, lantern-jawed man with the air of (yes) the heartland about him. He was born on a farm, and he used to say that his first therapist was a cosset lamb. Whitaker was radical in his technique and determinedly conventional in his view of the family. For example, he thought it was insane to try to raise a child without two active parents. And at some level he did not believe in divorce, thought people stayed emotionally tied to whomever they had married. Whitaker liked a crowd in the room when he did therapy; typically he would refuse to start a session with a couple unless all their ex-spouses were present, as well, perhaps, as the couple's children and the couple's parents. He would not mind having the ex-spouses' parents, either. Whitaker had faith in the power of groups and mostly considered differentiation to be an illusion. For Whitaker, the question was less Should you leave? than Can you leave? His answer was, No. There is only self-in-relation, and the "relation" is all the relationships you have ever entered.

I ran into Whitaker and told him about the Bowen-inspired "work" I had inadvertently done in my own family, my taking distance from my great-aunt. Oh, Whitaker scoffed, Bowen makes too much fuss about autonomy. The thing to do with beloved aunts is to regress and let them spoil you.

It is easy enough to demonstrate the irrationality of intimate relationships, and of family life with its myths, its hidden lines of control, its futile repetitive behaviors and conflicts, its overtones, on occasion, of exploitation. It is easy enough to admire the capacity to sever the ties that bind. But autonomy is finally illusory—the seemingly autonomous are often those who demand the most support. Connection requires its own special talents and brings its own special benefits. To scrutinize beloved relations may buy freedom at a cost of oddness, awkwardness, a lingering sense of the mechanical and unnatural.

Though hardly a believer in self-reliance, Whitaker was Emersonian in his nonconformity and in his responsiveness to the command, "Leave your theory as Joseph his coat in the hand of the harlot, and flee." Whitaker had written an essay on the hindrance of theory in clinical practice, one that advises the family therapist to "learn to retreat and advance from every position you take" and reminds the therapist that the family has a right to find life inexplicable, and even the right to self-destruct.

The unexamined life is well worth living, Whitaker was telling me; there are illusions worth retaining. Take what is offered, he was saying. Let the drink taste of generosity. That is another reason that Lou asks for iced tea when we get together, to remind me that autonomy is often its own punishment and connection its own reward.

11

Imperatives

O<small>VER THE FAX</small> machine comes a cryptic note in Lou's scrawl. In its entirety, it reads: No maxims? No metaphors?

I have been sending Lou selected manuscript pages, ones about the authors we read together those many years ago: Sullivan, Bowen, Kaiser, Horney, Rogers, Miller, Whitaker, Freud. I take Lou to be asking whether that material can be said to comprise a book of advice at all.

Lou knows me well. Looking forward to my meeting with you, I have been playing with two sets of notes that look like more straightforward self-help: One is a list of precepts about differentiated behavior in couples ("Change yourself first," and so on); the other is a sort of "Everything I know about relationships I learned on the ski slopes." I have held off on those notes because when I recall advice I have valued in my own life, I see it has never turned on fixed maxims or canned metaphors.

I think, for instance, of three pieces of advice that affected my development as a writer. All were modest, colorless remarks, but each was tailored to my needs. I hold them as images of the sort of advice I would be content to give.

*   *   *

Toward the end of my college undergraduate career, I came to feel I had lost all ability to write. I had just finished a draft of my senior thesis, an extended argument about ideas implicit in the novels of Charles Dickens. Aspects of the essay were solid enough, but the body of the thing seemed lifeless and unrevivable. To my horror—there was a thrill in the thought, too—I learned that my tutor had passed the manuscript on to Lionel Trilling, the literary critic, who was spending a semester in town.

To me, Trilling was a cultural hero. His loves were my loves: Matthew Arnold, social justice pursued without fanaticism, Rousseau and Diderot, Freud, the Russian writers of moral novels. Trilling himself had produced a novel, *The Middle of the Journey,* that I admired and a short story, "Of This Time, of That Place," that captured tensions of the world I lived in. He had succeeded as a Jew in the most hostile corner of the Ivy League. He had sat amongst the New York intelligentsia when membership required the capacity to Say a Good Thing. But mostly, I adored the style of Trilling's essays. Trilling could make simple clarity act as epiphany. It was Trilling's sort of writing that mine did not match up to. I had only a talent for taking odd perspectives and elaborating them. I had fought this tendency in the senior thesis, had tried to say what was exactly right, but since I was not Trilling, that effort only stripped my work of any quirky particularity.

Presently, I was summoned to meet the great man. I tramped the streets of town like a defendant on whom a grave verdict is to be pronounced. That walk sticks in memory better than the encounter, which lasted perhaps ten minutes. I imagine five were spent defusing my anxiety. Trilling spoke respectfully of the original ideas he recognized in the thesis. Then he gave me a word of advice: I might try dividing the essay into three parts.

If someone were to say that any words of Trilling's would have hit me with the force of revelation, I could not demur. But the form of what Trilling did say was especially apt. By mentioning only technique, Trilling seemed to indicate that the content of my thesis was acceptable. Certainly there was enough content—too much to be encompassed by a single line of argument:

Targeted advice opens hidden stores of knowledge in the listener. I took Trilling's few words as an entire writing course. I heard him to say: Take care not to overwhelm the reader, give each idea the space it needs, postpone closure on the big issues while achieving it on the small. The message of the advice, that the reader need not be hurried along to an airtight conclusion but can be allowed rests and pauses, seemed to me yet broader: that the reader is not hostile, but rather someone who trusts the writer; that the writer can begin anywhere and head anywhere, so long as finally the journey makes sense; that it never hurts to hold something in reserve; that each phase of an essay has its own technical requirements, so that different styles and rhythms can be mixed in a single effort.

Each of those precepts might be listed in a how-to book about writing, but that sort of book would not have served me in the way that a sentence from Trilling did. There is nothing so helpful as a small, generous, corrective comment that applies to one's own performance. A judicious word translates self-defeating anxiety into focused, enthusiastic effort. For the eager and serious learner, a simple directive may generate a set of insights: Now I see what sort of game it is, what sort of effort is required, what sort of other I am confronting.

I can imagine advice about leaving that parallels Trilling's about revising the thesis. Why not divide the process of leaving (or recommitting) in three? In the right circumstances, that targeted advice might seem to have multiple meanings, causing the advisee to think about effecting change deliberately rather than catastrophically, raising the possibility that what seems an all-or-none choice can be a reversible process in which observations and decisions are made sequentially. Is the goal to astonish and hurt the partner, as an element in a tumultuous relationship, or to part in a way that assures a stable ending?

More generally, advice regarding interpersonal behavior—I am thinking now of the suggestion to a patient that she or he is overurgent in a love affair—may communicate a great deal concisely. There are implicit messages about the patient's worth, the role of tactics, the image and substance of the other, and so on. In shining light on a defined lesion, circumscribed advice indicates a larger sector of health. There is sometimes great kindness in targeted advice, as well as a key to action: Begin here.

*   *   *

In raising the question of structure, Trilling took me, however minimally, to be a writer. This tentative blessing is one apprentices seek out repeatedly. Toward the end of psychiatric residency, I found myself deep into the sort of writing project that young professionals undertake, an account of my training. An accomplished editor took an interest in my work, and the collaborative process went smoothly enough. Then in one of our consultations the editor took on the guru role. He said, without elaboration, that he was not sure this was the book I wanted to write.

That sentence, too, was well-targeted advice, like a glassworker's tap that shatters a pane along just the right planes. I heard the editor to be saying that writing should emerge from desire, that I had the right to my own desires, that a warping or an insufficiency of desire showed through the text of this memoir, that I must be the judge of my wants since even a discriminating editor might for reasons of his own publish what was not quite mine. I decided that the editor was right. I was not doing just what I wanted, was not taking writing to be the free act it should be. I put the memoir aside and wrote a novel. Neither that editor nor any other chose to publish it. But I had been done a favor. Similar advice might be usefully disturbing in the interpersonal arena: Yes, the relationship is succeeding, thanks to your efforts; but is it the one you want to construct?

About three years after accepting the editor's advice, I found myself walking with Lou. It was a cool spring day, but late enough in the season for the leaves to be out. We hurried from one patch of sunlight to the next. I was in a university post now, making adequate progress in a psychiatric career. As a writer, I had to my credit only the unpublished novel, the unfinished memoir, a handful of research monographs, and a couple of essays printed in a trade paper. I told Lou I had thoughts about leaving academics to write, though it seemed the idea was crazy. I knew Lou valued the university and believed that psychiatrists at any distance from it were likely to be ungrounded.

That's who does write, Lou said.

Who?

People who are crazy.

Lou was reminding me that writing is a different sort of career than academics. There are no promotions, there is no tenure. Writing draws on special parts of the self. You cannot do it if you are ashamed of your craziness or afraid of being judged crazy. The advice was delphic, simultaneously naming the risk and mitigating the fear. To say, all right, call it crazy, was Lou's way of asking me to consider where my passion abided. Within weeks, I was out of academics and back to plotting a book.

Here, too, I can imagine similar advice in a matter of the heart: Yes, you would be crazy to cast your lot with that wild, eccentric man or woman. This is not to say that you must back off; but if you are to continue, it should be on the basis of passion, with a willingness to disregard opinion and an ability to enjoy the unconventional. Some relationships are likely to be more demanding than others.

Everyone has memories of advice that, whether it was followed or not, and whether if followed it turned out for good or ill, opened up an aspect of the world. It is this sort of advice that convinced me that a language devoid of advice, if that is how therapeutic language is meant to be, is impoverished. For me, the three modest bits of advice shaped and sustained a career choice and a sense of self. The last two, to follow desire and tolerate craziness, allowed me to be an exception to rules I had obeyed about a psychiatric career.

That sort of advice strikes me as diametrically opposite to most published self-help. To be sure, I can imagine a list that includes items like "If an essay seems at a dead end, try dividing it into parts," "Write only what you want to write," and "Trust your irrational leanings." In a lucky case, these precepts might serve one or another reader. As often, they would miss the mark, encouraging obsessionality in the writer whose essays are already too neatly framed or sloppiness in the writer who is already all over the place.

Like the Prozac-responsive depressed patient, the advisee has hidden competencies. Under the guise of a prescription of action, tailored advice opens the bundle of precepts a person already carries within. It creates a moment of engagement, by which I mean both exposure to a distinctive external perspective and elaboration of perspectives already owned. What begins perhaps as a narrow technical comment becomes the occasion for a dialectic and the synthesis of a novel point of view.

General and public advice might sometimes have this effect. "Go west, young man, and grow up with the country" taps into a collection of beliefs about independence, pioneering, national destiny, stages of life, and so forth, and I can imagine a person who is fruitfully disturbed, rather than affirmed in his prejudices, by the command. But I suspect that fixed precepts mostly do not enrich in that way, because they contain no assessment of the situation at hand—are you the sort of young man who can survive on the frontier, or one who already harbors too many romantic notions? When I read a self-help precept, invariably I think that the opposite advice might be equally apt, for someone.

More crucially, lists of precepts don't work like targeted advice because lists tend inherently to contain constraining messages. Unless carefully crafted, the list by its very existence implies the discoverability of right and wrong methods. It seems to say that complex matters are knowable, that process leads to foreseeable results. It implies a thin and predictable world, whereas the sort of advice that has mattered to me— disjoin arguments, monitor desires, respect craziness—bespeaks a quite tentative optimism, the optimism of the quest whose outcome is finally unknowable.

Such moments cannot be mimicked reliably in the encounter between unknown reader and the written page. Perhaps they most often arise in response to fiction, where a reader enters deeply enough into a creative world for useful strangeness to emerge. How often will a list of precepts or an extended metaphor surprise in this way?

I call up my list from the computer's memory. Taken in isolation, the precepts are conventional, but I have just been writing about Bowen's journey home and Emerson's response to his son's death. Perhaps in that context—surrounded by enough strangeness—these ordinary directives can take on qualities I value, of fleshing out a perspective and of being simultaneously stated and undermined:

Where you are is probably not far from where you ought to be. This is the principle of matched differentiation, which must be hedged to take account of capacities the culture undervalues, like skill at connection.

Still, it is a fair starting point, and it has useful corollaries: *Whom you have chosen speaks to who you are.* And: *There are limits to how different things will be if you exchange this partner for another.*

Focus on differentiation. Stand back from your needs and demands. Do you respect your partner's independence? This is a matter about which people deceive themselves. Do you respect your own feelings and values, do you maintain a sense of self? I might add: Do you offer, and elicit, the intimate give-and-take that Miller calls "mutuality"? Are you skilled at enhancing "levels of complexity, structure, and articulation within the context of human bonds?" Since real change is change in level of self, the logical target of change is your own level of differentiation—not change in partner.

Differentiation occurs within relationships. Especially if you are someone who tends to move from one relationship to another, change entails staying. It is the complexity, the impossibility, the dullness or painfulness of the current imperfect relationship that provides the context for change.

Change enough. If your efforts are to bear fruit in your current relationship, the degree of change must be marked and persistent. Remember with what tenacity Bowen worked within his family of origin. You might start with an achievable goal: Can you begin to enjoy what you disdain in your partner—in the way that Guy might begin to relax into an overstuffed sofa? For some people, progress might have a different direction: Can you moderate your tendency to give compulsively?

Change yourself first. Change means change in you—in the role you assume in the relationship—not insistence that the other change. Luckily. Because you are the person whom you are best suited to change. And because in applying this precept the frequent complaint, that your partner just will not change, disappears as an impediment to movement.

Expect discomfort. Your new posture need not feel natural or comfortable. It may need to be exaggerated. Though it must feel right in this sense: It should be chosen freely, from within, without compulsion.

Expect a response. Change entails tolerating the possibility that the other will also change or even leave. Indeed, persistence means holding constant while the other turns disturbingly reasonable or decamps.

Be self-centered. The other may benefit from your efforts at self-differentiation—may respond by himself or herself moving toward further differentiation. But effort in the relationship according to this model entails investment in your own self, just as in laissez-faire capitalism the overall system is said to work best if each actor tries to maximize his own gain. This selfishness is what is meant by being fair to the other, giving the relationship a chance.

Imagining you reading these precepts, I suspect you find them familiar. You know the rules. (You know alternative rules as well, that tell you never to tolerate discomfort in a relationship—to keep your bags packed at all times.) Writing down familiar rules has one important function—it allows them to be examined. Do you want to own them? You will note the list's limitations. It undervalues passion, intimacy, letting things alone. It directs you away from a posture you may enjoy, subordinating your personal interests to those of the relationship. You may find the list overly external, insufficiently responsive to what is special about your circumstances. It includes norms from which you wish to be exempted.

That sense of the list's insufficiency I take as welcome. I like imagining that when someone says the obvious—for example, that the way to make a relationship work is to be yourself—you find the statement a bit peculiar, recalling what connivance might be required for a person to get even a taste of autonomy. You are struck by how strangely the journey relates to the destination, how odd it is that autonomy should be held forth as the key to successful partnership. You find it unsettling that relationships, those havens for I-Thou in a world of I-It, should be seen first as greenhouses for individual growth. After all, the feeling you want to recapture in your relationship, if you are to stay, is the blind comfort or intimate arousal that makes affairs of the heart so precious.

Another problem with maxims is that it is not always clear how to take them. The commonplaces on my list apply only to certain sorts of relationships, like those of Guy and Lena, Iris and Randall, Jonnie and Adam, Asa and Nikki. There are compelling reasons to stay and go, emotional reasons, inherent in the relationship. The decision is not constrained by external factors, such as dramatic money troubles or young children or a need to impress the electorate. That is, the relationship can safely be considered simply as a relationship. And neither partner is frankly abusive, both are fundamentally decent, easy enough to love. Your problem may be knowing whether your relationship falls into that set. It is easy to fool oneself about questions of abuse or external constraint—is yours really a special problem, or are you kidding yourself?

Even if you take the precepts to apply, there is the question of what they mean. Like Guy, or like the overurgent undergraduate, you may want to say that you have changed a good deal and your partner did not respond at all. What the list leaves unclear is the sort of question that matters most, What constitutes adequate change?

I have been fiddling with an extended metaphor to address my sense of how much change is enough:

Imagine that you are a plateaued skier trying to learn how to use skis the way they are meant to be used, with an element of grace. You are standing atop an intermediate trail which you have just skied almost, but not quite, the way the instructor asked you to. What holds you back? The instructor says it is fear. You protest. You have skied steeper slopes than this one, and under worse conditions, and at higher speeds. And you have skied them in the most dangerous way, with bad technique. Now you are being asked to ski a modest slope with good technique. You will admit to being uncoordinated. But how can you be said to be afraid?

The misunderstanding concerns the object of your fear. You are not afraid of steep slopes, you are afraid of skiing them. You have perfected a way of getting down without really skiing. You clench your thigh muscles and dig in your edges to give yourself a moment-to-moment sensation of control, when true control requires trust in the shape of the ski and of the turn. You hold your weight "back"—back on the tails of your skis and back toward the slope of the mountain. Instructors call this "being in the back seat." What holds you in the back seat is intimate bodily fear.

I hope that you hear in this set of images a vague correspondence with your role in your troubled relationship. You are not afraid of your partner so long as you retain the right to handle the relationship all wrong. You may send messages about your lack of commitment, for example, by flirting vigorously with any new person who comes your

way. Or, on the contrary, you may assume a position of extreme dependency when what you fear is demanding that you be treated with
respect. You are willing to make sacrifices when what is called for is self-
assertion or to assert yourself when what is called for is self-sacrifice. You
will make all sorts of accommodations to the relationship, so long as
they are not useful ones. Or you will, like the undergraduate who now
waits slightly longer to phone, or like Guy with Lena, make appropriate
accommodations but tentatively and inconsistently.

I notice that in her recent and funny book *Fear of Fifty,* Erica Jong
asks what her analyst means by saying that Jong is afraid of marriage.
After all, Jong had three marriages, to that point in the narrative, so she
must not be afraid of marrying; and the marriages had horrible results,
so she is justified in being leery. I take the analyst possibly to mean what
a ski instructor means in saying that you are afraid of skiing, even
though you often ski steep slopes; you are afraid of skiing them in a way
that is committed and demanding and appropriately trusting. Yes, terrible things may happen to skiers, but it is not apposite fears that are at
issue. Though you are not afraid of slopes, or are only reasonably afraid
of injury, you have an intimate fear concerning loss of control—in a way
that a person might not avoid men or weddings, and might also have
many well-justified apprehensions, but might still be irrationally afraid
of full participation in a marriage. I take fear of skiing to resemble Jong's
own early metaphor, fear of flying, though the issue may also be fear of
standing quietly still.

The problem with skiing beyond the intermediate level is that,
except for those to whom balance comes naturally, it requires the simultaneous application of disparate skills. Balance demands adjustments in
edging, pressuring, alignment, angulation, and so on. The skier needs to
get all of them right. If you do most of what the instructor asks but stick
your butt out to hold your weight back, all your changes in stance will
be for naught. The skis will squirt forward, and you will try to skid and
brake. You will not feel what it is to ski.

Let us say that you add a skill: You set your hands in the right spot.
Nothing much happens. Adding a single skill does not improve performance. Even adding three or four new skills has no effect. Now you are
doing a number of things that feel unnatural and even dangerous, and

you are skiing as badly as ever. You may need to do eight or ten things better, and only then will your performance change in any way that you notice. Ski instructors speak of the eighty-twenty rule. The first eighty percent of change in form results in a twenty percent change in performance. It is the last twenty percent of correction that gives what you want, the great leap forward, the eighty percent gain. As one ski manual puts it: "If you are way in the back seat, and you move up a little in the back seat, *you are still in the back seat.*"

Also: To practice a new stance at all, you must exaggerate. You have to attempt twice what you think is necessary in order to do half. Your fearful brain is telling you that you are far forward when you are still far back. And then there is the problem of habit; each ineffectual self-protective maneuver has been overlearned, so that breaking out of the plateau involves unlearning.

Similar considerations apply to the risk sport you care about, extended intimacy. There are naturals at intimacy, of course, just as there are natural athletes. (And sometimes naturals crash. That may have been the therapist's assessment of Connie, in Lou's story "You Will Be Fine . . ."; Connie had skills aplenty and just needed to resume exercising them.) There are those who are content to do the thing badly, and those who are content not to do it at all. You are floundering and you are not content to flounder, which is why you are going outside the relationship, to ask whether it is time to leave. Assessing whether you should leave may require assessing whether you have tried to stay. For you, trying to stay will entail a number of changes in posture. You ought not to expect a response until you have changed substantially—until you are out of the back seat.

In the end, though, I am as wary of metaphors as I am of lists. If I am lucky, you will know about the dynamic equilibrium inherent in good skiing, and you will see just how to apply that sort of constant minor adjustment to your stance in the relationship. But perhaps you associate ski lessons with graded exercises, to be practiced in invariant sequence, one size fits all. Or for you skiing is self-indulgent, so that this metaphor seems to go beyond even the Bowen story in celebrating the individual.

Extended metaphors meet their limitations rapidly. To say that skiing and marriage both entail risk is at once apt and misleading. The risks
are of quite different sorts, as are the attendant obligations. And a
metaphor, however attractive, can just be wrong. The physical laws that
govern skiing differ from the psychic laws, if they can be called laws,
that govern relationships. Perhaps a small and symbolic change in your
behavior—the sort of change that would avail you nothing as a struggling intermediate skier—will, at home, elicit a small and symbolic
response from your partner, one that satisfies you deeply.

Whatever the attraction of maxims and metaphors, both finally are
too distant from my own discipline, which relies on immediate
responses to the person before me. I prefer the path Lou set me on at the
beginning, constructing you, and in the process defining a perspective
through overlapping stories. The result will not always be crisp, but my
sense is that the apt perspective must have a soft focus. Certainty—I
have in mind Freud's certainty—is too often destructive. So I will set
Lou's wry fax aside and continue to conjure you. It occurs to me that
you may be at an impasse that is not at all rare. You are in the sort of
relationship I call two-peas-in-a-pod. Male and female, I will name you
Francis and Frances. Your concerns are so similar that I can imagine
either of you showing up for a consultation.

12

Like As

Y OU ARE IN YOUR middle thirties, married six years. Elements of a true partnership are absent from your relationship. Since it has not been decided who gets to read the front section first, you have ordered a second copy of the morning paper. You have no joint bank accounts. Disagreements about timing have led you to postpone parenthood. And then there are the business trips.

Traveling, you meet colleagues who enthrall you, colleagues who embody the virtues your spouse lacks. Emotional generosity, where Francis is implacably just and measured; though sometimes it is reason where he is merely rigid. Levelheadedness, where Frances is frivolous; though sometimes it is sweetness where she is tough and unbending. You enter into intense platonic affairs. Even when these affairs extend beyond the platonic, they do not end the marriage. But they lead to further dissatisfaction and further acrimony. Your friends know none of this. From the outside, things look fine.

It is time to decide whether to have a child. That or divorce, since you want children. It seems unfair to start a family before answering certain basic questions. Is family life possible with one another? Is Francis trustworthy? Is Frances? Is this a family in which a child can grow up happy?

If you were to come for advice, you would tell me a story of frustration, doubt, mistakes made.

Before you met Francis, you dated warm and empathic men, modern men, men you could talk with. Although each disappointed you in his own way. One took drugs. Another failed at jobs and leaned on you financially. One lost his keys continually and called you out of work to rescue him. These men knew how to relate to you, but they had no sense of how to navigate life. When you met Francis, you knew you would marry him. In contrast to the others, he was competent. At the same time, he took your viewpoint into account, talked issues through at length. He was, you knew, a little less empathic—more mechanical in his considerateness—than the men you were used to. From the start you were aware in yourself of a whisper of concern not quite silenced by the thrill you felt in the face of his decided masculinity.

That whisper is now clearly audible. Francis's insistence on control has loomed ever larger as the years pass. He decides how the drawers in the living room desk must be arranged, how bills and correspondence must be filed. He will not attend gatherings with people he considers frivolous; go alone if you must. He hates it when you waste money, even if the money is yours. He rants if you fail to turn out the lights. Or if you leave the caps off soda bottles.

You have been in psychotherapy over your response to Francis. You know that his daily gestures arouse disproportionate fear in you, fear that he will be like your father, who dominated your mother mercilessly. You take after your father, and there is no man on earth who will turn you into your mother. Although sometimes you suspect she enjoyed her life—her marriage—more than you do yours. Anyway, when Francis steps on your toe, you repeat your mantra (the identical one supplied by three different therapists): He's not my father. The reminder helps for a minute, then all hell breaks loose. Often you wish you had not married Francis.

*   *

If you were to come for advice you would tell me a story of frustration, doubt, mistakes made.

Before you met Frances, you dated women who were reasonable, predictable, good chums. The sorts of women Henry Higgins longs for when he wonders "Why Can't a Woman Be More Like a Man?" You avoided anyone impulsive, anyone who played the scatterbrain and got what she needed through cuteness. It took you some years to see this pattern, since on the surface you liked a variety of women. Women with sultry voices, women with shy laughs. But in each case, you knew that the person beneath was sober and responsible, a trustworthy negotiating partner. Or else you left in a hurry. You were not going to subject yourself to the whims of a hysteric like your mother. In time, each girlfriend came to bore you. You prided yourself on the maturity of your separations. Romance would cede place to friendship. In your heart you knew that this success was due to your caution; you chose unimpassioned women and then threw cold water on whatever sparks you ignited in them.

Frances was different. Businesslike most of the time, but prone to tease, mock, flirt. Coquettish, demanding. She hurt you from the start, but you became obsessed with winning her. Now you cannot stand her impulsivity and her spending habits. You are afraid she will bleed you dry with womanly "needs" for frills, as your mother did your father. You feel helpless when Frances throws money away on gewgaws, or on expensive vacations that end in rage and tears. She resists any effort you make at rationalizing the domestic routine. You see future motherhood as making her only more self-indulgent. At the same time, it is her coldness that hurts you most. The women you turn to outside the marriage are at once more rational and more adoring. You are often ready to leave the marriage. At the same time, you know that your objections are petty. Frances pays her own freight. You like what she brings to the household. You have never loved anyone as, on good days, you love her.

The evening before the visit to my office, you have a blowup over nothing.

It is the night of your repertory theater subscription. You have prepared a thoughtful early dinner for Frances, a pasta dish you ate on your honeymoon. She acknowledges your effort but appears distracted. After dinner, you look in the desk drawer where you keep important slips of paper. The theater tickets are nowhere to be found. You notice that receipts from Frances's charge account at a clothing boutique have been stuffed in haphazardly.

You are annoyed at Frances for her prodigality and, worse, her slovenliness. You yell at her, she yells back at you. Frances has a hissy fit and marches out the door. You collect yourself and head to the theater, where you meet the friends with whom you share a subscription. You claim your seat without trouble and explain Frances's absence, but you find yourself unable to focus on the first act. At intermission you down two quick drinks and sidle up to a friend's wife; you have always considered her stiff, but tonight her reasonableness entrances you. You return home glum in the certainty that relations will be icy for days. To your surprise, you find yourself in tears before Frances, and she before you. The evening ends in not entirely unexpected fashion, with tender lovemaking.

Or: It is the night of your repertory theater subscription. For once Francis has bothered to give some thought to dinner. It annoys you that he wants credit for doing rarely what he should do regularly. He leaves the table with that martyr's face on, and then to top it all he has misplaced the tickets.

Predictably, he translates his frustration into an assault on you. You tolerate his fit of pique until he crosses the line and attacks your sense of reality. For a second you consider the possibility that you did misplace the tickets. Then you fly into a rage: This is just what men do, what your father did to your mother. Men appropriate reality. When Francis locks the desk drawer and pockets the key, he has gone too far. No man can control a woman in this way. You collect yourself, storm out the door, and head for a bar that an understanding co-worker frequents. He is not there tonight, so you return home and jimmy open the desk, crushing a few strips of veneer in the process. You calm yourself by going over business reports while in bed, but you are in despair over the marriage. Later, you catch yourself missing Francis's presence, are moved when his foolish, apologetic face peers round the door frame.

* * *

So, Frances or Francis, should you stay?

Let me begin by saying that I see the charm in your marriage. I like the way your childishness is laid out before us. I like the way that you both stick to your guns, and the way that you forgive each other substantial trespasses. As I listen, one measure I rely on is which impulse I am trying to control, smiling or tearing up. I find myself suppressing a smile. I mention the appeal of your squabbling also to diffuse your anxiety. Because I think the first element in your question "Should I leave?" is the couple equivalent of the plaint that pervades individual psychotherapy, "Am I crazy?" You want to know how bad things are.

I've seen much worse. You may have grown up in worse, and that standard is an important one, and exacting enough: to make your own marriage more humane than your parents'. It does seem, given your success in other areas, and given your warmth and vibrancy as you sit before me, that you might aim yet higher. Your marriage is like a promising graduate student who can never quite finish the thesis; its strong point is potential. The question is whether you are likely to let that potential develop.

Rather than prognosticate, let me tell you what I see, because I do have a single strong impression. You have pulled off the ultimate in matching. You have married your twin, your alter ego. Whichever of you is in front of me, I will say the same thing. I see two people each of whom mistrusts the stereotypical excesses of the opposite sex and each of whom avoids in the self the stereotypical excesses of the same sex. The two of you are, in terms of a traditional romantic culture, unisex—both orderly, driven, verbal, and empathic, appreciative of baseball, musical theater, domestic routine, and long walks in the fall woods.

And you are both focused on small differences. The least expression of a traditionally gender-related trait—Francis's taking the upper hand in a negotiation, Frances's subtle display of disorganization—arouses terror and rage in the partner. You bring to mind the problem of resonance in physics, where interacting systems of closely matched frequency give rise to wider oscillations and less self-correction than systems that are further out of sync.

Here's what's worrisome: You are barely married. You share little, you take your problems outside. You turn, perhaps not seriously, but still it is a pattern, to drink. You have been told, in therapy and by friends, that you have trouble tolerating intimacy and that the intolerance of intimacy is connected with the confusion of your spouse with a parent. To these I will add a third platitude. Your marriage is sustained by your arguments.

Anger is the lowest form of emotion, the one that remains when the capacity to tolerate love or even anxiety and depression disappears. Anger is a form of closeness. But for you, there is another element. Anger dampens fear: You have survived the worst a man, or a woman, can do; you are still intact. And anger is familiar, an affect that permeated the home you grew up in.

Reassured by anger, you can tolerate greater intimacy. (Self-pity plays a similar distance-modulating role. The sequence is approach, rejection, the comfortable solitude afforded by the feeling of having been wronged, and, once thus replenished, the security to approach again.) You tolerate even infidelity, knowing that your relationship is primary, the philandering is only one more way of modulating distance in the marriage. But if security cannot be assured in other ways, you will always require further arguments and betrayals. Of course, these platitudes apply only in a minor degree. You are at the mild end of the spectrum of emotionally unconsummated marriages. I have seen a couple sustained by frequent knife-throwing, a more concrete method for modulating distance.

None of this answers the question you have posed. Given your wish to have children soon, isn't it time to end this charade?

In anticipating my consultation with a seeker of advice, I have tried for the most part to avoid scenarios that involve children at home, because my opinion would turn more on their needs than on those of the parent. Research on the effects of divorce has made therapists less likely than they once were to predict that ending a difficult marriage will help children; given my own thoughts about spousal matching, I tend to worry that divorce and remarriage will provide a child with four underdeveloped parents instead of two. Altogether, consideration of children's welfare would make it too easy for me not to face my advisee. But your wish to have children is a different issue. It serves to lend urgency and perhaps to invalidate the contention that you should stay in this relationship, if for no other reason, to learn how to conduct yourself better in the next one. If you are going to judge that this relationship is hopeless, you will want to make that decision now and move on. So that the use of the relationship as a workshop or greenhouse—a place to grow—must be set aside.

Of course, the matter is not that simple. The image of a child in the house affects any take on this relationship. A key element in parenting, so we think nowadays, is allowing the child to be who he or she is. That talent for acceptance seems absent in this marriage. You require that the other be exactly like you. This marriage would not be a bad place to begin to acquire a talent for acceptance.

Your apprehensions are framed by the gender stereotypes that are the lingua franca of our social intercourse. You cannot tolerate Francis's attempts to make his environment neat and predictable because to you they are typically male efforts to expropriate reality. Or you cannot tolerate Frances's disorganization because to you a woman's messy desk drawer presages Circe-like seductiveness or attacks of the vapors—women's stratagems for controlling men. You fear stereotypical behavior.

The good news is that you have married someone who has few of the shortcomings you associate with his or her gender. Most of the time, Francis is sharing and nurturant. Most of the time, Frances is orderly and methodical. No need to worry. You won't be overwhelmed.

And here is the really good news: In a partner, you secretly enjoy the classical qualities of the other sex—in moderation. You married someone who was appealing precisely because of hints of gender-associated strengths that your earlier dates lacked. Contrary to what your therapist has told you, Frances is your mother. Or Francis is your father. I mean, Frances has a touch of your mother's flair. She makes life interesting. Francis has something of your father's decisiveness. He creates a world about him.

Understandably, you shy away from people who embody your mother's or father's characteristic flaws. In choosing a partner who shows hints of flair—or determination—you fear you have done something intensely neurotic. To the contrary, I see the choice as optimistic, a sign of self-confidence.

The simplistic way to deal with an intrusive parent is obliteration—creating a rigid triangle comprising you, your parent, and a spouse who is your parent's polar opposite. In choosing just the partner you have chosen, you have had the courage to acknowledge that, despite the excesses you witnessed in childhood, you know there is pleasure to be found in a spouse who is stylish—or bold. You are more flexible for trying to tolerate and even enjoy your parent's traits. You have skills in this area: You know how to handle this sort of person, really you do. You will fare better now than you did in childhood, and better than your same-sex parent did.

Often, exasperation with the opposite sex contains an element of envy. Women have it easy; all they have to do is be cute, and the world rushes to serve them. Men have it easy; the world lets them grab what they want without compunction. Isn't this a form of victory: when you have envied something for years, not to obliterate it but to enjoy it in your own life? Wouldn't it be a fine working out of your story for you to enjoy a (slightly) flamboyant wife or a (slightly) decisive husband? This sort of resolution implies a change in your own self, a growth in willingness to be "taken advantage of" (again, slightly) in the way that the victimized member of your parents' marriage was; there might be pleasure in that change, a relaxed feeling of diminished vigilance. Perhaps accommodating will be more satisfying than leaving a demanding mate and finding a dull one.

I don't want to gloss over the challenge your marriage poses. No one can be enthusiastic about adding children to your small family as it stands now. My optimism has less to do with your current behavior than my assessment of where the problem lies. It resides within you. The problem is not your choice; the problem is how you live with that choice.

So the answer, stay or leave, turns on whether you think you can change. You say you have already tried, to no effect. The problem is that you are in a situation where small, inconsistent efforts make matters worse. They are read as feminine wiles—or further proof that men just don't get it.

There are, it seems to me, two sorts of change that would help your marriage: for you to be less afraid of the other sex, and for you to be less provocative, in terms of unnecessarily doing the very things that frighten your partner. If we are lucky, these two will be the same: You are the sort of person who when he feels more confident becomes less domineering; or you are the sort of person who when she feels more secure appears less flighty. But how can you feel secure when your spouse is always provocative? Your spouse feels the same way.

What does it mean to be less provocative? The key is consistency. It is not enough to be mostly nice and sometimes unnerving, or nice about the soda caps and vicious about the bills. That pattern is precisely the one your spouse fears, the one your spouse grew up with—reconciliations and betrayals. The poet and animal trainer Vicki Hearne has written about a common mistake people make with crazy horses. These horses fear niceness because early in their lives a human who at first seemed nice abused them. To approach such horses with niceness is to risk serious injury. Retraining begins with the assumption of a posture of utter reliability.

Your spouse is not crazy, and you are not engaged in retraining anyone but yourself. But it may be true that your initial efforts at reconciliation will arouse suspicion. If you then become upset, and especially if you react to rejection with provocation, you will worsen your predicament. You will have proved to your spouse that your niceness is the precursor to an attack and to yourself that effort does not avail.

I think of the list of maxims: You are not far from where you ought to be. Your choice says much about you. Change enough. Change yourself. Use the relationship as a place in which to grow. Expect discomfort.

You are stuck because of a series of automatic responses. A misplaced ticket, or the accusation that you misplaced it, can cause you to turn into a parody of yourself. You are hyperrational and outraged, the one who will not be pushed around. That retreat into a familiar family role is an automatism, a constrained expression of self to which you regress when challenged. It bespeaks lack of differentiation. To be able to experience your spouse without retreating, to admire what once you criticized, would constitute growth in differentiation of self.

Moving toward is not the same as obeying. The goal is not to be the person your spouse hoped you would be. That sort of servitude is a common, and dangerous, solution to marital discord. The task is not accommodating so much as appreciating—appreciating what you already observe, what you have always known to be true of your spouse—which I take to be the best assurance that you will not lapse into self-righteous exasperation. You don't have to compromise your values.

Another way to put the matter: It is time for commitment—commitment to the change you are attempting. It may be helpful to think of what "commitment" means in ski instruction. Skiing is done with almost all the weight on one ski at a time: commitment to the outside ski. If you are committed to the outside ski, you should be able to lift the inside ski off the snow at any point. It has no weight on it. Another test is, Can you jump from the weighted leg at any point in the turn? There are similar tests of commitment to your efforts in the marriage. To be committed is to be able to find the receipts a mess and be perfectly fine—still aware of Frances in all her aspects. Or, when Francis asks where the tickets are, not to feel that all the air has been sucked out of the room. Though perhaps, as in skiing, it is better to begin somewhere less challenging, to "drop back a level." Could you look at an uncapped soda bottle, or cap one, without feeling violated?

You are trying to build a "bombproof" stance. I am referring to your attitude toward your spouse. The essence of differentiation in a peas-in-a-pod marriage is the capacity to allow the other to be different, and to be unselfconsciously different yourself. (A suggestion often given by a colleague who counsels gay women is: Stop wearing your partner's clothes—and stop worrying when she fails to wear yours.) You might manage to convince yourself that your spouse's self-indulgence is attractive. You feel large and important—like you've bagged big game—when Frances plans a sybaritic weekend or when Francis helps you beg off an unpromising dinner invitation. The bombproof stance relates to enjoying what you have resented, taking pride in what you used to label Frances's hysteria or Francis's machismo. I'm asking you to remember what charmed and excited you in the first place.

This change in stance should lead to a change in the other. Beyond the "upward" pressure inherent in differentiation, there is this: The more you enjoy the other, the less the other has to defend or exaggerate the parts of the self you fear. Perhaps Frances, once you begin to appreciate her relaxed style, will back off from it, and she will neaten up. Perhaps Francis, once you approve of his organizing the household in small ways, will find the exercise tedious, and he will cede control. As you begin to enjoy the other's difference, it may diminish; and then a new negotiation will need to begin. Or perhaps the gender-related roles will become more fully elaborated. You will smile at Frances's spontaneity, and she will become more playful and heedless. Francis, under your tolerant gaze, will become yet more self-assured. You will enjoy the other's gender differentiation. Or the movement may be lateral, in some direction not obviously related to gender.

What if you can't change? On the way home, you prepare yourself. But when you look at the uncapped soda bottle, you think that Frances has only contempt for you. She is, to use Graham Greene's metaphor, like Brighton Rock candy, the same all the way through, inconsiderate and wasteful and empty-headed. And vicious. Really, she is vicious, knowing how uncomfortable you are with incompetent women, not to do the one thing you ask of her. And then you catch yourself—surely you will catch yourself, if you are well prepared—and you will think, we are talking about flavored water; you must smile at that. The uncapped soda is an aspect of what you have always loved in her, a charming distractibility. That reframing might help, if it occurs. But you may not have those counterbalancing thoughts, or, even with them, you may find you cannot get past the soda. Your efforts have failed at this easiest level. You have discovered a self-limitation you cannot transcend. To give the experience a too-grand description, you have glimpsed your existential dread.

These easy challenges can be devastating. I think of a couple, both popular and dedicated schoolteachers, who came to me when their marriage was on its last legs. The wife was the more conventional of the two. The husband carried with him into suburban life some of the shambling posture of his 1960s hippie days. He professed to be giving and, by external standards, he was—available and physically affectionate. But the wife found him stubborn. His generosity did not extend to what she wanted: predictability, conventional social behavior, willingness to include her in decisions. I asked whether we could not reopen negotiation around a simple and concrete issue.

The wife said, yes, she wanted for her husband once to come down on a Sunday morning and fix her blueberry pancakes, the way some men do. Perhaps she knew just why this suggestion was impossible; perhaps she knew only that it was. In the event, she demonstrated his rigidity. I asked the husband whether the request seemed reasonable. Though he would not elaborate, he said that the task turned him off, seemed to make him the sort of husband he was not. The very question made him feel I was ganging up on him, that I did not understand how he detested the stereotyped bourgeois gender role and any hint of servitude. Still, he said he would do what she asked.

He did not, and presently the wife moved out, and in with a more conventional, though perhaps equally difficult man. There were other reasons for the breakup, the reasons that had led them to seek help in the first place. But the clarity of the pancakes had played a part. I ran into the husband years later, and he said that not flipping those flapjacks was the best decision he ever made.

I tell this story to highlight the power of insubstantial acts fraught with emotional power—Adam's failed application for club membership, Lena's interior decorating, Frances's uncapped bottles. To observe one's incapacities in the face of these trivial matters is to confront one's boundedness. Sometimes I think that Bowen's method, displacing the effort back a generation, toward one's parents, shows a special genius. Hard though that exercise is, it may be easier than dealing here and now with flapjacks.

If you cannot find a way to reframe what the soda bottle says and to hold fast to that reframing, probably you will leave. But you will leave focused on limitations in yourself. People who leave that way may fare well, either alone or with another partner. My guess regarding the soda bottle problem is that once you see it not as a matter of compromising your values but of confronting your fears (of endlessly disorganized women, of endlessly controlling men), you might choose to stay and soldier on.

* * *

What if you change and the other does not reciprocate? As you reframe Francis's flaws, he takes ever more space, a territorial imperialist pushing on every front; or Frances sees your admiration as permission for extravagance. If you have made a decided adjustment in your stance, you may choose to stay and negotiate further. More likely, you will leave, because the relationship has lost its promise. A promising relationship is one in which, when you change enough, a reciprocal response occurs.

If you leave, you will leave with a new skill. A man or woman with new skills—differentiation of self, flexibility of perspective—should be better off. I suspect that you will, if this is the matter we are discussing, have better luck with future relationships. A psychologist friend of mine once reviewed his clinical experience with single men and women, with an eye to the question of luck; his conclusion was that luck is shorthand for clear-sightedness or learning from experience. Those who turned down opportunities to repeat their mistakes got lucky. Learning from experience—not being drawn to familiar impasses—is another way of characterizing growth in self-differentiation. A character in Joyce Carol Oates's novel *What I Lived For* says, "Courage *is* luck, sweetheart." Along the same lines, I would say that differentiation is luck.

My belief in that luck explains something about the approach I prefer for you. Perhaps you have been in a couple therapy that encourages you to "invest in the relationship." But people can invest too much and then stay to guard the investment, ignoring the gambling and investing principle that "money in the pot is the pot's money." Since you begin by wondering whether to leave—since you question whether the relationship is viable—I would want any investment you make to be one you can take with you. Investing in the relationship can be empowering to the extent that it teaches you how to refine your skills at connection. Or you might prefer, in the context of the relationship, to focus on autonomy. If I suggest you stay, I will want that staying to entail investment that enhances your luck.

I doubt you will need that sort of luck. Your efforts should find a response. Your occasional philandering, your resort now and then to an extra drink—these say more about limitations in your ability to tolerate closeness or deal with frustration than they do about the suitability of your marriage. You have helped create a marriage that is just at the limits of your social abilities, always a hopeful sign. And you are well matched with your spouse, in terms of differentiation of self, whether that phrase refers to autonomy or connection. Francis or Frances is the spouse you would want if only you could tolerate a bit of difference.

What if yours were not a peas-in-a-pod marriage but the other sort, the opposites-attract, division-of-psychic-labor, we-two-make-one-whole-person marriage? They exist, the sitcom marriages between insensitive, competent husbands and attuned, impractical wives. Would the assumptions I bring to the discussion be different? There, the priority might be less tolerating the other than allowing the self to resemble the other, reclaiming potential that has been denied.

In any relationship, anxiety or conflict tends to inspire a retreat to temperament—the slightly passive one becomes entirely passive, the active entirely active. Differentiation is often a move against the grain, against temperament, toward a greater repertory of responses. For the habitually giving and compliant, differentiation entails withholding; for the habitually passive and underengaged, taking the initiative. This sort of move seems especially appropriate—self-enhancing—in a culture that believes temperament is not so much an expression of unconscious fantasy as a matter of genetic happenstance; to go against temperament is not betrayal of carefully honed self. Appreciation of others' temperaments and one's own suppressed traits is not self-abnegation but an expansion of possibility. The trick is to act on the basis of the examination and transformation of needs, as an expression of hope, not surrender. These difficult efforts sometimes pay large dividends—allow the seemingly natural to emerge in the relationship.

In the end, the urgency of the ticking biological clock does little to alter what I might say to you in a brief consultation. Is there nothing at all I could learn about either of you that would cause me to advise you differently? Of course, the marriage might look vital to you and dead to me. Or a betrayal that strikes you as routine might seem to me a sign of irredeemably damaged character. There are all sorts of "close decisions"—like the fellow who comes home to find his wife in flagrante delicto with the neighbor and says, "*Now* I'm getting suspicious." But then, if you have really missed clear signals in your intimate life, or cho-sen to ignore them, we would have to understand why that is. In a cul-ture, or perhaps a species, where most people are so exact in finding a mate, why is it that you, who have the many strengths that led my men-tor to refer you for this odd one-shot consultative session, have managed to mistake yours?

MOODS

13
Force Majeure

CONSIDER THIS sequence: Bill and Hillary, George and Barb, Ron and Nancy, Jimmy and Rosalynn, Gerald and Betty, Dick and Pat, Lyndon and Lady Bird, Jack and Jackie. The pairs differ markedly from one another, and yet it is easy to attribute to each an aptness of fit, in terms of self-differentiation. There even seem, in many of these public couples, to be other correspondences, of overall level of insecurity or self-esteem, and such more particular traits as moral awareness, social comfort, greed, or ambition.

But the public library of images also contains incongruous pairs. If Murray Bowen is right that all marriages are between people at the same level of differentiation, it follows that Marilyn Monroe was as mature, psychologically, as Arthur Miller. One can make the case: She evinced mystical strengths, enchanted her biographers; nor is he without his self-confessed frailties. Many considerations—social class, education, the distorting lens of publicity—make it difficult to assess the comparative maturity of these two figures. Still, the thesis lacks face validity. Or mind and body validity—his mind being matched not so much with her mind as with her body.

Monroe appears to be a victim of lack of differentiation. She is driven by insecurity, uncertain in her values, eager to please, easily influenced by those around her, in need of drugs and drink and humiliating liaisons to stabilize an inchoate sense of self. Whereas Miller seems—at least in his public performance, say, in his writing *The Crucible* while Joseph McCarthy was still in power—to be a man who can maintain autonomy under extreme pressure. In ordinary light, 'their marriage concerns a woman with poor differentiation of self who uses her other assets—sex appeal, beauty, renown—to gain the support of someone who impresses her with his maturity; or, from the opposite angle, it concerns a man who peddles his self-differentiation to obtain not an equal but an icon.

We may be unable to assess this particular marriage, Monroe and Miller. But its public appearance represents something that surely occurs in private life: Self-differentiation cedes place to *force majeure*. People choose mates for reasons that have nothing to do with maturity, extraordinary beauty being the common example. When we say, "I wonder what she sees in him," and the disparity is one of looks, we have no need to wonder what he sees in her. He sees what we see, skin-deep, and we understand that he may have overlooked other qualities because of this one.

And yet I wonder how often beauty constitutes *force majeure*. When I see the tycoon and the trophy wife in treatment, they often strike me as precisely paired. Calm the agitated trophy wife, and the pigeon-chested executive husband will deflate right in the office. To look at the problem in terms of the bargain the physically attractive person makes: Generally, I am surprised at how little beauty buys. If anything, there seems to be some danger that a striking woman, if she has any weakness in her sense of self, will marry down emotionally in response to the concrete blandishments of narcissistic men who are expert at disguising their hollowness and who require a woman's beauty as a shield against their own insecurity.

Still, not only beauty but wealth, power, intellect, achievements, social class, and social skills must often cause incongruities of psychic matching. The sharing of an extreme experience that no one on the outside can understand—exposure to the horrors of war or political internment, or, on the domestic plane, the death of a spouse or a struggle with alcoholism—can sometimes act as a *force majeure*. But to my observation, much more frequent, and for the advisor more complex, problems of mismatching arise in response to broad swings in mood state. Depression is a common form of *force majeure*.

This is where I work. People with mood problems form the bulk of my psychiatric practice and did even before I wrote *Listening to Prozac*. Murray Bowen considered depression, or even a vulnerability for depression, to be a sign or a form of undifferentiation. His thesis is that the spectrum from health to illness is a spectrum of autonomy, that mental disorder is undifferentiation and differentiation is mental health. And that is one way of seeing the matter, to expect a depressive but otherwise mature man to marry a somewhat immature woman.

But often maturity and mood stability seem to exist on different axes, or to interrelate in complex ways. A depressive man may be mature—secure in his values, assertive, emotionally connected, and so forth—except when he is depressed. The man has two distinct levels of differentiation. The one he inhabits most of the time, when he is not depressed, feels to him and looks to me like "true self," leaving that admittedly untenable term undefined. The man is not likely to feel compatible with an immature wife, and why should he?

People often make choices, and even marry, when in extreme mood states. That is the nature of bonding in this cautious world; it takes euphoria or desperation to make a person cross the threshold. The narcissist, for whom no one is good enough, can sometimes deign to marry when depressed, and such a match can mean a happy end to years of isolation. Perhaps most mating takes place in euphoric states. It is when people ignore the big picture—lack perspective—that they take the plunge. In these heightened and overfocused conditions people may nonetheless choose with great precision. To say that a man was depressed, or even manic, when he chose a wife proves nothing. People prone to mood swings do sometimes choose badly, or at least in ways they later regret. But it may be the regret, and not the initial choice, that is a result of depression.

And, of course, depression may arise from marriage. People in unsatisfying marriages tend to be depressed. Research studies say so, and the numbers are high: Half of women unhappy with their primary relationship are depressed; both men and women in difficult relationships are twenty-five times as likely to be depressed as spouses in well-functioning relationships. And these results do not count low-level depressions, or mania, or the instances where a mismarriage took place during a prior episode of depression. So the combination of marital disaffection and mood disorder is exceedingly common. Given that you are asking whether you should leave, there is a much better than fifty-fifty chance that you or your partner is, or has been, depressed.

Any account of troubled couples that omits an understanding of depression is on its face inadequate. In each instance the chicken-and-egg question is crucial. Will separation make matters better or worse? (Freud misjudged this issue in the Frink case, when he convinced a manic-depressive patient to leave an apparently unexciting wife, only to see the man descend into a paranoid psychosis.) Evaluating marriage when mood fluctuation is at issue requires a highly external perspective. The premise of the person seeking help is that his or her judgment is or has been unreliable.

Beyond major depression and mania lies a broad field of minor and often chronic mood disorder. Many people suffer "rejection sensitivity" or adult "separation anxiety," which is to say that the end of a relationship will bring a period of deeply painful affect. These tendencies create diseconomies in the marketplace of intimacy: People get stuck in trial relationships they know are wrong for them. (The same is true for people with extreme shyness or social phobia. They may find it hard to leave a relationship because they know it will be painful to initiate the next one.) A rejection-sensitive woman grows emotionally, and when that growth is not reciprocated, still she cannot move on.

People subject to these minor variants of mood disorder cannot carry out their own wishes. Like battered spouses, they are afraid of what will follow if they try to leave; like sufferers from Parkinson's disease, they cannot muster the drive to initiate action. They need loaned and borrowed self, affirmation and encouragement. Iris's anticipation of distress on leaving—her memory of the painfulness of her divorce—may be one reason to favor advising her to end the affair with Randall; when someone who fears endings has any inclination to leave, she should be given a push.

For years, the social consequences of mood have fascinated me. What am I to make of a depressed woman's complaint that her relationship is at fault, or of a depressed man's claim that all that sustains him is his shaky marriage? There is something moving about the interaction between mood disturbance and troubled intimacy. I find it upsetting to see a marriage fall apart because of unrecognized mood disorder or, on the contrary, to sense that unrecognized mood disorder is making a destructive relationship drag on. It would not surprise me if this were the sort of problem Lou sent my way.

Perhaps the effect of mood on romantic choice is so disquieting because it gives rise to stories open to such disparate readings.

At a moment when she is feeling steady and resilient, a woman—Amanda—comes to believe that for years she has suffered from intermittent bouts of depression. This conclusion colors Amanda's view of her marital discontent. In retrospect, she wedded when she was depressed. She was in an altered state: viscerally insecure, unattractive to herself in body and spirit. In this vulnerable condition, she made a decision to join forces with a man who appeared stable, honest, and unthreatening. Now that Amanda feels better, Toby looks different. His rectitude she sees as mulishness.

Toby is continually outraged at others' ingratitude. But where Toby sees black-and-white betrayal, Amanda sees shades of gray; she can understand the situation from each party's point of view. Amanda takes Toby's extreme responses as signals about how he might deal with disloyalty from her. She is grateful for the support Toby offered when she needed it, but there are limits to obligation. She has a dream of finding a soul mate, and she knows it will not be Toby.

Occasionally Amanda perceives a modest loosening in Toby's posture, a movement to meet her own newfound resilience. It is hardly enough. Especially since she also suspects he is willing to drag her down in order to return to life as it was when she was more devoted.

Back when depression gripped her, Amanda believes, she sold herself cheap. Desperation made her convince herself that she loved Toby. Free of depression and out of love, she suspects that she has no business in this relationship. She wants out now. But having chosen badly once, she has doubts about her judgment in matters of the heart. It seems altogether reasonable, does it not, for Amanda to turn to someone knowledgeable about depression and ask, Is it time to leave Toby?

Amanda's account provides what must be the single most suitable occasion for advice: a mismatch in levels of differentiation, based on a transient disturbance of self. But this story, even sketchily imagined, contains room for doubt. Amanda's epiphany about her mood disorder makes me uneasy, as does her wish to be quick in cutting her losses. Before advising Amanda over Toby, I would want to hear more about her history of moods and liaisons.

It might emerge, as we talk, that for the whole of her adult life Amanda has ricocheted from one romantic relationship to another. Her tendency since adolescence has been to feel needy, lean on a lover, move toward commitment, and then pull back. Her shifting feelings toward Toby represent an old pattern. If so, I might imagine that Amanda would do well to gain the ability to feel comfortable in the presence of a flawed man to whom she has obligations, or to tolerate a range of affects without acting impulsively. Staying and rotating the self might suit Amanda, especially if the past state she calls depression can equally be understood as a set of panicky feelings brought on by loneliness, feelings that are replaced by other panicky feelings (of superiority, of mismatch) once the loneliness has given way to intimacy. Perhaps with a more stable wife Toby would focus less on duty and behave in ways Amanda finds appealing. Amanda's efforts to sit with her feelings, especially if they elicit a responsive adjustment on Toby's part, might even diminish the amplitude of her mood swings.

Then again, they might not. I have seen what looks like flightiness disappear only with medication. There are occasional patients in whom a repetitive sequence of approach and avoidance is best understood simply as a cyclical mood disorder. To imagine the most mechanical of correlations: Amanda might move close to men in winter and separate each spring, or the reverse. The alternation is unlikely to be quite so exact, but sometimes careful history-taking will reveal a pattern.

Why did Amanda go so far as to marry Toby? Surely he, more than past boyfriends, has qualities that correspond to her needs and desires.

But perhaps it is only that, while involved with Toby, by happenstance Amanda experienced a change in the depth and duration of her recurrent depression—a change in her level of demoralization and impulsivity—and that the extended mood state caused her to move from flighty courtship to marriage.

Amanda asks to be joined in a perspective, one that attributes her social problems to an autonomous mood disorder. Her account must be taken fictively; perhaps it is oversimple. And yet Amanda's version must be respected not only because it is hers but also because it might be right and right in a way that would overwhelm a host of other considerations.

14

Enfant de Bohème

W HAT APPEARS to be a problem in socializing is really a problem
in mood. This sort of statement emerges from a core psychiatric perspective, one that treats mood state as a discrete phenomenon. In
its extreme version, that perspective amounts to psychological material-
ism, the contention that aberrant mood is most usefully understood as
the expression of disordered brain biology. Depression or mania, or an
alternation between the two, is seen as the expression of a physiological
condition, one that gives rise to a typical sequence of social behaviors.
Even psychiatrists with a more complex or agnostic view of the origins of
depression are likely to see certain mood states as stable, hard to alter, and
profound in their effects on social functioning. The psychiatrist explains
it all simply: When you are depressed, you lose differentiation. When
you are yourself again, you realize that your depressed behavior has not
served you well. But which is the disservice? Depressed mood can lead
you to settle for an inappropriate mate; it can also cause you to leave an
appropriate one.

Many studies indicate that divorce results in depression. My belief
is that, at least as often, undiagnosed depression antedates and causes
divorce. When a patient discovers all sorts of faults in a spouse or lover,

or when long-standing complaints suddenly become urgent, I find it useful to consider mood disorder as a possible explanation. Even minor mood disorders can result in a deep sense of dissatisfaction with relationships, and minor mood disorders can be insidious. When Amanda says she has no use for Toby, I may even wonder whether she is not depressed again, in some partial or atypical fashion.

It often seems that I could fill a practice with cases of falling out of love, so common is the complaint. The usual scenario is this: A young couple is well into the phase of family formation—though it is only from a distance that the family formation appears long-standing. The two have recently had their second child, and to one spouse—it could be either, but I shall choose the husband—this state represents the start of family life. Until that point, the husband experienced himself as single, a wife and first child being elegant accoutrements to psychological bachelorhood. With the birth of the second child, he discovers that he is permanently a husband and father. And then one day he comes home and announces he is out of love and leaving forever.

He may be unable to remember why he was ever in love, unable to remember what love felt like, and certain that his wife is a burden, a stick-in-the-mud, an unfortunate victim of his past illusion that he knew what love was. Or he may be out of love with his wife and in love with someone wilder and less encumbered. And this love may be requited or not.

Marriages are marriages of families. The children's grandparents will become involved. Perhaps they will happily widen the rift. More likely, they will try to patch things over. In time, they will insist that the couple try to work things out in counseling. The husband will attend, not because he expects the sessions to be of any use but out of a formal obligation to the wife or other family members. He knows that it is unseemly for a man in the prime of life to up and leave his wife and children because he is no longer in love.

The couple counselor will formulate the case in one or more of a number of terms: the husband's anxiety about commitment, his fear of fatherhood, his Oedipal anxiety about marriage now that his wife is a mother, his unwillingness to give up the freedoms of adolescence, his feeling unattended to now that his wife expends energy on the children. Any or all of these explanations will seem right and tailor-made to the situation. In response to the therapist's interpretations, the wife may change her behavior so as to flirt with her husband again, the worried grandparents baby-sitting for the children in hopes that a second honeymoon will rekindle love or at least renew attachment.

But all is in vain. Unmoved by the efforts on his behalf, the husband assures whoever will listen that it is not a matter of anxiety, Oedipal or otherwise, but of what he says it is, falling out of love. How to respond? Everyone secretly knows that within couples infatuation in time cedes place to more domestic emotions. Why doesn't the husband do what most people do, settle for the possible? Some friends may secretly envy the husband his insistence on passion.

The couple counseling fails, and yet it still seems to the wife and grandparents that something is wrong and could be made right. Perhaps the grandparents will offer to pay for a consultation with a psychiatrist. Perhaps the husband will make the choice himself, to prove once and for all that nothing is the matter. Or because all this fuss has finally kindled a flicker of doubt. Although he remains pretty secure in his feelings—no glimmer of love—he is willing, before he files the separation papers, to entertain one more outside opinion.

If you are the long-suffering husband, long-suffering in the sense that you have put up with unwanted attention from parents and in-laws and mental health professionals, none of whom is willing to see matters as you see them, namely as a question of falling out of love, you may find yourself contacting me, asking for confirmation of what you know to be the case, the marriage is over.

As you tell your story, I will listen for evidence of mood disorder. You do not meet standard criteria for major depression, nor even for dysthymia, the prevailing term for chronic minor depression. Nor do you complain of depression, only of being out of love and of being sent from pillar to post because no one believes you. And still I will say my little mantra, "Depression causes divorce as often as divorce causes depression," and try to see matters through the simple lens of mood disorder.

In other words, I will be like the others, assessing matters differently than you do. I will begin with the medical presumption that common things are common, and in these circumstances mood disorder is a common thing. For the moment, I am only secondarily concerned about what caused the depression, though if someone before me has not already done so, I will order tests of thyroid function and other physical contributors to altered mood. I may well believe one or more of the couple therapist's hypotheses; family formation arouses difficult feelings, and difficult feelings can trigger depression, by which I mean some substantial entity that goes beyond an aggregation of feelings. My focus is on that entity, I want to free you of it. My aim is to get you back in shape fast, before your wife and children have turned against you and we have that problem to deal with. I want you to have the choice of returning when you are yourself again, presuming, as I am for the moment, that you are not quite yourself.

Here is how I expect to see your situation. Your falling out of love is a sort of anhedonia—an inability to experience pleasure—and this anhedonia is a biological relative, or even an equivalent, of depression. Nobody has identified your problem as anhedonia because you say you look forward to activities and take pleasure in them. But my inclination is to insist that you are suffering a quite dense anhedonia.

You will object. You may protest that you still have an interest in your business, but I will say that you are merely withdrawing from social intercourse, "burying yourself in your work." Moreover, what draws you to this work is not pleasure but compulsion, which is another concomitant of depression.

You will argue that you are not anhedonic in matters of the heart; witness your passion for the unencumbered woman down the street. I know this neighbor; other patients of mine have given me a clear impression of her. Though she is no gypsy—actually, she manages a boutique and has lived for years in the same suburban house—I call her La Carmencita. This Carmen likes action, complications, intrigue, attached men. Once your family turmoil is resolved and you are out in the cold, you will not last a month with her. When you say that you need Carmen to arouse you, you are saying that your hedonic capacity is turned way down low so that it takes enormous stimulation to move you at all. We know that older men need younger women not because the men still have it but because they don't; it takes something special to get them started. I might add that in this case it is your diffidence (read anhedonia) that has caused this mercurial woman to take notice of you. I take Carmen to be the most skilled of diagnosticians, a hundredfold more sensitive to stirrings of depression than any algorithm.

Also, in your slightly depressed state, you have lost differentiation of self. Though you will never admit it, you feel unworthy of your wife, and less capable than she is to make good decisions; you cede vast territories to her because you feel dull-witted and slow, and then you resent her for taking too much control. You feel especially vulnerable in the family because your wife, whose feistiness once gave you pleasure, has not wakened to the fact that you are too damaged to defend yourself, that she is crushing you by taking over in areas where you once resisted her encroachments. In your mildly depressed state, you have slid, temporarily, to Carmen's emotional level.

It will be the same for any other objections you raise. You still enjoy time with your old friends? Yes, but that is because you drink and gamble together, more compulsion and overstimulation. What you find with them is not pleasure but momentary surcease from pain and emptiness.

And what are we to make of your readiness to withdraw from contact with your children, whom you say you adore? The truth is, you can no longer feel pleasure in any sphere. When you report that you enjoy yourself in this or that context, it is because you no longer remember what pleasure is.

Your very willingness to show up in the offices of this series of caregivers is indication of a certain complaisance or automaticity that suffices to make the informal diagnosis. Protest though you may, I will have you anhedonic, I will have you depressed.

At least this is one perspective I will adopt. The notion that depression, even minor depression, often has a life of its own, that it can be addressed directly—sometimes even addressed independent of its psychological causes—is one of the few distinctive contributions of biological psychiatry to advice in matters of the heart.

The contribution is important because it overwhelms all the usual considerations that we are likely to mention when we discuss the viability of relationships. A patient may tell me that he and his wife communicate poorly, find sex together pedestrian, disagree over career or parenting goals or religious or moral precepts, no longer share common interests, and squabble incessantly over issues of power and control. I will take those claims of incompatibility to be·as nothing if I believe that he or his wife is at base depressed. My working hypothesis is that every complaint will look different once the depressed or anhedonic spouse can again feel pleasure.

The idea that anhedonia is a discrete entity—an "essence," a nugget of reality, an intrinsic aspect of self that you carry with you to any activity—I want to call the essentialist perspective. At its extreme, essentialism says that a given trait will not usefully succumb to psychological analysis but is best accepted simply as an illness, an aspect of (biologically based) temperament, or a level of aptitude. Even complex psychologies presume a natural bedrock that is to be taken as a given—for example, basic drives or the pleasure principle or death instinct in Freudianism. The essentialist approach is often grounded in biology, and attempts to alter essential traits sometimes employ biological means: If your interpersonal crisis is a manifestation of mood disorder, it may make sense to approach it through psychopharmacology. But today there are also psychotherapists who would see your disaffection with your wife as anhedonia. They might not treat the anhedonia as bedrock—it has its psychological causes—but they would consider it an important, stable aspect of your makeup. In therapy, they would target the depression, not the marital discord.

The essentialist approach looms large not because it always helps but because occasionally it helps so completely. The focus on mood is thoroughly fictive. It doubts your premise, that you have made a mistake in marrying, and substitutes fresh ones. The essentialist approach offers a distinctive form of hope. And it specifies a means of attack for solving your dilemma: target the depression.

I should clarify one matter. When I refer to biology I am not thinking only about genetics, although some psychologists do believe that people may be born with low levels of "cerebral joy-juice." There are parenting styles that can beat a child down. Children raised in states of psychological deprivation may carry an acquired physiological vulnerability to anhedonia later in life; it seems to me that in my practice the most obdurate cases of joylessness have been of this sort. The distant origin of the condition—nature or nurture or, as is likely most common, an interactive combination of the two, vulnerable nature stressed by hostile or neglectful nurture—is of less interest here than the current effect. In those predisposed to anhedonia, a modest strain in a marriage may result in a solid impediment to ordinary pleasure and then to all sorts of compensatory behaviors.

I will keep in mind your plea: People do fall out of love, don't they? But my first thought is that the effective response to your marital dissatisfaction will be to address your anhedonia. Just as you are insistent on your viewpoint, I am passionate about mine. I hate the insidiousness of mood disorder as a cancer surgeon hates the insidiousness of cigarettes. It disturbs me that families should be torn asunder because people fail to think about depression as the cause, rather than the result, of trouble. Facing you, there are moments when I feel like Cassandra, prescient but unheard. I suspect that given time and your trust I might with the simplest of interventions spare you, your wife, and your children years of pain.

The perspective of altered mood is utterly convincing to the person who inhabits it. You know that you once thought you loved your wife, but you cannot for the life of you remember why, not in any way that matters. Past reasons seem distant and mechanical. Your current understanding is the only one that counts. Once you were mistaken, self-deluding, a menace to women and to yourself. Now you are honest, open, set on the righteous course toward a new life, an Emersonian idealist turning away from lies.

Is one perspective privileged? Mine, that you are something just short of ill? Yours, that you are enlightened? For the moment, that question is irresolvable, though in time we may come to see each other's point of view, even come to agree.

Let us say that I make my case to you, and out of consideration to the family, you decide to give the marriage a last chance. Because I seem reliable in other ways, and because you are beginning to feel stirrings of doubt, perhaps an unacknowledged hint of panic in the presence of Carmen, you agree to take an antidepressant medication. This is my advice. You ask whether you should leave, and I say that you should seek out a psychiatrist who sees things as I do and get yourself properly treated. Or perhaps we will go beyond advice, and I will treat you myself.

And let us say that after a few weeks you begin to feel different: more comfortable with the children and tougher with your wife—not tougher in your insisting on leaving but in your insisting on staying and having it your way. You will find yourself spending more time with the children. Soon you will move back home. La Carmencita will seem in retrospect a strange diversion. Early midlife crisis, you will say, as will the many concerned relations.

Or perhaps your recovery will occur through a psychotherapy focused on depression—although psychotherapy might be difficult since you are unmotivated, clear in your own mind about the marriage, and unaware of your diminished capacity for joy.

However it occurs, your willing return to the marriage will feel wondrous to all concerned. Gently, and knocking on wood, we will celebrate. And whether or not psychotherapy was involved, you will rethink the episode. You and your wife may conclude that in retrospect your disorder of desire went back to well before the conception of your younger child. In an attempt to prevent further fallings out of love, you and I will go on to examine your apprehensions about family life and fatherhood, and your arrangements with your wife about who makes what decisions. You or I will remind your wife that when you look weak is not the time for her to press her advantage. We will talk about adults' need for time to play childishly together. In short, we will do the things the couple therapist hoped to do many weeks ago. But we will do them after the fact, when you are back in love again, or at least contented to be in an ordinary state of marital comfort.

Alternatively, nothing will work, and you will remain distant from your wife, and she will regroup and move on. Carmen will drop you, your friends will grow up and get married, you will be overwhelmed with depression, and it will seem that you became depressed because of the trauma of your divorce, preceded by the prior grand mistakes, your marriage and your decision to have children together; so it will appear that the depression arose from the realization that you were not in love and the acts that logically followed. I will look very bad, arbitrary in my use of medication. Who is this charlatan who sees mood disorder behind every tree? Perhaps I will modify my opinion. More likely, despite the failure of my treatment methods, I will remain fixed in my impression that your falling out of love was, in essence, depression.

Or perhaps you will marry Carmen and live happily ever after. You and I know that this outcome is unlikely—there are elements of self-hatred, despair, and defiance in your move toward her. But unlikely things do occasionally happen. And surely aspects of you and of Carmen are hidden from me. I have my limited role, which in this case is to say that minor mood disorders are very common, and tending to them often helps life make more sense. That role is important enough. As a therapist, some of my most satisfying treatments have begun with the suspicion that what looks like marital discord is best conceptualized as depression in one or the other spouse.

15

Howard's End

FOR THE SAKE of completeness, I should add that I will also be on the lookout for minor variants of mania. You are someone who wishes to be an exception: You want to leave a relationship that all your friends believe to be working well. Your decision is created or sustained by a degree of certainty, a sense of urgency, a level of determination, and a narrowness of vision that, though not strictly foreign, constitute an exaggeration of your customary manner. If you were open to it, you might benefit from a word of advice.

Here is how I picture you: You are a working mother with remarkable verve and zest. Spry, sprightly, feisty, is how you have always been described. You have your own little advertising firm. You do it all, soliciting accounts, drafting copy, arranging photo shoots, laying out, pasting up. (It helps that you need next to no sleep.) You are known for your originality, your cleverness, your ability to talk up and land outsize clients. You could expand your shop, or run a division of a bigger firm. But you treasure your independence and, more especially, your time at home. You are enormously important in your children's lives, demand of yourself that you be.

Your own parents were alcoholic, indifferent at their work, unreliable in the family. Your only image of them together involves the degeneration of wit into sarcasm and then open fights. They divorced when you were approaching adolescence. You have married in such a way as to prevent your children from experiencing what you did. Howard is no Romeo and a bit bumbling in his work, but never mind. You provide the spark. You are content for him to serve as ballast, stabilizing the family.

In the past, you have come to me for psychotherapy now and then. Not because much is going wrong, but prophylactically, to inoculate yourself against the possibility that neurosis might interfere with the perfect home life you are creating. I am sympathetic with this effort, hope you will find your way. I never get to know you well, because you dart in and out of treatment. Once, as you return for a visit, I interrupt your presentation and ask how long you intend for the therapy to last. I note that you end our encounters abruptly, as if you were apprehensive that you might discover something quite dreadful about yourself. This speculation is too pointed. You lash out, attack my character, the arrangement of the furniture in my office, and the level of my intelligence.

You do seem smarter than anyone around you. It is as if you had chosen me the way you chose your husband, as a drone who will support your dreams and talents. I am willing to play this role. But I wonder whether I should make something of the sharpness of your assault. It has the feel of paranoia, as if you were tightly coiled, full of venom, ready to dart out at potential attackers who venture too close.

In accomplished, energetic people, paranoia is, to a psychiatrist, a likely component of a near manic state. There are formal criteria for mania and its lesser cousin hypomania: grandiosity, talkativeness, distractibility, motoric and psychic agitation, a scattering of thought. You have none of these individually, and certainly not the whole package. But given your level of wit and energy, and your sleep pattern, and the way you are coiled, the disorder you don't have but cause me to think about is mania.

* * *

Today you come in not for psychotherapy but advice. You have a plan, one that goes against your lifelong determination never to divorce. You need to hear from me that your reasoning is sound—though you have not waited for anyone's approval. Already, you have set your plan in motion: to leave Howard for Bart.

You are breathtaking in your decisiveness. You have made your commitment to Bart, have convinced him to put his house on the·market in anticipation of moving into yours once you kick Howard out. With your impressive energy, you have devised a daily schedule that allows you to spend extensive time with Bart while attending to your usual duties at work and home. You have a lawyer researching the best venue for filing. You have sequestered the family financial records and coached the baby-sitter as a potential witness regarding your extreme competency as a parent and Howard's shortcomings. You have even called the police and ascertained how they respond to allegations of domestic violence; not that you would necessarily act on such a scheme, but you have considered finding a way to provoke Howard, in hopes that he will strike you, enabling you to have him evicted instantly. Howard knows nothing, other than that you are finding constant fault with him, where once you were attentive to his needs before he expressed them.

You lay out for me a formulation more detailed, and certainly more blunt, than any I have entertained. You married Howard for security, to defend against the possibility of turmoil in your and your children's lives. But you have always shouldered the burden of motivating and directing the family. For what? The children are secure, but they are plodding, like their father. Change would not harm them, and it might help. Divorce would be no worse for them than life with a chronically discontented mother.

And you have been discontented. Haven't you turned to me periodically for that very reason? A person can't go on cheating herself in this way, robbing herself of passion. Which is just what you have been doing, depriving yourself of the one thing your parents did have, for all their failings, an ability to take the tide at its crest, to fill the heart to overflowing. In retrospect, you have loved Bart for years. He is a commercial photographer, you have used him in any number of campaigns. A free spirit, an artist, a kindred soul. And sex with him is indescribable.

I have a little trouble attending to your list of Bart's virtues. I hear that sex is good in mania—further evidence that the brain is the primary sexual organ. For the rest, Bart sounds to me a good deal like Howard, a man who can be handled. Weaker than Howard, if he would latch on to you when you are in this odd condition. Over the years, your stories about Howard have made me fond of him; for the children, his quiet and accepting style must be a nice counterbalance to your incisiveness. The way you now devalue one man and overvalue the other says to me more about you than them.

The style of your discourse disturbs me. You rely on clichés: how men are, how children of divorce are, how the modern family is. You confide: "You know how a woman who comes from a dysfunctional family will look for an overly stable man. That sort of compromise tends to break down. Half the women in this town are getting divorced for that very reason." You shoehorn your own circumstances into these clichés and then look at me in a kindly way, as if I were a co-conspirator.

I feel, I must confess, rather like Howard and Bart. I am hardly quick enough to answer you, and not a little afraid of what would happen if I were. I can see it your way. You all but close the deal with me—except that my psychiatric attitude has intervened. With the clinical part of my brain I am thinking, This poor woman has gone off the deep end.

Let me be more exact. By strict standards you are not mentally ill. You are not even much different than you have been for many years—quick, intuitive, self-assured. The family court judge will not find you worse off than any number of focused and insistent women who have come before her. If your husband requests that you be examined psychologically, you will pass with flying colors. You are not spending money unwisely—or if you are spending money fast, you have an explanation for everything. And I believe that you may stay in this frenetic, decided state indefinitely, without its deteriorating into anything worse. But you are walled off from me. You use the vocabulary of intimacy, but there is no reaching you, nor will there be for some time.

*   *   *

I think, as you try to sweep me off my feet with your reasoning, of one of Lou's short stories, "Lux et Veritas." It concerns a mid-century housewife who after many years of happy marriage has been deserted and then divorced by her businessman husband. The abandoned woman is disoriented. How did it happen? The marriage bonds were strong; her husband's love, profound.

The housewife consults a psychoanalyst. He is a rigid technician, a moralistic believer in the premise that the truth sets men, and more often women, free. He helps his patient review her life in the harsh light of reality. Throughout the marriage the husband had been hypomanic, which to the analyst (such was a widespread opinion in those years) means also emotionally shallow. What the wife mistook for love was merely the man's energy and intensity. In retrospect, it is clear that the woman's husband never saw her, was incapable of taking her into account. As episode after episode in the relationship is examined, it emerges that the wife supplied all the affect—hers and, through imagination and attribution, his. There was never a second person in the couple, only a busy screen onto which the wife has been projecting romance. The whole of her life is the marriage, and the whole is meaningless; she has not been loved.

This truth is, of course, too much for the poor woman to bear, and she responds by falling dependently in love with the process of psychoanalysis and with the analyst or an idealized image of him. He realizes—too late—that he mistook his job, that the only hope for this patient from the start was the strengthening of her illusions. Now he must sustain the illusion of psychoanalysis, or the patient will be utterly bereft. The hypermoral analyst is left, at the story's end, interminably involved with the naive patient, supporting her in a sham quest for depth. The effect is disquieting in a way that goes beyond the implicit critique of psychoanalysis and its meager tools, interpretation and insight. The story creates doubt about the presence of the other. How much are we just alone?

I fear you have some of that husband's blindness and some of that wife's tendency to imagine others in ways that serve your dreams. I have an opinion. Stay with Howard, by all means. Stay and get treatment.

Even though you meet no discrete criteria for diagnosis, I may consider asking you to try medicines ordinarily used for quite serious mental illness. At the very least, I want you to wait, to see whether this state remits.

Saying this would be like stepping in front of a runaway train, unhealthy for me, unlikely to slow things down. My strategy will be to play dumb, since you have already indicated a willingness to have me in that role.

I might say something conventional: What about marital counseling? You will have your reasons why not: I must know how dogged Howard is. If this is allowed to drag on, he'll pull the kids over to his side.

I will persist, also dogged in my conventionality: I have seen couple counseling help in cases like this. I will avoid giving reasons. I want to provide no ammunition for your putting me in the wrong—for your making me the object of paranoia. I am worried about your becoming isolated, perhaps isolated with Bart. I fear that you will have few friends when your plan unfolds.

I will be tempted, as I say something bland, to give you a knowing look that reveals how I see things, the look that says, we both know better. But you would turn on me in a flash. In order not to lose you, I will struggle to sit beside you, emotionally. To say, "Men!" or even, "All men are bastards!" when you tell me something Howard has done wrong. I am fully on your side—that is my job, to be on the side of people with a distinct perspective, and then to oscillate from that perspective to other ones—although in impugning men I am trying to make a little trouble. I want to hold myself at the edge of the circle of the scorned (men!) and edge Bart into it—in order to breach your certainty, unsettle you, introduce an element of self-reflection.

My play-acting alters the nature of our dialogue. What matters is not the advice I give—you are hardly likely to listen—but how I place myself with regard to you. You will be right to suspect me. I am trying gently to manipulate you, to slow you down. It might be more honest simply to tell you how I see things and have you throw me over; but I care about you too much to be honest in this narrow fashion, believe in this instance that authenticity consists in dissembling.

I doubt that I or anyone can reach you. My belief is that you cannot hear advice. Are shut to it, as Martin Buber said, indicating that in certain conditions, such as paranoia, isolation of perspective is not a choice but an imposed state; the paranoid person "does not open himself and does not shut himself. He *is* shut." Your contention will be that it is I who am paranoid, paranoid to mistrust you when everything you say is reasonable. People do discover that they have made mistakes; people do find passion. One perspective faces another, and there is no way to judge between them. Unless your mood state changes, and you return to the office to say, "You know, something was very wrong with me back then; I'm surprised you didn't pick up on it." Or unless you fall into clear-cut mental illness and then recover. Very likely, neither development will occur, and we will remain shut from one another.

You ask for advice, but what you expect is affirmation. If I fail to provide it, if I demur over the least detail, you will dismiss me. "You know shrinks, how they make an illness out of the most ordinary human impulse." You see yourself as healthy—true self at last. You are an energetic woman who has fallen out of love with one man and into love with another. And even if you are a bit disturbed, don't you have a right to be, given how withholding your husband is?

If I raised the issue, you would make the case that you have grown immeasurably in differentiation of self and level of connectedness. You are busily involved with your family—immersed in the sculpting of family relationships—and yet you are certain of your values. You are impervious to the suasion of the group, indeed, unshakable in the face of any doubts your friends or relatives might have. You say with Ralph Waldo Emerson that you will no longer hide your aversions; you intend henceforward to live in truth.

From the outside, as a psychiatrist attuned to mood disorder, I see you as inhabited by a dybbuk, one I can barely name but would nonetheless love to exorcise. I agree that with your unshakable perspective you meet the technical·definition of the thoroughly differentiated person. Since you do, you call the validity of that definition into question. I see you as the least mature you have ever been. Not so much "cut off" from a particular person as cut off from anything outside yourself. You are locked into your viewpoint, differentiated in a way that verges on the psychotic.

Still, I am burdened, as you are not, by moments of ambivalence and uncertainty. Though I see you as uncharacteristically shut from others, I recognize that you have always held your own views in high regard, always shielded them from outside influence. And you are right that there is an element of continuity in your assessment of the marriage. In your earlier visits to me, you did often complain about Howard's stodginess, and you often wondered aloud whether the way you constructed your family life in opposition to your parents' was not extreme. If Howard were to say that there is a different woman in his house, not the one he married, I would be inclined to agree with him. Except that this woman is quite like you; for the whole of the marriage you were almost this way.

16
Unequivocal Eye

YOU DRESS PLAINLY and greet me quietly. You are unprepossessing. But as you enter my office, I am aware of a critical sensibility. You approve, I think, of the framed photographs on the walls, though you squint at one—you have seen it before and judge it prosaic. When you notice the computer, you back away, as if its presence here, in a room devoted to private encounters, were an affront. When you sit down, you are slow to speak. You need to take in the atmosphere.

In your soft voice, you say that it will be hard for you to tell your story. You have known almost from the start that there were problems in your marriage. Now that you have the chance, you are determined to get a little help in making up your mind about whether to stay on.

Your account is rich. There are many characters; you realize them deftly, with words or facial pantomime. You are a keen observer of your surroundings, and your presentation has a texture that a close reader, a psychoanalyst, could think about for hours. I try to stay tuned to detail, but since I will be called on shortly to advise, for the most part I am listening with the gain turned down, seeking out broad patterns.

You and Mark married just after high school and then moved from your hometown. No one you see now remembers you apart. It has always been Mark and Sandy. People run the words together, like warm and sunny or, lately, cool and cloudy.

You married because you were soul mates. In class, you were the kids who understood why Emily Dickinson's work endures. You both agreed with the sentiment about it being dreary to be somebody. Alcohol, which obsessed your schoolmates, had no allure for you. You had seen enough of striving and fighting and drinking in your own families. You held yourselves apart from other kids. Sometimes they frightened you. It was not that anything anyone was likely to do could surprise you, but you had faced enough indignities, and you promised implicitly to protect each other from any more.

You have often since questioned whether shared sensibility—and now you see it more as shared hypersensitivity—is an adequate basis for marriage. Neither of you wanted to compete with others in the workplace. For the usual societal reasons, Mark had the more substantial career, and he resented both the stress of competition on the job and the pressures associated with being a breadwinner. He would come home feeling unappreciated.

Too early in childhood, you had responsibility for your brothers, and you never felt you could do right by them. So you panicked when Mark, who had also been relied on too young, leaned on you in his childish way. You lacked confidence you could make another person feel better. Merely to think of Mark heading home worn out and hungry for affection made your day seem black. When he walked through the door and saw you already drained, he would shrink away. Having forsworn anger, he could translate his hurt only into distance. You felt his withdrawal as another sign of your inability to give or elicit nurturance. In the face of that failure and rejection, you became hopeless and more needy than Mark could bear.

You delayed having children. Thank goodness for that. You both felt overburdened as it was. Mark must often have considered leaving. You know you did. Part of what held you back was a terror of living alone, and a sense that you could not bear the process of disentanglement from Mark. You have something like a phobia for separations. But what did most to maintain the marriage in its early years was a series of affairs you carried on with married men.

You depict these men precisely, their transparent attempts to look caring, their emotional greed, their vanity. You describe an almost invariant pattern. A man, perhaps the husband of someone you know, catches you, as this sort of man is skilled at doing, at your bluest. For him, your vulnerability is an aphrodisiac. To you, an adoring man is solace from the isolation Mark imposes. But you feel dirty, since you are engaged in one of the many things you had vowed as a child never to do, the very thing your father did. At the same time, you feel you have no choice, life is too bleak without at least the pretense of admiration. You give the man what he wants, and it really amazes you how easy men other than Mark are to please.

Despite your awareness of what you are up to, you feel well and truly held. You are buoyed by these dalliances. In your happier state, you are more emotionally available for Mark, able to face him even when he is enervated by work. Your support allows Mark to do better at the office, appear more resilient, request and sometimes receive promotions.

Mark remains distant at home. How can you complain, knowing that you are hurting him? Surely a sensitive husband must have a sub-liminal reading of where his wife's energy is directed. You do not want to drive him crazy, *Gaslight*-style, by demanding commitment while you betray the marriage.

In time, Mark's newfound confidence at work spills over into the home. Mark asks less of you and gives slightly more. Feeling stronger yourself, you end your affair with the current married man, to the relief of both. But then something slips, as you or Mark face a challenge that causes one of you to demand more or give less. And there is some other married man who seems necessary. You wonder whether there are any honest marriages left.

What surprises you through the course of these cycles is how much tenderness you continue to feel for Mark. He tries hard in a world he is not made for, and sometimes he succeeds. His demands on you, those he openly expresses, are few and reasonable. He sticks with you through what must seem extreme unpredictability and moodiness. And he displays fine taste, an appreciation of the arts and of the art in daily life, that continually endears him to you. The more you know of lovers, the more you like your husband.

You look charmed as you describe Mark's virtues, and charming; I can see how you grow on men. Just what is your question, I wonder, since my experience is not that something must change. Quite the contrary, after years of seeing troubled couples function, my observation is that, once brought into being, these complex equilibria can sustain themselves indefinitely.

As if responding to my thought, you indicate that the balance has begun to shift recently and in unexpected ways.

Throughout the marriage, you have moved from one part-time job to another: making up gift packages in pharmacies and florist shops; arranging and restocking food displays in a specialty store; doing windows for boutiques in a neighboring upscale suburb. Always you put more time into these jobs than you are paid for, and, given your taste and dedication, you are underpaid to begin with. Egged on by one or another lover, sometimes you walk away from jobs, because a storeowner does not have the vision to follow your lead, or because she is competitive or jealous and you do not have the inclination to straighten the relationship out. You dislike the work world anyway, the way it takes advantage of people who don't happen to be squeaky wheels. You prefer to be at home.

But over the past couple of years your odd jobs have turned into a career. Your work in a fabric shop led to requests that you consult informally on interior design. You took courses in the local art school, learning how to marbleize, wood-grain, paint trompe l'oeil. To your surprise, you are now in demand. You have been commissioned to hand-paint chair rails, window frames, and fireplace surrounds for the local private library. A former lover has begun to put your designs into small-scale commercial production, a line of decorated mirrors and boxes and picture frames stamped with a modest "Sandy" logo of your making. You have managed—best of fortunes—to earn rewards for being who you are.

This good luck, or perhaps it is only your growing older, has allowed you to feel secure month in, month out. There are no more lovers, though with your entrepreneur friend the door is open, especially now that his own marriage is headed for divorce. You are better able to handle Mark, he seems less of a burden. But lately your relationship with him has been subject to extreme ups and downs. For a while, just as your work took off, you disdained Mark. He turned whiny and petulant, beyond what the pressures of his job could justify. He seemed to disapprove of your commercial success, as if you had gone over to the enemy, the movers and shakers, in a way that was disloyal to your joint view of the world. And then Mark began to show his other side: perceptiveness, openness, enthusiasm for your creativity. Though the last phase may have just been explained in a funny way.

Mark has a lover. Or almost a lover. A platonic girlfriend. He told you only weeks ago. He needs for you to know of his near-peccadillo, because for him it throws the marriage into question. He does not want to sneak about, wishes to include you in the important decisions in his life, even this one. As you tell me about Mark's confession, you put your hand to your mouth and catch your breath, smiling the self-effacing and mischievous smile that Meryl Streep or Emma Thompson favors when she is playing at being pleasantly surprised.

Lately you have found yourself thinking, Here is an opportune moment to leave, to make an honest and independent woman of myself. Though you know you would be taking advantage of Mark. He does not really want a lover. He is simultaneously pleading with you and protecting himself against losing you. He is asking for reassurance that you, with your success, still want him.

You think you do want to leave. But you cannot quite see yourself taking the leap. It is scary. At the same time, you would hate to reassure Mark and then walk away from him in a year or two. If you are to leave, now is the time.

I hope you will not feel diminished when I say I recognize this crisis. To put the matter in shorthand, yours has been a marriage between melancholics. Now you are over your depression—substantially changed—and the question is whether you should stay.

People with serious mood disorders tend to mate "assortively." Manic-depressives marry manic-depressives and the like. So that while mood disorder may interfere with matching, it may also make it more precise, depressives going beyond differentiation of self to find someone with signs of a similar vulnerability. This selection process is apparent in clinical practice. I have treated patients who are hell-bent on teaming up with recurrently depressive mates, in the way that certain children of alcoholics seek out alcoholics. The combination you describe is common, the mildly melancholic with the mildly melancholic, or the coupling of two young adults with difficult childhoods.

To come through a difficult childhood makes you special and different, and one solution to your needs is to pair off early, with someone who is enough like you to understand your experiences and promise not to reproduce them. Such marriages have inherent problems. You and Mark had each failed already, as children must fail, at parenting younger siblings in stormy households. That experience left you with a sense of inadequacy in the face of neediness. But when you marry young, you marry with strong dependency needs. You and Mark came together with a horror of each other's longings.

Yours is a particularly stifling sort of peas-in-a-pod marriage, one made overly stable by an implicit promise never to change, never to move toward the wider world. Your shared trait is not mistrust of the other gender but heightened sensitivity, and a vulnerability to despondency. People prone to depression need to keep in check an amalgam of insecurities, compulsions, and mood instability. Marriage can be stabilizing. Marriages between emotionally sensitive people can be models of the best that human beings are capable of. But the result can also be the one you describe, ordinary stressors being felt as threats, threats leading to demoralization, demoralization in one spouse then acting as a stressor for the other. This ping-ponging of perceived slights and felt inadequacies leads the relationship to slip downward. It is not at all unusual to reach outside for stabilization, as you have done with your lovers and as Mark seems to be doing now.

The marriage has its complexities and dissatisfactions, and then one of the members changes—moves into the social surround and away from the constrained perspective of melancholy. You no longer experience events as you once did and as your husband still does. Your marriage is no longer peas-in-a-pod. There is no returning to the old marriage, at least I do not see that as a good outcome.

Today, when depression is treated so vigorously, this crisis—change in a member of a depressive couple—is especially likely. I am thinking here of patients "transformed" by medication. You made your move on your own, through success in a career. Successful work often has this function of altering self-image, breaking stalemates, focusing issues at home. When a person is paralyzed in the sphere of intimacy, I some-times press (as Lou taught me to do) for attention to the work front, where change may be easier; the hope is that movement in one arena will lead to movement in the other. But whether recovery is through pill or job, the question is the same: What is to be done, now that your hus-band's melancholy has lost its appeal, or its hold over you?

You will weigh your obligation. Obligation is at issue in any separa-tion, but there are special considerations where depression is involved. I will ask you about your values, of course, and your inclinations. But I will tune my ear a certain way, knowing that melancholics tend to be guilt-ridden and rigidly idealistic. The situation here resembles those involving "rejection-sensitive" spouses or people who are anxious in the face of transitions—perhaps if you have any inclination to leave, you should run with it.

Might you first suggest to Mark that he seek treatment for depres-sion? That question is difficult when what is at issue is personality style rather than illness. This much is worth asking: Is there any likelihood that Mark will change? It seems a shame to continue the marriage as it is, with resentment on both sides and constant recourse to lovers.

It is not hard to make the case for leaving. Your marriage was a solu-tion to problems of adolescence. (You may think of it as a long interval of recovery, to use the movement's word, from your parents' alco-holism.) There is no reason to assume that such an arrangement will suit adulthood—unless you adduce one, such as your affection for Mark. This does seem an instance where you must assess who you are, and then consider the marriage in light of that assessment. That is to say, it is a moment for remarriage or separation.

The case against leaving involves considerations of differentiation. In changing your relationship to the workplace, and to your lovers, you have made a differentiating move. Mark is reacting. It is not unusual that his early responses should be awkward. The temptation for him is to pull away from you, or to pull you back toward a familiar level of immaturity and depression.

If you stay put and remain focused on the relationship, you may next find Mark turning angry, which I would consider progress. You may find instead that he will move forward to join you, and you will be able to judge, after these many years together, whether a period of real marriage is possible. There would be a victory in completing the task you began, guiding each other through life. The question is whether that is Mark's sort of victory—whether he wants to accompany you as you are now, or whether he prefers to stay where he is, perhaps with this new lover, or another, who shares his old values.

There are particular grounds for optimism. Mark's responses to your behavior are precise. When you do a little better at home, he does better at work. His holding back from you is a reasonable behavior if he understands that you are not fully present. Even his current gesture, taking a platonic lover, has a gracious quality; as you begin to reenter the world, he offers you a way out of the marriage.

There is a sense in which you can be said to have created Mark. He is just what you have been able to bear. A companion who is perceptive without being intrusive. An unthreatening husband, who will tolerate almost any behavior on your part. You have kept him in his place, demanding always that he assume a bit more financial responsibility than he can comfortably handle, giving him a little less of his due as a man than would be necessary to make him whole. Perhaps if you are able to give more, he will prove able to be more.

We could tell the story the other way as well, say that he created you. He gave signals that he did not want responsibility for the whole of a woman, and for many years he made the work world seem more daunting than it needs to be. But recently, he has in some fashion allowed you to grow. We might even speculate that your amazing progress as a designer owes something to an emergent ability in Mark to tolerate a wife who succeeds at the crass work of the world. Because of both of your efforts, the marriage is beginning to function, and the question is whether either of you can let it.

Since you care so deeply for Mark and admire so many of his qualities, and since you have come so far with him, you may choose to let the marriage play itself out a bit further. True, you may be missing a golden opportunity to leave at a point when you are feeling strong and when Mark is unlikely to make a fuss. But if you really have a new level of independence, you can leave at any time; and that independence may work wonders within the marriage.

Are you thinking of divorce and then marriage to your patron entrepreneur? How could you not be? This is a frequent response to recovery from prolonged depression—entry, with intense relief, into a highly "normal" marriage, one focused on pleasure rather than ideals, on the future rather than the past. That solution has its dangers. The patron may be someone who enjoys and demands dependency in a wife. Your autonomy is hard-earned, along with your new strengths—quiet toughness, firm balance. I would hate to see you take a step backward. And yet, inhabiting my role as a (Sullivanian) reporter on likelihoods, I will say that I have seen it work, have seen people with difficult childhoods finally enter into mainstream, success- and consumption-driven, optimistic marriages with great contentment. Perhaps your entrepreneur will treasure you and challenge you and rejoice with you in the bounty of life, and you will hold on to what is precious in your sadness without having sadness possess you.

I am reassured by your unequivocal eye. You are a keen observer of objects and of men. In your career, you have found a way, without self-betrayal, to translate your vision into action. Guided by your aesthetic sensibility, you have managed to discover a path. It strikes me that the only apt advice is to say that you will need to fiddle with this problem as you have with others, quietly, from around the edges, at your own pace. You will need to be an artisan, here as elsewhere, and to rely on your unerring sense of the fitting. Yes, you must consider whether to leave—it is that sort of moment—but I am not sure you want to fix on Mark's platonic lover as a pretext. You seem someone who would prefer to find just the right time for leaving and to craft your exit in a way that pleases you, if you are to leave at all.

17
Mixed Signals

ONCE YOU had a conversation with your brother in which he asked, How do people choose?

The question was so bald that it took you unawares. What did he mean?

He said, Other than through desire?

For a moment you glimpsed what it is to live his life, life without access to cues about the character of other people. He was saying that he has a handicap, a color blindness or tone deafness for interpersonal nuance. You thought: That explains his choice of wives. As you continued the conversation, he pulled away from what he had asked, denied your interpretation of it. But ever since, you have suspected that he lacks a sense you thought everyone must have, of aptness of fit.

Your brother's problem is not one of mood, but I will want to set his story alongside those of Sandy and Amanda and Howard's wife and the man who fell out of love. Your fear is that there is a hard nugget of reality, some faulty essence in your brother's makeup, that interferes with the process of matching.

Here is how you present yourself.

You march into the consulting room and seat yourself in my chair. But for its placement—central, flanked by a side table where I rest my notepad—my chair looks much the same as the others. Still, the placement is distinctive enough that in ten years only two other patients have made a move to sit where you are seated now. One was a dazzling narcissist, the other a gifted swindler. You have neither the con artist's smoothness nor the egotist's air of entitlement. To the contrary, you look retiring and uncertain and eager for counsel. You begin to talk about your brother, Donny. Should I interrupt and remind you that we are here to discuss your dilemma, not his? Perhaps it's best to follow where you lead.

Donny, you say, is the nicest guy anyone would want to meet, but his taste in women is beyond explaining. The sort of thing that will happen is this: Donny shows up for dinner at your house with a date who is self-centered and shallow. She preens, laughs shrilly, flits from topic to topic, demands attention. She talks proudly about how she took advantage of a loophole in a business deal and how she uses sexual teasing to coax discounts from repairmen. When you ask how she and Donny are getting along, she lists the gifts he's given and the places he's taken her to eat. You smile to yourself. Your brother's had his share of trouble with women. Why shouldn't he find himself a night on the town?

Then the next day Donny phones and asks, "So, what did you think?"

And you say, "Donny, what do you mean what did I think?"

And he says, "Of Belinda." Luckily you hesitate in replying, because he confides, "I'm going to marry her."

You are devastated. The jerk—he does it to himself time after time. Should you warn him? You spoke your mind about the last fiancée. He married her anyway, and months later, after the woman ran off, Donny implied that your poisoning his mind had something to do with the failure of the marriage. Still, you don't know whether he can afford another of these adventures. You collect yourself and say, "Donny, would you like to have lunch Friday?"

He says, "Belinda adores you. She'll be eager."

And you disabuse him: "Not with Belinda, Donny. Just you and me."

*   *   *

You know how the lunch will go. You will say, "Donny, what is it you like about her?"

He will say, "How open she is." Or, "The way she communicates." He will give examples. "She told me all about her family." Or, "She says what she values in a relationship is mutuality." Or, "When I reveal something about myself, she reveals something about herself."

Donny is not the world's best reporter. Even so, it will be clear that his conversations with Belinda are hollow. The two people talking have read the same scripts about intimacy. However often anyone tries to tell Donny about openness or communication or mutuality or the sharing of confidences, he will never understand what those words mean. He is like a computer program that responds to key phrases. If a vacuous woman uses the right vocabulary, Donny concludes that she has content. Hearing Donny praise Belinda, you will be overcome by a sense of futility.

Often in psychotherapy a patient will relate a friend's troubles and, in the process, skirt and approach difficult truths about the self. I wonder whether your discussion of your brother is of this sort—you are taking the indirect route to your own concerns—or whether Donny's is the "matter of the heart" over which you want advice. I decide that in either case the prudent course is to let you continue.

Futility? I ask.

Donny has always been this way—your mother said as much recently. The context was a conversation about your nephew, your sister's son, who just turned five. Your sister wondered, Should the boy enter kindergarten? Your nephew does not have a good sense of the flow of classroom life, needs to be told rules explicitly. The problem with holding him back is that he already reads and adds numbers. He was tested by a child psychologist, who labeled the boy a "superior immature" and said your sister should think seriously about "retaining" the boy in pre-K.

Your mother laughed at the suggestion. Remember how Donny was? she said. If ever there was a "superior immature" child it was Donny. But when he was in school, the ideal student was one who could sit quietly and fill out mimeographed worksheets. Donny skipped a grade. Now the focus is on group play, and they're holding boys like Donny back. At what age, she wanted to know, would Donny have qualified for today's kindergarten? Ten years old? Twenty? He still needs for things to be spelled out explicitly. You know, your mother said, I'm not sure "immature" is the word for what troubles the men in this family; if it's immaturity, they ought eventually to grow out of it.

Your mother has always been dismissive and undermining of all her children. And she likes nothing better than to drive wedges between them. You began to protest—look how well Donny does in groups now—but even as you countered your mother's arguments, you believed that this time she was right; Donny misses the flow of feeling in groups. People have to make allowances for him.

It seems you are here to talk about Donny. Donny's a solid guy, you say. Romance aside, he does well, has friends.

Donny makes friends readily?

Everybody likes him. He can fill a big hall if he throws a party. But in terms of an inner circle, he sticks with guys he met in high school. When it comes to new acquaintances, Donny's a bit indiscriminate. He lets many people into his life, and those who prove loyal over time become friends. Everyone says Donny is easygoing; a less generous take on it is that he has no quick way to make social judgments.

Still "superior immature"? I ask.

When it comes to romance. What makes it hard to call him immature is that on the job, Donny is recognized as a leader. He never dithers. He is good at heading up projects, getting colleagues to focus on a task, eliciting unconventional solutions. And in the defense of a good idea, Donny is persistent, not easily swayed. But the independence of judgment that serves him well at work gets Donny into trouble in his private life. The women he picks! Anyone but Donny can see that they are shells of persons; nobody home. When you hear the expression "poor judge of character," you think of Donny. But is it judgment exactly? It seems almost to be a matter of perception. He has no ear for the overtones of phoniness that would tell anyone else that these romantic prospects are bad news.

When a man makes repeated bad choices in marriage, he is deemed neuroticaIly self-destructive. You don't see Donny that way—there's nothing neurotic about him. Like a person with monocular vision, Donny has difficulty judging depth. This is your defense of Donny from the implicit charge that he must have flaws that correspond to his ex-wives' flaws, or now to Belinda's shallowness and greed. His partners do not speak to who Donny is, you argue, because the factors that ordinarily dominate choice do not exist for him. You want to know whether I buy your version—whether anyone ever looks to me the way Donny looks to you.

Like everyone who works with problems of intimacy, I have run into people who seem never to get it right. And I wonder, as you are wondering, whether they are socially blind or whether, as psychoanalysis would have it, such people see perfectly well but use their vision in the service of a compulsion to fail.

I practice in a university town, and often I am asked to evaluate students who are worse off than Donny. In the consulting room, these young men and women appear well-spoken and personable. But they are confused by the society around them. Its intentions and demands seem uninterpretable. Their friends are limited to a few social outsiders like themselves; or they may have no close friends. And their romantic relations with the opposite sex are painful to all concerned. These students have an inability to anticipate the course of friendships, to foresee betrayals.

Among these students are those who have transgressed the social code in specific ways, young men who have pushed themselves on young women. These young men are not the heedless, self-centered sorts you think of when you hear "date rape." Rather, they appear bewildered at what has befallen them and generally out of their depth in social settings, unable to interpret interpersonal messages of any subtlety. And I wonder whether they have blundered into trouble through a failure to appreciate the ambivalence of a hard-to-read young woman or whether in an unhappy moment they have lashed out, in frustration at their inability ever to understand what transpires between two people.

*   *   *

There is mounting evidence, not entirely mainstream in psychiatry, that certain people handle social cues poorly, with harsh consequences for their happiness. We have no word for the capacity to pick up social nuance, but a name—dyssemia—has been proposed for the condition in which a person lacks it. Dyssemia is a recent coinage of Stephen Nowicki, Jr., and Marshall Duke, psychologists at Emory University. They built the term on the Greek word *semes*—sign or signal, as in semiotics or semaphore—using the models of dyslexia (difficulty with reading), dysgraphia (difficulty with writing), and dysthymia (difficulty with the "thymus," which the Greeks considered the seat of the emotions). Dyssemia is an abnormality in displaying or understanding nonverbal cues employed in social intercourse.

The notion of dyssemia arises from the observation that many children who don't "fit" socially also display one or another problem with nonverbal communication. They misinterpret the signals by which children recognize one another, or they project signals poorly regarding their own intentions. Nowicki and Duke believe that a primary problem with nonverbal communication—understanding it or producing it—underlies a host of social difficulties in childhood. The Emory group recognizes six areas of nonverbal language in which children can be handicapped: use of space (such as standing too near); gesture (signaling rejection when acceptance is intended); rhythm (failure to "read" when a situation calls for hurrying); facial expression (inability to distinguish signs of emotion); "paralanguage" (misusing or misinterpreting voice tone, rate of speech, or word emphasis); and "objectics" (inattention to such concrete factors as others' style of dress or their own body odor).

This list corresponds to traits I observe in young adults. The university students I mentioned, when you asked whether I had seen anyone like Donny, may speak too loudly or in a monotone, or they may lecture rather than converse. They may have trouble deciding what I expect of them or how I have responded to a comment of theirs. And they are baffled by the challenges of campus life. These students voice familiar woes—there are so many cliques; no one else is like me; my roommate is inconsiderate; old-fashioned values are no longer respected; you can't meet anyone unless you drink and put out. But for these students, the complaints are more intense and more paralyzing.

It is as if these lonely students cannot make use of the many markers that should allow them to distinguish potential friends, and even when they can, they have trouble making themselves understood. A body of research that stretches back to the Second World War finds that relatively simple tests of the capacity to grasp nonverbal signals—rating students' accuracy in judging the emotion an actor is expressing—are fair predictors of social integration. Even students who are bright and emotionally balanced tend to have few friends if they mistake nonverbal cues.

Problems in social judgment tend not to stay simple. Differing levels of sensitivity to nonverbal communication are established early in life. Often dyssemic students arrive at college with a history of social failure and a sense of inadequacy. Some find ways to cope, as Donny evidently did. But for others, the communicative problems become masked by an overlay of resentment, insecurity, despair, anxiety, and even paranoia. The idea of dyssemia allows a therapist to look past what appear to be grave psychiatric symptoms and focus with certain students on the goal of adjustment to campus life in the face of a definable problem in coding and decoding.

Perhaps in the early years dyssemia can be remedied directly. There is evidence that schoolchildren can be trained to do better in the specific areas where they score poorly on a dyssemia index and that this improvement results in better social integration. But I find my university-age population challenging. There are so many layers to peel back, and their difficulties with self-expression make these students hard to read.

Some years ago, a momentary fantasy brought home for me how devastating even small disabilities in social signaling must be. I had just read about the new sexual offense policy at Antioch College, the "Can I do this? Can I do that?" rules that generated nationwide discussion in 1993. (I remember a *New Yorker* cartoon of a praying mantis embracing her worried consort and coaxing him, "If I have to ask permission for every bite, dearest, we'll be mating all day.") By requiring verbal consent to each individual sex act and prohibiting action based on nonverbal cues, Antioch had created a whole campus of de jure dyssemics. At the time, I was treating a number of uncomfortable students, and my fantasy was that the solution to their problems would be a transfer to Antioch.

Anyone might feel safer dating under the new rules, but imagine how important the banning of attention to nonverbal signals could be for someone who knows she misreads them. I had in my practice unconfident young women who were in the habit of running away from a man as soon as courtship became confusing. Despite their uncertainty about the nonverbal messages they were sending or receiving, these women might be able, under the Antioch regime, to allow a perplexing approach by a man to play itself out. Only the words would count. The result might be more sex on campus, not less, since the rules would allow students like my patients to be permissive in the early stages of sexual contact, thereby also gaining practice in social intimacy. And think of the benefits to the bewildered young men. Clarity is a saving virtue for those who misread complexity.

My fantasy was that the legal imposition of a universal handicap might help those who happen to have the handicap already. But as soon as I fiddled with specific scenarios, my optimism waned. There are too many pitfalls for dyssemics. If a woman cannot gauge whom she is with, the requirement to answer yes or no to a series of questions will only unmask her confusion. As for doing the asking, the awkward will appear all the more awkward when forced to specify what they want. We are too much a species of signalers for any limited set of rules to relieve us of the requirement to send and process messages on multiple levels. The Antioch rules may succeed as a mechanical means to alter power relations between the genders; but the gap between fluent and nonfluent signalers is too vast to remedy through law.

Having worked with socially awkward students, I am able to entertain the perspective you propose: Donny misreads the data most people use to judge compatibility. He is an exception to the rule of matched differentiation of self. Donny hasn't a clue about how immature, needy, demanding, empty, and capricious Belinda will turn out to be. The kindest thing you can do is to make him aware of what he is overlooking. Like Harry Stack Sullivan, you will want to interrupt a disastrous plan with the exclamation, "Merciful God! Let us consider what will follow that!"

I see that you are discouraged. It is one thing for you and your mother to say that Donny is different, quite another for me to agree and attach a word to that difference. The fear that psychiatry will have no name for what ails those we love is counterbalanced by the fear that it will. The model of the concrete entity—illness, handicap, defect—tends to shape psychiatry's approach even to ordinary diversity. You ask that Donny be seen as exceptional, but you want the vision to be less categorical.

In truth, the psychiatric view of social difference can be yet more worrisome. There are reasons to believe that the concept of dyssemia is incomplete or inexact—that flaws in simple functions like perception are not at the root of social misunderstanding. Years ago, psychologists looked at the difficulties schizophrenic patients have with nonverbal cues. The patients did a fair job of identifying affect in videotapes of facial expressions; but if the experimenter added further cues, such as gesture and tone of voice, that were of use to most observers, the schizophrenic subjects did not improve their judgment. They could see any one sort of cue, but they failed to integrate multiple cues or to take in complex patterns of social information. Donny's problem, and those of my student patients, may be more of this sort. Though they do not have schizophrenia, they share the schizophrenic patients' difficulty in integrating social signals.

They may share other aspects of schizophrenia as well. Imagine that you have a second brother, Donny's identical twin, and this twin is afflicted with schizophrenia. Even during intervals when he is free of hallucinations and delusions, the schizophrenic twin is socially isolative, ungainly and stiff in his mannerisms, concrete in his understanding of metaphorical language, guarded and suspicious, altogether unsubtle in his response to social intercourse. In that case, we might ask whether Donny's social handicap has some relationship to his twin brother's schizophrenia. Because of genetics or perhaps an aspect of the family environment (parenting styles, exposure to viruses or bacteria, maternal health during pregnancy), your relatives have a particular difficulty in social communication, one that shows itself in mild form even in some who are in no sense mentally ill. Of course, you do not need an identical twin to have a partial presentation of schizophrenia; what looks like dyssemia in Donny is most usefully understood as lying on a continuum with mental illness.

The essentialist perspective in psychiatry often takes this form, conceptualizing normal behaviors as the healthy end of a spectrum that stretches to mental illness. And there is no shortage of mental illnesses to consider. Here is yet another way of thinking about Donny's handicap: As important as knowing what a given affect looks like is knowing what it *feels* like. Perhaps Donny's problem is less an absence of gross information about the other (there are many ways to know that the person across from us is sad) · than an inability to gather information through the subtlest of routes, empathy. Empathy is a resonance with the other that depends on familiarity with one's own feelings. Empathic data can be unreliable—sociopaths or even skilled salespeople can sometimes mislead the empathic by sending false signals—but in ordinary circumstances empathic attunement captures overtones of affect: the quality of sadness, its intensity, the sincerity that attaches to it, the degree of unspoken desperation or stoicism. And people differ greatly in their capacities for empathic attunement. Looking to mental illness, a central feature of autism is an apparent absence of empathic response.

Autism and its less severe variants encompass a range of dyssemic traits. There is a variant of autism, Asperger's disorder, one of whose features is pedantic speech. Adults with Asperger's disorder do not so much converse as lecture; they have no sense of the amount of detail, length of response, or level of vocabulary that will be comfortable for others. Everyone has met people with mild forms of this tendency. Often they will be, in a colloquial sense, obsessional, pursuing hobbies in great depth. They may seem more interested in facts, machines, or the routine of work than in the fine points of relationships. To say that such people have an expressive dyssemia tells a very partial story. Their personality contains a mixture of distinctive traits—fragments of dyssemia, social avoidance, obsessionality, and limitations in empathy. A psychiatrist is likely to imagine that such a person is at the healthy end of a spectrum that includes autism and Asperger's disorder.

If you look for dyssemia, you can find it in a variety of conditions.

Children with attention deficits, hyperactivity, and learning handicaps often have associated social problems; these problems may persist even when impulsivity, academic problems, and issues of self-esteem have been addressed. The bedrock disability often looks like difficulty interpreting social cues. Certain patients with obsessive-compulsive disorder lack intuition in interpersonal interactions and deal poorly with ambiguity. The mild end of the "OCD spectrum" includes "obsessional" types who, though normal, have similar constraints in their social functioning. Psychic trauma, especially severe stress in childhood, may impair social perception. There is evidence on this point from primate research. Monkeys isolated at critical stages of early development, even if they behave normally otherwise, will be prone as adults to misread social cues such as threats by dominant males. And they will do poorly in the social setting.

Perhaps a biological marker will be discovered—a blood test—that shows one of these illnesses to be an all-or-none phenomenon; either you have the disorder or you don't. But for the moment, it looks as if most psychiatric ailments have partial presentations. Some healthy people are hypersensitive to minor stressors and also misperceive, in the manner of post-traumatic disorder; others are hypervigilant and misperceive, in the manner of paranoid schizophrenia; and so forth. Rather than merely label Donny's problem "dyssemia," I may want to ask how he behaves once a relationship is under way. What does it mean that he blames you for the breakup of one of his marriages? Why is it that once you named his wife's flaws he could not get them out of his mind? Is there a touch of obsessionality here, or even paranoia? If I am to respond to your request for help in planning your forthcoming lunch—crafting an approach that might reach Donny—I will want to have formed an opinion. Maybe Donny is doing well to have snagged Belinda.

Here is the familiar dilemma that arises out of the essentialist psychiatric perspective: Is dyssemia (with or without such accompanying traits as minor levels of obsessionality, paranoia, hypersensitivity, or a need for social distance) merely an impediment to accurate social choice, or is it an aspect of low differentiation of self? In his arguments with you, Donny does sound a bit immature. Donny and Belinda may have more in common than you are willing to recognize.

Belinda's frequent references to meals and gifts make you think she is in it for the money. When you say she has bad character, you mean she deserves the sort of labels I applied to those who have sat where you are sitting now, narcissistic or even sociopathic. But sometimes people who look narcissistic and sociopathic are better seen as dyssemic. Belinda may have trouble assessing affection without its material concomitants. When Belinda boasts about her sexual manipulativeness, you cringe; but perhaps she can't gauge how she sounds to others, and perhaps she relies on sexual appeal because she is not skilled at other means of persuasion.

I don't say that Donny will have an easy time of it with Belinda. A union of two people who read social signals poorly—one of them underinvolved and prone to blaming, the other demanding and accustomed to making connections by using her sexuality—can spell trouble. Donny's other wives left him, and Belinda does seem a flight risk. But Donny's match with Belinda no longer seems inexplicable.

We are considering two opposing ways to look at Donny's decision to marry Belinda: He has chosen poorly because he is handicapped; or because he is handicapped, the choice is more appropriate than it at first appears. But these formulations overstate Donny's problems. He is not paranoid, he has always had friends. So what if Donny filters out social signals that are of importance to others? Calling that style an impairment or disability betrays an unwillingness to judge Donny according to his own values.

Donny has strengths—as you say, at work he looks mature. You have mentioned your brother's social eclecticism. He is slow to judge, and people like that in him. Even Donny's blandness, his failure to notice indicators of hostility, jealousy, or self-consciousness in others, makes him attractive. People don't feel stripped naked by him. He gives people space, allows them to prove themselves through their deeds. There are forms of rivalry Donny does not elicit. His matter-of-factness encourages his group to complete tasks without the constant reference to ego that might infect a team led by a more perceptive person. Donny's capacities are reflected in his beliefs. He thinks it unfair when managers rely on "feel" to evaluate workers; results should speak, not considerations of personality.

Donny embodies a certain American masculine ideal. He is decisive. He understands that some problems are best dispatched quickly,
because further evidence is unlikely to change the ultimate resolution.
He does not worry or regret much or say he's sorry. In his freedom from
neuroticism, Donny is not handicapped but advantaged. When I meet
someone like Donny, I realize how much better he works in groups than
I do. If he were evaluating me as a leader, Donny would find me oversensitive. He would advise me to set aside much of what I think I see,
allow people to go about their business. And he would be right. Here is
one area where the euphemism "differently abled" describes the situation well; sensitive and insensitive people are differently abled, and neither type has all the virtues.

After all, social acuity has its excesses. I sometimes think I see
patients who suffer from hypersemia. A woman may know just what is
going on with a man. When he says he adores her, she sees to what
extent this sentiment is due to his compulsive need to place women on
pedestals and attribute to them traits like docility and sweetness. She
considers the man insecure and mistaken. His hidden potential for rage
is apparent to her, as are his narcissism, his difficulty with commitment,
and his excessive need for control. She is easily hurt by small gestures of
neglect, gestures of which the man is unaware unless she points them
out, something she avoids doing, knowing she would only be thought
petty. She senses that he is never fully present, not even during lovemaking.

This woman's world is full of such men, and full of the signals of
ambivalence and unreliability that they emit. To her, many men are
blind to their own needs; others are frankly hypocrites. She holds these
beliefs resentfully and with a constant awareness of her difference from
men. The myriad of cues overwhelms her; she can scarcely distinguish
the more solid man from the less. Facing a man who is only slightly
deluded, she cannot smile at his shortcomings and hope for growth. The
flaws stand forth too vividly. For the hypersemic, to enter a relationship
requires a conscious effort to ignore what she perceives with great accuracy. Any liaison takes a leap of faith, and either she does not leap at all
or she leaps at the wrong moment, toward a man who is not subtly but

grossly unreliable. For all her discernment, she may be as much in need of advice as Donny.

Watching hypersemics in action gives the lie to any simple notion of "emotional intelligence" as a quantity that might be measured, say, by noting how well a person can identify the affective content of a videotape. Your brother Donny misses detail, but in many settings his inattention to the extraneous makes him effective. Regarding emotional intelligence, isn't the overarching consideration what you do with what you see? Many sensitive, perceptive people appear exquisitely self-destructive. As for Donny, do you really want to make the case that he has no notion of who Belinda is?

Belinda approaches Donny carrying big signs, with bold block letters that say sexy, demanding, passionate, emotional. He can read those signs, and they appeal to him. Your concern is that he misses all sorts of other indicators, that Belinda is unreliable, shallow, selfish. Regarding unreliability, even Donny must understand that flashy women, or men, can be trouble. You don't have to be a close reader of social conduct to hold this belief. If Donny chooses to marry Belinda, he must want trouble. Although trouble is too harsh a word. Donny wants a sense of connection.

At least this is my impression about people like Donny. They are not mentally ill, and they have enough alternate ways of gathering information to be generally in touch with consensual social reality. But they do overlook subtle cues, and they feel a bit on the outs. They are sensible of what they are missing and want someone who can give it to them. The problem that Donny is trying to solve is not how to bring stability to his life; he has stability. What he is missing is intensity of feeling. And Belinda promises that.

In worrying over Donny, you underestimate the otherness of the other. Donny doesn't approach marriage as you do. For all that you share some of the same genes and upbringing, he differs from you in his values. He is not so intent on getting it right as you are. His work matters to him, and his old buddies. Marital concerns may never be central to his life. He does not have the impression that marriages are made in heaven or that only one woman will do. He knows that part of him comes to life when he is with Belinda; he hopes he will be able to handle whatever else she brings.

Taken in this way, Donny's story illustrates the complexity of assessing differentiation of self and its matching in relationships. If we construe differentiation as the capacity for autonomy, we will say that Donny is better differentiated than Belinda. But his choosing her may not be a mistake. People who are bound up emotionally and out of touch with passion often "marry down," in terms of the capacity for autonomy or self-control.

Arthur Miller marries Marilyn Monroe because maturity isn't everything. In his autobiography, Miller writes: "[S]he had taken on an imminence in my imagination, the vitality of a force one does not understand but that seems on the verge of lighting up a vast surrounding plain of darkness." She brought back, Miller writes, the "myths of childhood," and the sanction to write. Perhaps he is lying to himself, and it is only sex, beauty, and fame that attract Miller to Monroe, but he presents her as a muse, a link to forces that are necessarily chaotic and even infantile. The moment he first envisages her suicide is the moment he knows he must marry her. He is overly differentiated—not so in touch with chaos as a writer might reasonably wish to be—so he seeks out her open instability. Monroe addresses Miller as "Papa," sees him as a shield against mental illness. Miller's tie to Monroe is built on the gap in their capacities for autonomy; the distance between the partners' ways of apprehending life is the basis for the romance.

Mightn't Donny's connection to Belinda be like that? Such alliances are difficult, likely to be plagued by a mutual idealization that is perpetually disappointed; but they are as compelling as the many relationships grounded in precise matching. And these marriages may be "matches," if we understand the capacity for connection to be an element in differentiation. The very markers of immaturity—impulsivity, spontaneity, lust, vitality, immediacy, loudness, neediness—are also markers of connectedness, and perhaps of a certain sort of independence as well.

We have spent so long on Donny's relationship that we have not had time to discuss yours. You ask if you can return for a second meeting. It takes you time to get comfortable. You do want advice. You are confused by the way your partner acts—a little dishonest at work, a little selfish at home. You live with the reality Hitchcock captured in *Suspicion,* of marriage as life with an unknowable other whose acts are explainable on each particular occasion but whose overall intentions are opaque.

I do want to meet with you again. I am guessing that you have a yet more minor variant of whatever Donny has. You are only passably good at reading the social world. That is how many people are, less accurate judges of others than the theory of matched differentiation of self says they should be. For them especially, intimacy entails uncertainty. Your unspoken concern, that you just do not read intricate situations well, makes the case for your getting advice—what you see as a minor degree of selfishness, I might see as something much worse. Like you, I hope to be protective of those who have trouble interpreting social cues.

As for Donny, you might suggest he go slow, though I doubt he will listen. The passage of time may help him judge whether Belinda meets his needs. Or he may mistake her entirely, in which case he is in for trouble. It is difficult to help those who fail to grasp social signals; decisions in matters of the heart are so subtle—this is the main thrust of our discussion—that one person can hardly make them for another. There will be more trial and error in Donny's searching than in most people's. You should not be surprised if it takes a few marriages for him to get it right. My own experience in these matters is that when people cannot see things as you do, it is difficult to spare them pain.

Matched differentiation of self is finally as fallible—as liable to exceptions—as any criterion that might serve as a starting point for assessing relationships. Perhaps it serves best as a metaphor for our remarkable capacity to locate one another. This capacity has limitations. Not everyone is clear-sighted. Humans give off ambiguous signals and engage in deception, so that skill at detection competes with skill at concealment. To these intricacies are added the variety of our appetites and the discontinuity of our character. Personality is in part a function of fluctuating mood. Judgment is clouded by our inertia once we have bonded and by our fear of loneliness, which causes us selectively to ignore unpleasant truths. Our ambivalence over values—autonomy versus connection—complicates mutual evaluation. It is finally hard to say which is more remarkable, our perceptiveness or our talent for living a hidden life. And yet I find that combining two flawed perspectives—the view of human limitations expressed by essentialist psychiatry and the view of human possibility expressed in a (modified) ideal of the differentiated self—creates a usable, if modest, structure on which to drape fictions that may help make sense of a relationship and its alternatives.

For anyone schooled in psychoanalytic thought, those fictions will seem superficial. Psychoanalysis holds that social difficulties arise from the individual unconscious made manifest. The very world a person encounters is shaped by his or her inner fears and longings. To speak only of overview concepts like "differentiation of self" or fixed essences like dysthymia and dyssemia mistakes the way relationships are inspired and sustained. Your individual history compels you to create idiosyncratic scenarios in matters of the heart. I have shied away from the analytic paradigm, not least because of my sense that in requesting advice you have signaled that you do not want to be intruded upon and "analyzed." But it is fruitless to limit ourselves to an external assessment of your circumstances if those circumstances are a product of irrational forces that lie within.

MISGIVINGS

18

Abie's Irish Rose

THE INSIDE shapes the outside. Who you are determines whom you encounter. At the first level this process is a matter of perception. A paranoid person is surrounded by enemies because he sees others that way. Understanding this process—how people create idiosyncratic versions of external reality—is one of psychology's most basic tasks. Partly for that reason, Freud chose paranoia as the subject of some of his earliest theorizing. He came to believe that paranoia is characterized by projection—a tendency to take disturbing thoughts, traits, feelings, or wishes and attribute them to others. Rather than own his self-accusations, the paranoid perceives others as accusing him. Projection is a defense, a way to protect the self against the full impact of disorganizing inner states.

Your projection ought to provide a means to locate you. The way you see me reflects your private fantasies. I will use this tool; I will try to track your sonar. But I will treat the results of that inquiry skeptically, because projection is a deceptively simple concept that leads to all kinds of trouble. Just how is a therapist to determine which repressed thoughts or wishes a projection represents?

That problem has been with psychoanalysis from its earliest days. Here is the first case in which Freud employs the concept of projection, a case that exemplifies his tendency to grasp the "obvious" in ways that exasperate modern readers: An unmarried young woman develops delusions of observation and persecution. She believes that the neighbors pity her, hinting that she was jilted by a former boarder, a social acquaintance who some years prior had taken a room in the family home. The woman's older sister informs Freud of an incident involving the boarder, which Freud reports: "[The younger sister] had been doing out the room when [the boarder] was still lying in bed. He had called her up to the bed, and, when she had unsuspectingly obeyed, put his penis in her hand. There had been no sequel to this scene. . . ." The man moved out of town, and in time the woman was troubled by periodic paranoid symptoms. For Freud, the connection is apparent: "[S]omething was repressed. And we can guess what that was. She had probably in fact been excited by what she had seen and by recollecting it. So what she was sparing herself was the self-reproach of being 'a bad woman.' " It is this self-accusation that she transposes and projects onto others.

A century later, this account of projection expresses all that separates us from Freud. In the era of the false memory debate, we will be less convinced than Freud was that the sexual episode took place at all. Perhaps the younger sister's illness extends further back than the older sister knows, so that the bedroom scene is not the cause but the expression of paranoia. Or perhaps aspects of the story are missing. The younger sister may have been approached by the boarder more often than the older sister says. From today's vantage, the boarder's behavior looks abusive rather than inviting, and even then this may have been a conventional view of the matter. The younger sister was molested, and rarely are instances of molestation isolated; the molestation may be a return to prior trauma. Taking the other side of the false memory debate, we will be open to the possibility that the younger sister was traumatized in childhood as well and that the paranoia is the result of repeated psychic injuries.

The modern reader will likely generate a series of alternative accounts, involving the role of the older sister, the neighbors, and even Freud, who has been accused in other instances of doctoring the facts rather than the patient. A range of histories including those I have outlined—that the younger sister was never molested but simply has a progressive paranoid disorder, or that she was molested repeatedly and has something like a post-traumatic stress disorder—seem more likely than Freud's version, that the whole of the illness can be traced to a single morning. A mental disturbance—an "essence," either paranoia or post-traumatic stress disorder—brings the relationship with the boarder to the fore of the patient's imagination or leads her to latch on to gossip over the boarder as a way of explaining disorganizing inner feelings.

How dangerous it is to rely on projection as a way of understanding the woman's hidden thoughts and feelings becomes clear when we turn our attention to what Freud says was repressed: "She had probably in fact been excited. . . ." Well, Freud may have been excited. As for the young woman, it seems more probable that she was humiliated or terrorized. If she had any foolish hopes, they were dashed, rather than awakened. Here Freud seems cruelly blind to the circumstances of women, exactly as critics make him out to be. He attributes to the victim intolerable self-accusations over her impulses when the problem is that she has been left crushed and hopeless. The young woman, like every person, does have a distinct perspective; as Leston Havens says, "We all stare forth from an individually shaped and genetically different nervous system onto a world seen from this time and place by no one else." But what does that perspective signal? From the many possible causes of the woman's discomfort in the neighborhood, Freud selects one; and the selection seems grounded less in her imagination than in his. Analyzing projection has just this difficulty, that what is discovered may say more about the doctor than about the patient.

Even for the modern analyst, who before venturing a hypothesis would spend extended time in discussion with the patient, Freud's version of projection is flawed. Freud assumes the existence of a stable self that can be readily located—a self built around a "structured mind," a repository of thoughts, traits, feelings, or wishes that can be traced by the projections to which they give rise. Freud grasps the thread and is led through the labyrinth to the patient's core. Psychoanalysis no longer trusts that there is a discernible core; perhaps all that exists is tangled thread. It is the interaction between patient and analyst that brings apparent order. Contemporary theory emphasizes the many unintended ways in which the therapist affects the patient. Authentic self is not discovered but created, as a result of the patient's efforts in the emotional presence of the analyst.

But the greatest difficulty for "projection," in terms of its use within psychoanalysis, is that it does not reflect what the analyst experiences in the consulting room. In intimate relationships—including the analytic relationship—what is at issue is less perception than action. The paranoid patient goes beyond perceiving a hostile world; he or she creates one.

A paranoid patient may speak so guardedly that the analyst finds herself acting like a prosecuting attorney, ferreting out details and speculating wildly, in order to attain the levels of information and authority she needs to feel comfortable. This effective sort of projection, the type where, for example, a patient not only sees the doctor as intrusive but treats her as intrusive, makes her feel intrusive, and even pushes her to respond intrusively, is called projective identification. Here, the patient does not merely disown unacceptable thoughts, traits, feelings, or wishes and attribute them to other people; he actively makes something like his inner reality appear around him.

Meanwhile, the analyst is influencing the patient. She may want to say that she has assumed an unresponsive "neutral" stance so as to let the patient "be himself." But there is no neutral stance. Psychologists have performed experiments in which a mother responds to an infant's overtures with a "still face." The still face arouses and frustrates and ultimately enrages or depresses the infant. For some adults, behaviors reminiscent of the still face evoke similar reactions. The analyst's passivity may well have elicited the patient's anxiety. And the analyst has her own needs: a flow of free association sufficient to produce the data she requires to construct hypotheses, adequate emotional contact, a certain level of open distress to which to respond. In short, she needs a "patient." By withholding and questioning, by observing and poking and prodding, she has created a person who meets her image, namely someone suffering from paranoia.

On the surface, neither patient nor analyst has gotten what he or she wants, and both may complain. The analyst may say she would prefer a more trusting patient, and the patient may say he wants a more supportive analyst. But each has gotten something familiar and compelling enough to allow the relationship to continue. The analyst is thoroughly committed to the treatment because she is badly needed by the disturbed patient. The patient is attached to the imperfect analyst because he recognizes how disorganized and helpless he is, and because in his current distressed state he would be even more mistrustful of someone new.

What is odd about this relationship is how much of each person is absent from it. The participants have not so much located one another as provoked new and arguably inauthentic selves who are engaged in a process that feels necessary, urgent, and vital. Yet each imagines it might be a relief for the whole thing to end.

You can see how short a leap it is from this account of psychoanalysis to an account of troubled marriages.

■   ■   ■

You are Francis's friend, the man whose wife Francis approached at intermission at the repertory theater. You have had it with your marriage. Your wife is an ice maiden—rejecting and sexually withholding. Mutual seduction was an enjoyable part of courtship. You married Linnea because she was sensible and capable of warmth, not cool and arbitrarily dismissive like your mother. The good sex lasted through the early phases of the marriage. But for the past couple of years, you've been getting the cold shoulder, and the cold hip and buttock. Isn't it time to leave?

Your complaint is clear enough. And yet on hearing it, I wonder— as many in this culture would wonder—whether you do not have ambivalence in this very area, sexual intimacy. Or ambivalence about warmth from women.

As part of my reconnaissance, with your permission I interview Linnea. She says it is hard to be turned on by a man who carps at just the wrong moment. When I ask her to elaborate, she indicates that she is often open to sex as she gets ready for bed, but you typically choose that time of day to pick a fight. Money is your favorite topic. As you brush your teeth, you notice her charge card bill, open on the bathroom counter. And then the tongue-lashing begins: How can one person spend so much? And the finance charges—she is like a vampire bleeding you dry.

Once you have recited your litany, Linnea is in no mood to do the things she was in a mood to do when you were dating. More to the point, she is no longer in the mood she was in half an hour ago, when she turned off the television and suggested you make an early night of it.

She hates the way you perseverate about money, because it is exactly what her father did. Failure to turn off the lights was a federal crime, and this was long before there were ecology police. She cannot bear to remember the way her father treated her mother—and the family was by no means poor. No wonder her mother became sharp-tongued and bitter. "Vampire" was the very word Linnea's father used—how did you find that word, and the gall to use it? Speak about disappointments. Before the wedding you were tender, so unlike her cynical, sarcastic parents. Of course Linnea no longer enjoys sex.

There is no shortage of approaches to a problem of this sort. I don't hold with your impression that the right next step is separation. I might think about a referral for specific counseling around sexual engagement. Or a behavioral intervention—suggesting you set aside an earlier time to discuss finances. I might say simply: If you care about sex, don't pick fights at bedtime.

Any of these recommendations might prove useful. But however I approach the relationship, I will be inclined to try to understand it in terms of projective identification. You and Linnea are enacting a drama in which each assigns the other an unappealing but recognizable role. How else to explain her leaving the bill in the bathroom? How else to understand your using just the word that turns you into her father? You each have found the perfect chilling effect. How can I avoid the suspicion that you are intent on creating a frigid wife and she a hypercritical husband?

I don't have an absolute conviction that projective identification is at work, know almost nothing yet about your family of origin, your fantasies, your hopes and fears. But it does not take much to cause me to wonder whether the sexual indifference you encounter in Linnea begins in your own imagination, whether the carving of ice maidens is an unwanted specialty of yours, just as the molding of martinets may be a specialty of Linnea's. This speculation has the flaws of the Freudian method—the possibility of mistaking fixed temperament for socially responsive character, the reliance on unverified historical accounts, the likelihood of blaming the victim. Flawed though projective identification may be, it is part of the obvious in our culture. And like other of the perspectives we apply, mutual projective identification has roots in mid-century psychiatry.

• • •

In 1967, the year Murray Bowen surprised his colleagues with his tale of the sojourn in Waverly, a British psychoanalyst named Henry Dicks published a book that was to attract its own devoted following. *Marital Tensions* is a sober and restrained account of the workings of the Marital Unit of the Tavistock Clinic in London, a psychoanalytic institute built largely around the work of Anna Freud's rival Melanie Klein.

Klein founded one of the principal schools of psychoanalysis, "object relations," the word "object" referring to an emotionally important person, as in "object of affection." Object relations theorists believe that what motivates people is not so much the forbidden drives that populate the Freudian unconscious as whole emotional constellations— large chunks of feeling and fantasy taken from charged relationships between the self and an important figure. In this model, self-destructive behavior is often traced to an unresolved attachment to a parent who elicited strong feelings of frustration. At its most pessimistic, the theory says that men are not just out to "marry their mother," but to marry the pain they felt in the least satisfying aspect of the relationship with her. Hidden in this theory is a notion of creative compulsion—these men must keep working on it until they get it right.

It was Klein who yoked two Freudian concepts to coin "projective identification." She focused on circumstances in which a person induces a disliked part of the self to appear in another person, usually an intimate, thereby at once getting rid of and remaining in touch with what is repudiated. Projective identification is Klein's account of a common way that people keep the images of emotionally charged relationships alive. When men don't marry their mother, they make whomever they marry into her.

Like Freudian psychoanalysis, object relations theory is interested in structure—how aspects of ambivalently held relationships are stably encoded in the individual mind. But object relations is also the early form of psychoanalysis most concerned with the interpersonal. It is no wonder that it should give rise to a theory of couples, arguably the predominant couple theory of our time.

That process begins with Henry Dicks. Dicks was a short, vital, immensely likable man. In a time of sectarianism in psychoanalysis, he was able to maintain friendships in all camps. After serving in the Second World War, Dicks built a clinic around the notion that marriage and its vicissitudes are most readily understood in terms of mutual projective identification. Between 1949 and 1967, Dicks worked with over two thousand couples, and he wrote convincingly about his findings. Techniques for treatment have evolved. But what distinguished *Marital Tensions* was Dicks's compelling description of people in crisis and his application of theory to couple functioning. As regards description and analysis, *Marital Tensions* has not been surpassed or superseded.

The vignettes in *Marital Tensions* take the form of charmingly concise case notes, with husbands referred to as H. and wives as W. From the start, Dicks was working on the Bianca and Hank problem. Here is his account of the first patient he looked at from a couple perspective, in 1949:

> A glamorous "peroxide blonde" of 35, of working class Irish origin, she impressed one as a primitive, temperamental, but essentially straight woman, more mature and intelligent than H., with capacity for warm feelings both of love and hate.
>
> . . . Of her only sister, W. said: "She likes Germans and Nazis—I am for the Eastern and Southern types; she married a rotter." It would seem exogamy was strongly marked.
>
> W.'s first marriage was to a "flashy boy" when she was 18. She was innocent and loved him and her three children deeply. Somewhat pathetically, she said she "would not now be impressed" by such a type, but she obviously idealized him still. . . .

After one of the children died, the woman left the flashy boy. While depressed, she married the current husband, "a romantically handsome

London Jew, shabbily elegant, the typical small-time 'spiv' of those days," whom Dicks diagnoses as an "inadequate paranoid psychopath." (A spiv is an unemployed man who lives by his wits; the word can also mean a shirker or slacker, and there are overtones of dandification, as in "spiffy." "Inadequate paranoid psychopath" is harder to define, but it does not signify a good catch.)

The wife has complained to her social worker about the second husband's violent attacks on her, and the couple have been referred to Dicks's clinic for an innovative service, a marital evaluation consisting of separate psychoanalytic interviews. Dicks's question is why the wife stays with the husband, despite his violence, her lack of feeling for him, and a judge's advice that she should leave. Equally: Given the evident strength of the partners' attachment, why is the marriage so turbulent? Dicks's answer begins with the hypothesis that despite the husband's evident shortcomings the wife contributes "*her full quota of ambivalence and retaliatory motivation*" to the drama. We hear the wife's mixed feelings in her own words:

[At first] I liked him, he didn't seem to be much after sex. . . . He seemed neglected—I started looking after him . . . but I was disappointed and started to despise him; he seemed cold, without real desire. . . . I like a man who is rough and dominates me, even if he is crooked. I would have loved to have him knocking me about—I was hungry for a real man. . . . I mistook him: I thought he was Spanish and passionate—but he was soppy and sentimental. . . . So I made spiteful remarks—yes, I goaded him. Now I *know* I am like his mother. . . .

A woman chooses a man who will let her be strong and maternal, but soon she is goading him into rough masculinity. Despite his assessment of the wife as more mature and intelligent than the husband, Dicks recognizes strong elements of "matching" in the marriage. With precision, each member has located or created a partner corresponding to a set of powerful, if maladaptive, erotic, and emotional needs.

What the spiv sees in the warm, temperamental blonde is no mystery, a glamorous mother figure; the problem is that in order to mask his dependency and his sexual inadequacy, he turns violent. More precisely, he alternates between sadism and apologetic tearfulness. But what does she see in him?

Dicks decides that the wife began by looking for an idealized version of her father—for a man who has her father's ability to provide protection but without the father's contempt for women's sexuality. The wife wants security leavened by romance. She has actually taken in many of her father's values—she is domineering, and she mistrusts her own drives. Her hope is to invest a man with her strength, to have that strong man value her feminine sexuality, and thereby to come to value it herself. Although she says she once liked her new husband's lack of sexual pushiness, she selected a Mediterranean type because she thought he would be liberated from traditional scruples. It is when the new husband disappoints in this regard that the troubles begin. The wife's complaint is not that the husband beats her but that he weeps. The husband is not manly enough.

This vignette illustrates Dicks's principle: Marital tension results from disappointment, and disappointment arises from spouses' failure to act like preconceived models in each other's imagination. The husband hopes the maternal and sensual wife will make him a man, as his undermining mother would not. The wife hopes the husband will make her a woman by accepting her projection of strength and then approving of her appetites. Each is intended to help the other with a task, growing up. But the wife's independence is too threatening to the husband, and the husband is too meek for the wife. The result is what Dicks calls a cat-and-dog marriage.

What Dicks does not say in his consideration of this early case, but what he comes to believe as his experience broadens, is that the cat and the dog create one another, in order to fill deeply felt needs. The full sequence of events is:

A person enters a relationship burdened with an unconscious image or group of feelings derived from a troubled early relationship. The wife, for example, has taken in aspects of difficult encounters with her dismissive, judgmental, forceful father.

The person then falls in love with someone onto whom he or she can project an idealization. In this instance, despite early indicators to the contrary, the wife sees the husband as highly masculine and also appreciative of female sexuality. This projection may include attempts to reshape the other, to make him as he should be, perhaps through the manner in which the wife nurtures the husband and offers herself sexually.

If the mutual idealization breaks down, disappointment ensues. The husband only imperfectly accepts the idealizing projection, and the wife realizes that he is neither manly nor romantic. Indeed, the husband is dismissive, as the wife's father was, and as the wife is toward herself.

In a resilient couple, where the initial idealization was not desperate and the level of subsequent disappointment is workable, efforts will be made to accept or alter the rejected part of the self that appears in the other. Less flexible couples respond to disappointed expectations by engaging in destructive forms of mutual projective identification. Each member of the couple will behave in just such a way as to induce in the partner exaggerated features of a frustrating parent. By goading the husband, the wife helps create a violent man, a parody of her forceful father. The husband, in frustrating the wife, replicates his hypercritical mother.

This is Dicks's account of marital tensions. Each partner was chosen in partial contrast to a parent and then idealized; both partners disappoint expectations; through mutual projective identification, partners are made into hurtful parodies of parents; this transformation establishes a destructive relationship that has great stability, in part because each spouse embodies unacceptable traits that, so long as the marriage persists, need not be experienced or dealt with as parts of the self. Many aspects of self and other remain hidden. The troubled marriage is the domain of altered creatures created by mutual projection.

Laid out baldly, Dicks's schema may seemed forced, but it is one that people use all the time in assessing relationships. Think back to the story of Iris, the publisher who finds her e-mailbox stuffed with evidence of her lover's emotional betrayal. Whatever else they believe, Iris and her friends will conclude what I also conclude: that Randall needs Iris to be a prickly pear and that through his indiscretions he aims to make her one. Simultaneously, Iris's friends and I will ask why Iris has given Randall so much room. The man of integrity who disappoints at home—that may well be a figure from Iris's imagination.

Or think of sleek Lena and her shaggy Guy: Lena passively accepts Guy's superior posture, and we may wonder whether she does not quietly goad him as well, stimulating his self-doubt and activating his contempt. Certainly Guy seems to need a dismissible woman, an image of Lena he clings to even as she demonstrates that she is nothing of the kind.

Awareness of mutual projective identification is today's common sense. Without the concept's having been made explicit, I (and I suspect, you) have seen every story through the lens of mutual projective identification: Asa makes Nikki bellicose; she makes him appallingly reasonable. Frances amplifies the domineering qualities of the man she is with; Francis, the self-indulgence and irrationality of the woman. The delicacy of Mark and Sandy proves to be not so much a solid fact as a mutually required role.

Murray Bowen's claim to self-differentiation can be seen equally as a claim that he is immune to projections. Through extensive preparation, Bowen avoids allowing himself to be inhabited by his mother's or brother's images of him. At the same time, he declines all opportunities to remake his relatives according to his own needs. Differentiation of self is very largely the capacity to resist, and to resist employing, projective identification.

As a perspective on couples, the idea of mutual projective identification is workable because it goes beyond the ostensibly blameworthy traits of each individual. The approach suggests the likelihood of joint responsibility for any trait and then asks an illuminating question: What drama does that trait serve? Regarding your current relationship, your partner's makeup does more than indicate your level of differentiation. The most distressing aspects of your partner provide a starting point for considering your needs and fantasies. Your own hard-to-change, provocative behavior speaks to your partner's needs and fantasies. You reap what you have sown.

But projective identification does not escape the limitations of its progenitor, projection. Granted, each person shapes the surrounding world, but must the manner of that reshaping always reveal the psychological imprint of early relationships? As with so much else in the theory of psychotherapy, mutual projective identification meets its limit in the essentialist perspective: The way a person "just is"—anhedonic, manic, dyssemic—also creates needs and evokes responses.

Perhaps this limitation is best illustrated by an example drawn directly from the field of child development. David Reiss, a psychiatrist and family theorist at George Washington University, has collaborated with geneticists to examine the settings in which children are reared. Comparing the familial experiences of siblings of different degrees of genetic propinquity, Reiss has found that a child's genes shape the child's environment. This result is counterintuitive. Ordinarily we imagine that parents mold children, much more than the reverse. But Reiss's work points to genetically modulated "child effects" on parental warmth, control, consistency, and especially conflict—extending to severe punishment and verbal violence. Part of what looks like nurture may be the child's nature, expressed in parental reactions.

The genes may increase the odds that a child will be a certain way— hypersensitive, impulsive, obsessional, aggressive, or timid—and each way of being selects different behaviors from the parental repertory. To look at a limited example that Reiss poses: Hyperactivity in children is in part hereditary. Parents of a hyperactive child will tend to be controlling and negative; they may become unresponsive even to positive communication from the child. If a medication reduces the child's symptoms, thus mitigating heredity, the parents will become more flexible and accepting.

This sort of analysis restricts the applicability of projective identification. One could hypothesize that a hyperactive child has an inner template of the unresponsive caregiver and projects that template onto parents, inducing the relevant behavior; but that idea seems disrespectful to the child—as with Freud's take on the paranoid younger sister, it blames the victim. When impulsive behaviors are said to be unconsciously motivated, the usual claim is that the children want more intense, not less intense, parental responses. An alternative and more plausible account says that the parents a hyperactive child gets have little to do with the child's internal wishes. The child does influence his environment, through behaviors that arise from the child's neurological makeup and that elicit the limited array of responses, for parents in this culture, to persistent impulsivity. When medication or behavioral treatment reshapes the family, it is through decreasing the child's hyperactivity and without any reference to the child's fantasies—although the child's ideals, images, and needs certainly will change as the child focuses better.

The genetically based "child effect" stands as a stark example of intimate interpersonal influence that has nothing to do with projective identification. Analogously, in adulthood you may sculpt your partner's behavior in ways that do not reflect unconscious conflict or internal images. The tension in your relationship will say something about your "individually shaped and genetically different nervous system," but it may not reflect the disappointed idealization that Dicks deemed so important.

Dicks is known for applying the theory of mutual projective identification to couples. But like Harry Stack Sullivan, and like Freud when he was on target, Dicks was so aware of the practicalities of daily living that his everyday wisdom overwhelms his theory. When Dicks says that disappointed expectation is what plagues difficult relationships, he opens the door to the outside world. There are all sorts of expectations and disappointments in life. A husband loses his job and disappoints expectations of security. (Imagine how the story of Linnea and her overbearing husband would look if we knew he had just lost his job to downsizing and that she had been pushed unwillingly into the workforce. We might still turn to mutual projective identification to explain the form of their bickering, but not before alluding to the stressors, external to the psychology of the marriage, that have disappointed their expectations of security and personal freedom.) A wife develops vaginal pain on intercourse and disappoints certain expectations of sexual fulfillment. Emigration to a new culture alters standards for the balance of effort and power between husband and wife. People have expectations, and life has a way of supplying disappointments.

Dicks recognized as much. He became involved with couples largely in response to the epidemic of divorce in postwar England. Dicks saw frequent divorce as inevitable in society's progress toward a less authoritarian and more permissive form of organization, especially as regards women's sexuality. But Dicks did see divorce as a source of pain, and of turmoil for children, and therefore worthy of doctorly attention. In *Marital Tensions,* he looks at the factors that changed rapidly in the first half of the century: norms for marriage and family structure, the role of women, the mixing of cultures, the distribution of earnings, the balance of rural and urban life, patterns of housing, and supports for the nuclear family. People complain of similar stressors at the end of the century. Social upheaval poses problems even for straightforward, conscious expectations. The spouse you get can never quite be the one you expect, because the culture is ever-changing.

Dicks's awareness of social likelihoods serves to undermine the claims of theory. His story of the glamorous peroxide blonde and the shabbily elegant spiv can be seen as a drama of cultural mixing. Dicks leads with the wife's Irishness and the husband's Jewishness because stereotyping plays a central role in their expectations. Cross-culturally dyssemic, they misread cues. The husband is not the Mediterranean lover he looks; the wife is not the lighthearted colleen. There is nothing subtle or inaccessible to consciousness here; ask the wife and she will tell you. She misread the husband. She mistook the form of his corruption; he is lazy and self-pitying, where she likes her men rough and driven, on the model of the flashy boy. Of course the wife goads her husband—to express her disappointment, to "make a man of him." We can call her goading projective identification, but the phrase brings excess baggage to our understanding of a marriage whose difficulties are apparent once Dicks points to their origins in cross-cultural confusion.

As for why disappointed people stay together, there are all sorts of reasons, including practical ones, such as the wish to give children two parents. As observers, our (and perhaps Dicks's) distress is in response to the husband's violence. If we adopt the wife's stated perspective—that the violence is of only intermittent concern—the continuation of the marriage is perhaps not so very remarkable. Or we may take an opposing perspective: The husband's violence is debilitating and addictive. In that case we will also understand the marriage's duration, and with no particular need to refer to the wife's creation of the husband according to her wishes.

In any relationship there is so much going on—the influence of personality traits that have nothing to do with unconscious imagination, the fulfillment or disappointment of expectations that arise from changes in the ambient society, the effect of cross-cultural misreading of signals (and every "family of origin" is a separate culture), fluctuations in health and mood—that "mutual projective identification" must take its turn alongside more mundane and less imaginatively appealing contributors to the fictive attitude. Dicks himself wrote about a trait he called "relational potential," and, elsewhere, "fitness for marriage," a global measure (not altogether dissimilar to differentiation of self) of a couple's commitment, flexibility, insight, sexual confidence, and so forth—one that makes mutual projective identification a less central factor than it might otherwise seem.

And yet I am unlikely to hear your presentation without listening for patterns of mutual projective identification. On the positive side, mutual projective identification is one of the glories of intimacy. In the best case, marriage lends you desirable qualities: You are credited, via idealization, with a new range of strengths; and you assume them, just as children come in time to assume the strengths imagined in their parents' appropriate fantasies. Mutual projective identification, taken this way, is one of the arguments for connectedness and against extreme differentiation—an instance of loss-of-self as gain-in-possibility.

But if you and your partner have reshaped one another through a crueler version of mutual projective identification, should you leave? Some of what you complain about in your partner is of your own making. It may make sense for you to stay and struggle, especially since in moving toward the other you are simultaneously moving toward an acceptance of aspects of self and freeing the other to be otherwise. Like Heraclitus, psychoanalysis says character is destiny; wherever you go, you will take along your fantasies and your need to project them. It might be as well to come to terms with them here and now.

There is another side to this argument, and often it is decisive. Some of who you are—provocative and withholding, impotent and rageful, ice maiden or martinet—results from the pressure of your partner's fantasies. In a destructive relationship, mutual projective identification assures that the sum of a couple's resources will be diminished; both members are denied their strengths. You might do well to get out. Even without much wrestling and struggling with the self, you might find you are luckier the next time round. As an advisor, if I think your trouble is a case of destructive mutual projective identification, I may well encourage you to leave.

Much of the powerful sense of decompression after separation or divorce relates to the reexperiencing of self outside the force field of the spouse—the feeling Hank expresses on leaving Bianca. Even quite mentally ill patients may do markedly better when a complex marriage ends, not so much because they are relieved of disappointments as because they regain scope of personality. They no longer have to conform to the imaginative requirements of the marriage. This effect is most powerful in instances of abuse—where one spouse has been enslaved by and addicted to mistreatment. Unfortunately, those relationships are the hardest to help people change or end. The person a therapist would like to negotiate with is absent; in her place is the skittish creation of her dominator's imagination.

The ethnically Irish wife says she knowingly provokes violence. How trustworthy is her account of her desires? Dicks has the reputation of a reliable interviewer, and we would do well to remember that generations differ and that people are diverse in their wishes. Variety is implicit in the concept of projective identification; it is meant to explain how people create and tolerate strange relationships. Still, we might easily imagine that the wife is more despairing than her self-report implies, and less comfortable with violence. After all, she has come for help. How might the wife—a free spirit by her own account—appear outside the marriage? We never learn. If she had therapy, it did not set her free from a marriage she claims to have despised. Nor was advice effective. Despite the repeated recommendations of judges and social workers, the wife never left her shiftless husband. Or rather, she left and returned eight or nine times over the following eight years. Then she and the husband and their ten-year-old child were lost to follow-up.

19
Simple Gifts

Y OU ASK: Do I want to know how you left that man? One day he
came home and asked you to hand over your engagement ring so
he could use it as a present for his mistress. If she was unhappy, he
would be unhappy, and he knew you wanted him to be happy. You had
been out of your body, looking down at yourself as you washed the
kitchen floor, terrified that he would find a spot of dirt and yell at you,
calling you a slob and a failure. And then he asked for the ring, and
you reentered your body, reentered laughing. And no nervous, hysterical titter, but a booming, just-whom-do-you-think-you're-dealing-with
laugh. You remember thanking the Lord for giving you the gift of that
man's foolish request. You were blind and now you saw. All you could do
was shake your head, at him and that dross-and-glass engagement ring
and that poor woman he was deluding and the foolish years of your life
that you were about to walk away from. You had not been eating for
some time, and so your fingers were thin; you could slide the ring off
easily. You tossed it on the table. And as he grabbed for it, you slipped
past him and across the lawn to your neighbors' house. You called the
police and had him thrown out of your life.

*   *   *

You ask: Do I want to know how you left that man? You saw him arguing with a client. He had no case to make, but he was arguing anyway, just the way he did at home. You saw him reach into his pocket and palm a handful of diet pills. He swigged them down with coffee and began to lay into the guy. Pure threat and swagger. And you thought to yourself, That's his magic, the frigging pills. And you realized you were in a relationship with a brain fried on uppers. This is what you're in bed with every night, this is where you expect love and security to come from. Suddenly you felt free. It took you a while to leave—arranging the new job, engaging the lawyer, finding a place to live. In the meanwhile, you started seeking out his stashes and flushing them away. One day, right before you walked out, you were in the office with him and you saw him reach into that pocket and come up empty. Then and there you picked a fight and said what you'd been afraid to say. Up yours, buddy, find yourself another bimbo. Get off my project, get out of my life. You could not imagine why it had taken you so long, you think of yourself as a tough broad. You felt like crap, though. And it took you years to trust anyone again.

There it is. After twenty-odd years in the field, the only distinctive thing I know about ending enslavement is that sometimes you get a gift, and if you do, you had better recognize and accept it.

Usually I hear about gifts in retrospect. A woman who is now doing well and wants to do better recalls a period of enslavement. How did she leave? She will tell me about an incredible act of overstepping by her possessor. He knocked up a single mother with four kids and wanted to move them in, while things sorted themselves out. Or the act may be so trivial as to seem indistinguishable from the man's habitual behavior. He made a pass at her special childhood chum. He insulted her in front of people she had hoped would be shielded from her misery.

It is hard to know what to make of the notion of the gift. Perhaps it is a representation, in story form, of a more gradual change in circumstance—new support from friends, the success of psychotherapy, a shift of power in the family of origin, spontaneous alteration in the possessed woman's mood, improvements in the political standing of women.

Men can be possessed, too, as *The Blue Angel* and *Of Human*

Bondage testify, but in my practice more often the victim has been a woman. A good while ago, I evaluated a woman who had spent years in a demeaning relationship. In a preliminary screening, she proved to have a previously undiagnosed thyroid disorder. Once on replacement hormone, she became enraged over an incident in which her boyfriend demeaned her son by telling the boy he was too ugly to be seen in public and too clumsy to be left at home. The boyfriend had applied these very words repeatedly to my patient. This time, and on her son's behalf, the woman was able to tell the man he had gone too far. She ended the relationship. Which was the gift, the insult or the thyroid medication?

And when is it a gift? For Iris, is Randall's suggestion that she take in Shatzi a gift? Is the bundle of e-mail letters gift enough? Can Iris reasonably risk Randall's promised efforts at fidelity?

Cases of possession raise a challenge for the prospect of advising. Henry Dicks's early vignette can be seen as a story of possession: the woman who cannot leave, despite repeated advice from everyone around her. If advice does not work in these instances, where the whole society is in agreement, of what use is it? And yet among psychotherapists even purists will often advise when it is a matter of abuse: Here is the location of a women's shelter, here is the name of a lawyer, I am phoning the police right now. Still, the degrading couple relationship is likely to persist.

In some ways the problems are harder if it is not a matter of physical violence but of what Leston Havens calls mental trespass and psychological possession. I have said that some of my most satisfying clinical work has been with patients hampered by insidious forms of depression. Some of the most frustrating is with the psychologically possessed. They are skittish. A wrong word, and they are gone—out the door to a life whose horrors are apparent to me—and there are no police to call.

One trap to avoid is the temptation to become another possessor—to try to substitute the therapist's control for the enslaver's. Judith Lewis Herman, an outspoken psychiatrist working with severely traumatized patients, warns that the possessed woman "must be the author and arbiter of her own recovery. Others may offer advice, support, assistance, affection, and care, but not cure." Herman recommends delicate psychotherapy, focused on providing a safe environment, naming the enslavement and reconstructing or remembering its causes, and creating a community in which the possessed can feel connected. Both advice and the gift seem puny tools in the face of what is required. But for more subtly enslaved patients, I have seen the gift work, and when I spot a gift I do not hesitate to point it out.

Where there is no gift, if I give advice I may worry whether it is for my own sake, so that I am on record as having outlined certain dangers. If I do advise in this formal fashion, the woman will say, But you don't understand. There are so many reasons, concrete reasons relating to money or career or children and psychological reasons related to how she sees him and how she experiences herself. To advise her to leave is to ignore her constrained perspective, which is her central problem. To advise her to leave is to deny the existence of mental trespass and psychological possession. The first question is not whether to advise but how to find standing in her narrow world. The next task is to help construct or reconstruct a self, perhaps the self that can leave. Often it seems that the cases where advice is least controversial are also the ones where it is least productive.

When it is time to advise, how is it to be done? We need a rhetoric of advice. How shall the opinion be framed, given the hypnotic power of the possessor and the paralysis of the possessed?

Thinking of Dicks's case, of the Irish-born wife I will now call Rose, I realize that I do not know enough about her circumstances. Perhaps she would not leave her husband, call him Abie, because the courts kept awarding him custody of their child. Perhaps she was realistic in seeing the marriage to Abie as the best she could do in life. She had a tolerance for being struck. And she may have enjoyed her power in the relationship.

According to recent research, domestic violence by men is more likely to occur in marriages where the man has little power, in terms of daily decision-making, and the woman's communication style—she withdraws and stonewalls—is stereotypically masculine. Rose and Abie's relationship might have been like that. The finding that it is powerless husbands who strike their wives seems counterintuitive until one thinks of violence as compensatory, for the man's inability to make his wishes prevail by nonviolent means. It is hard to know whether, within the marriage, Rose is powerful or possessed. Dicks's account leaves room to believe she may be both.

If I were Rose's caseworker and she came to me about Abie; if I thought Rose's inability to leave was an instance of psychological possession; if I knew that straightforward advice had failed eight or nine times; if Abie was still violent; and if Rose was a good-enough mother and the courts were willing to grant her custody of the child—the many ifs required to make the matter "obvious"—then what would I do? I might just listen for the sound of the gift. I would direct my empathy toward hearing what it is that still has the power to shock. If Rose did at last mention a moment when Abie challenged her to accept a distinctly deeper level of degradation, I would gasp in pained disbelief. Throughout Rose's telling of her story, my empathic posture would have allowed me to absorb Abie's violent blows with equanimity, just as Rose did; only the final insult would take my breath away. That gasp would contain the whole of my advice, though some might object that gasping is not quite advising.

In conjuring you, I have so far imagined that you will not be seeking advice over an abusive relationship. I have assumed that you are self-possessed and self-sufficient. This anticipation has been as much an expression of hope as of conviction. Because trespass is insidious. Havens says that some who think they are giants do not realize that they are in the belly of the whale, "confined and being psychologically digested." Certainly the confinement and digestion may be inapparent to those who meet the possessed. Perhaps Lou mistook your dilemma. Or else behind your bland request Lou heard the desperation of the caged and referred you on the principle that in these matters a doctor welcomes whatever opening is offered.

* * *

You come through my door, Donny's sister, now here to discuss your own marriage. You begin by saying you don't want me to get the wrong impression. You and Philip have a lovely relationship. What made you ask for a consultation is something that will sound trivial. Philip gave you a tongue-lashing at a recent party, and the hostess, Jonnie, took you aside. Nora, she said, if you will not stay here with me tonight and tell Philip good-bye, you must at least promise that you will see someone. You know how it looked to Jonnie. But don't I agree with you that there is too much talk these days of abuse, too much jumping to conclusions?

Occasionally you do feel hopeless about the relationship. And Philip's outburst did put you into a funk, mostly because he had upset the hostess. When later at the same party you found yourself speaking to a senior psychiatrist, you asked whether there was not someone to give you straightforward advice. You have seen therapists, recently and in the past. They dredge up ancient history, which leads nowhere; or they advise mutual accommodation. Philip is not about to accommodate, and how you could accommodate any further you do not know. So in the end, there is only one question: Should you leave?

You want me to understand how decent Philip can be. You insist that this be my starting point, Philip as you knew him when you first met, a man capable of considerateness. Often you wonder what is wrong with you that you cannot bring that Philip back. You know you have been a disappointment to him. You believe in the inherent value of duration in relationships. If there is any hope at all for you and Philip, you want to stay. But sometimes you want to know how crazy you are for being such an idealist.

God bless the unreliable narrator. I mean, we are all unreliable narrators, not just the sons of bitches, like in Ford Madox Ford. In the end isn't "unreliable" redundant? And we are imperfectly self-possessed. The premise behind "differentiation of self," and behind "mutual projective identification," is that everyone is, to some degree, under the influence of others.

I do take you, Nora, to be an idealist of a sort. But I know I'm going to hate the ideal you are serving, know that your story will be excruciating to hear. And that it will involve, beyond ideals, all sorts of mixed motivation—fear, apprehension, and yes, the sort of addiction Jonnie glimpsed in your response to Philip.

Matters are worse than I had thought. Your sitting in my chair the other day—when you worried over your brother Donny's fascination with Belinda—that little error wasn't a sign of dyssemia, not a bit of it. You are someone who usually gets by on facade, and your distractedly choosing the wrong seat was an indication that you can no longer quite hold it together. Your clothes were fashionable but wrinkled, and piled on in layers, as if you had dressed yourself out of the hamper. I thought you lacked a sense of how outfits are worn, but I realize now that you must just have been demoralized and inattentive to details that ordinarily matter to you. I see today that you are capable of elegance, and I wonder, as I get a look at you in a tailored suit, whether you are not a bit anorexic as well. Shame on me for having missed so much. It was an instance of selective inattention—your skill at denying your circumstances to yourself and my willingness to share your blind spot.

It is the contrast of the presentations of self in the two meetings that gives a fuller picture: Dependent on appearance, you are no longer able always to keep up appearances. You have lapses in concentration. You are falling into what has been called a smiling depression, and you are not always on your game.

I intend no criticism. I am an admirer of facades, which have their own beauty. They are often used generously, to protect others. The issue is what you are doing behind the facade and how seriously you take it when you look in the mirror. No doubt I should begin by seeing you as you are struggling to appear, contented and in control; Havens's constant admonition to trainees is to work from the image to the person suppressed. For the moment, I will ignore your undertone of desperation and encourage you to tell your story as you choose.

What you loved in Philip was his self-assurance, his calm in the face of turmoil, his self-containment. You know you have let yourself go, such a disappointment to Philip. But back then you were attractive and—you wonder whether I can believe this—accustomed to avid responses from men. In Philip, you met a man who looked past appearances to genuine worth. He made you want to earn his admiration. Sometimes you think you have been at that task since you met.

You remember the moment: the low boom of crowd noise in the

convention center, topped by an odd slapping sound, the ricochet of exclamations off concrete walls. You feel dwarfed in outsize buildings. And then before you stood Philip, crisp and confident. You knew his name from articles he had co-authored. You felt lucky to have the chance to speak with him. He was reassuringly formal. Men can be so intrusive. You showed Philip how you had worked his approach into your own, on the little jobs you bid on as an independent consultant. You hoped you were coherent. You felt unsteady on your feet, uncertain of how loudly to speak and in what detail.

Days later, Philip surprised you by phoning—would you join him on a project? You were bowled over. Already you had been thinking of no one but him. You gladly merged your business into his—so much easier to get work with his name atop the proposals. Those were the happy months. You were starry-eyed, he seemed to be moving, however slowly, from business relationship to courtship. It was good to meet a man who did not burden you with overvaluation.

Philip was well spoken, promising, presentable. He pleased your family. Your best friend, on the other hand, accused him of trading on the creativity of others and taking the credit. Philip's acid tongue, which in an odd way made you feel at home, angered her. In time, you cut her off: She did not appreciate his understated kindness to those without talent.

When you discovered you were pregnant by Philip, you were secretly thrilled. You had believed you were infertile, because in years of unprotected sex with an old boyfriend you had never conceived. Now you were carrying the child of a good man.

Philip turned icy cold—how could you do this to him? Only in time did you realize what he demanded. He would marry you, but on the condition that you abort the pregnancy. You were not religiously opposed to abortions, they just made you queasy. And you had been so concerned that you were barren.

You understood that if you kept the baby, you would lose Philip. What choice, really, did you have? You aborted, which was more horrible for you than Philip could know, or than you would let him know, since you wanted him to enter the marriage with the sort of woman he demanded, a happy woman.

He did marry you, he kept his bargain in that way, but grudgingly. You had hastened his schedule. What was funny was that you loved him all the more, loved his little-boy squeamishness about intimacy, loved his going off into the world selling his ideas. If he criticized you, it was with good cause. After the marriage you started falling apart, failing him in small but important ways. You might miss a deadline, or forget to pass on a phone message, or in the middle of a meeting make the sort of comment that infuriated him. He began to shield you from clients, to demand—with every reason—that you stay in the office and do grunt work.

You know you have not made him happy. You are not the looker you once were. When he was finally ready to have children, you failed to give him any. There has been unspoken resentment about that, you suspect. Sometimes you wonder whether he is turning his attention elsewhere.

Who can blame him? If Philip says hurtful things, the way he did at the party, it's your fault. His exasperation with you has driven the refinement out of him. You like that he cares enough to correct you. Sometimes you go for days without eating after he calls you a fat bag. But then you take your calories through liquor.

You are terrified that he will leave. You feel flabby and debilitated, no longer capable of attracting a man and not the least bit suited to isolation. You fear being alone, have adopted three cats, drink yourself to sleep when Philip is away on business. You don't accompany him because you can't travel, are afraid you will vomit. At first, you could handle it if you had an aisle seat and constant access to the bathroom. Philip despises your fussiness. It has proved easier to stay at home.

Are there other women? Sometimes after a trip, he brings his own clothes to the cleaner. And you came across an odd document that seems to show he co-owns a condominium with a woman who works with one of your business competitors as an idea person. He yells at you so much over little things, you can't imagine what would happen if you asked him about the condo. These problems concern some wives more than others. You are of so little use to Philip or anyone.

You feel foolish asking for advice. What put you up to it was a word in Philip's diatribe at the party: Philip called you a dried-up prune. You knew what he meant. Infertile. You don't know why, but that one epithet seemed to step over the line. You realized, in a confused moment, that some of what has kept you in the marriage is loyalty to your lost pregnancy—your lost unborn child, you sometimes think. After what you sacrificed, the marriage has to work.

Now that you are here, you see that your sensitivity about Philip's language is petty. People do not understand how kind he has been to stay with you this long. You feel foolish asking whether you should leave a man you love and who has put up with so much from you.

The only rhetoric at my service is the look on my face when you say "prune." Not horror or astonishment. Any strong reaction would risk driving you to the other pole of your ambivalence. What I am aiming for is your affect, a wondering whether perhaps it is not finally all too much. Your affect plus a little extra. I want to underline what you have said, to ask you to linger at the thought about loyalty to the baby and what that entails.

If I thought I could get away with it, if you were not too skittish, I would also advise you to leave—not in hopes of your taking that advice, but in order to plant a seed and because it is important, in your presence, to show that someone can be clear and direct. But I suspect it is too early for open advising.

Leston Havens's specialty is reaching the hard-to-reach, through the less verbal rhetoric of psychotherapy, its gasps and grunts and brief statements of surprise. Havens is also interested in what linguistic philosophers call performative language—the difference between a fan's yelling "Strike three" and the ump's yelling the same thing. Context, as much as grammar and vocabulary, determines what language means and does. Sometimes a psychiatrist's words make things happen, as when in the course of a hearing he pronounces a person psychotic and dangerous and therefore legally committable. Similarly, it might be effective for a psychiatrist to say to you, Your partner is abusive—but only if your willingness to believe it is so has given the psychiatrist the authority to make language performative, and only if there is a route out.

Because I have convictions about your relationship with Philip—

because its destructiveness falls well into the range of the obvious—I will want to make my gesture and comportment effective. Later, when words can reach you, I will say that Philip is abusive and you must leave. For the moment, I might only venture: You do look worn out; I would like to see you a few more times, to help build your strength for the challenges you face.

You say you want advice, but I am afraid that if I give you advice in full measure you will bolt. My first goal is not to lose you; my second is to make you less shut, less isolated within your fearful perspective.

Regarding enslavement, there are theories, but no one has explained it satisfactorily. In his early work, Freud argued that the key motivation is pleasure, in particular sexual pleasure or libido; he believed that self-destructive behavior resulted largely from guilt over illicit desire. But so prevalent is the tendency to tolerate or even seek out pain that in later years Freud felt compelled to look beyond the pleasure principle and to propose a death instinct and a compulsion to repeat. Freud's is an essentialist perspective—people "just are" self-defeating on an unspecified basis grounded in the human constitution. "Death instinct" and "repetition compulsion" are mostly ways of expressing ignorance and wonder. When so much of ordinary life is governed by the seeking of rewards and the avoidance of punishment, why should some of the grandest decisions, concerning love and even the attachment to life, be governed by renunciation?

Today, we take it for granted that people will repeatedly enter or become stuck in destructive relationships. We expect that children who are abused will as adults seek out abuse, if they do not themselves become abusers. Some graduates of painful childhoods enact all the permutations of the abusive relationship: beating one lover and then accepting beatings from another, undermining the first child and then making outlandish sacrifices for the second. Portions of this behavior are apparent in other species, traumatized young growing into traumatizing or submissive adults. Oddly, some humans who have had seemingly happy childhoods also tolerate emotional enslavement.

Vulnerability to enslavement is so striking and so maladaptive that it requires explanation. How can such a trait survive? Sometimes I think of enslavement as a hypnotic phenomenon. The enslavers induce a substitution of wills, their will for their subject's. They are vampires, gaining strength as their victim wastes away; the commanding and decisive executive you see by day flourishes on the blood of the wife he drains by night, his dominance fed by her submission. This view of enslavement as quasi-hypnotic brings to mind traits seen in other spheres—loyalty to leaders, mass hysteria, religious ecstasy, the loss of self that occurs in listening to a tale. Perhaps enslavement arises from qualities that more often serve an adaptive function, capacities for attachment, loyalty, and creative transcendence.

Certainly attachment is an essential drive, as basic as sex or hunger. It is four decades since the psychologist Harry Harlow showed that baby monkeys will prefer a cloth-covered dummy—one to which they can cling—over a wire "mother" that supplies milk; and aspects of the need for attachment persist throughout the life cycle. No one knows how to supply the attachment drive; at their best, psychiatric interventions remove impediments to attachment or (in cases of possession) modify or deflect attachments that are maladaptive. Given the instinctual nature of bonding, it is hard to know which is more mysterious, that enslavement occurs or that it does not occur more regularly.

In animal species organized by hierarchy dominance (and this is a widespread and ancient social arrangement; not only monkeys, wolves, and lions but even lobsters and crayfish have the brain structures in place for dominance and submission), the majority of animals are submissive. Submissiveness is sustained biochemically, through the laying down of neuronal pathways and through stable changes in brain levels of neurotransmitters and hormones. Levels are influenced by genetics and by trauma. Perhaps enslavement is an extreme form of submission.

In our species, it is easy to imagine systems getting stuck in such a way that extreme submissiveness feels like true self. Occasionally people experience an increase in self-worth when they respond to an antidepressant. When the affect changes, thought and willpower do as well. Here is an approach to enslavement to go along with grunts and gestures. If you are more amenable to psychopharmacology than to advice, and especially if depression is part of your presentation, it might make sense to see whether medication broadens your range of perspective.

*   *   *

Some people seem altogether desperate and disorganized, eager to be possessed as a way of avoiding the effort that would be required to take life into their own hands. But in others, self-dispossession is more mysterious. Outside the home, they are productive and attuned, considered in their judgment. Only in their intimate relationship are they obsequious and terrorized. Among these latter dispossessed, vulnerability to trespass seems a specific flaw, out of sync with who they otherwise are. At home, they meet Murray Bowen's definition of low self-differentiation—they cannot hold on to their beliefs or values; but once beyond the influence of the possessor they have a high level of competency.

I have seen instances of possession that are exceedingly subtle. The possession is not based on violence nor on intimidation. A romantic, insecure woman is in what seems a loveless relationship with a haughty man. Why does she stay? Because he is sometimes so caring, she says. Further inquiry will reveal that the "sometimes" is infrequent. Once ten weeks ago, and then again just before the session with the psychiatrist, as if to weaken the woman's resolve to change. A random and intermittent reinforcement is at work. The woman rarely gets what she wants; she is at once increasingly bound to the man and increasingly hopeless. Couple therapy seems to work—the man responds immediately—but its effects are fleeting, part of the intermittent reinforcement schedule that maintains the woman's deprivation. This sort of marriage may be quite common.

■   ■   ■

Leston Havens takes enslavement to be an ordinary aspect of the human condition, a corollary of the reality of power. His is an intelligently paranoid perspective—the perspective of a child of a judgmental father who was slippery, withholding, unknowable, and too clever by half, a contemptuous father who, in Havens's words, "found the ordinary boring, when in fact it is often extraordinary." In Havens's universe, there are victims and victimizers, trespassers and those trespassed upon. For the most part Havens's sympathies are with victims. In order to avoid discovery and possession, many who are threatened by others' power assume roles and masks or even remain inchoate. One of my favorite

Havens metaphors says that some people in psychotherapy are like frag-
mented nation-states: You have to create an interim government in
order to have someone to negotiate with.

The patients Havens writes about are often beautiful women—
simultaneously possessed and prepossessing. With their chestnut manes,
natural grace, long-fingered hands, and their capacity to move with still-
ness, these women are prisoners both of a particular man and of their
image. A woman's regal bearing will lead men to mistake her lack of self-
ownership and to wish all the more to own her. For such a patient,
Havens hopes to catalyze self-possession, a concept that has elements in
common with self-differentiation.

Meanwhile, Havens admires these women for their solicitousness.
They seem more concerned for the doctor than for themselves. Havens
responds with an attitude that says, "Thank you, how kind, but let me
do as well for you." His task is to make these self-deprecating patients
feel worthy of his attention. The therapy is positional. Metaphorically,
Havens sits beside the patient, looks out at the world with her. He gives
her room, lets her be, takes care not to usurp judgment. Havens is ever
aware of the question of agency: "In my heart I felt she should raise hell,
shout out, 'No one will treat me this way!' But she had to do it, not I."
He is careful not to impose his will, since he is treating a disorder of the
will. The key to change is creating a setting in which the remaining
spark of will can kindle.

A Havens vignette supplies a definition of possession, or its lack:
"she was not in possession of herself, that is, hers were incomplete and
unacknowledged goals and unaccepted facts." (For Havens, too, dispos-
session is close kin to undifferentiation.) Havens is writing about a
privileged nineteen-year-old, Jeanne, whose parents have offered her a
persona, that of a rich and beautiful young woman, and also a goal,
marriage to Prince Charming. Jeanne is not (as classical Freudianism
might have it) guilty over these attributes—not inhibited in her ability
to experience pleasure. Nor is she a fraud. The culture deems her rich
and beautiful. These are Sullivanian facts, apparent even to Jeanne.
When men say she is beautiful, she disconcerts them by accepting the
statement as the simple truth. But though they are facts, their implications do not attach to Jeanne. She does not own the romantic worth

attributed to her by adoring men. If anything, the images these men propose threaten Jeanne—like her parents, the men want to overwhelm her. Jeanne's resistance, her sense of unreality, is as close as she comes to self-possession.

Havens tries to sit beside his patient and look out with her at the Princes Charming. Part of that process involves saying, "I hope he is worth your while"—imitating and amplifying Jeanne's inner voice. Hearing her voice, Jeanne begins to organize, to brave a move toward a self she can own. And yet Havens remains tentative. He retains the fictive attitude, the sense that any story, even Jeanne's as she begins to express it, must be heard skeptically and that alternate versions must be entertained. Jeanne will wisely have concealed herself, and she must retain the right to reveal herself gradually, with false starts and instances of deception. It would be a mistake, for instance, to praise her for traits that will turn out to have been imposed on her. She must be helped to feel worthy, but first she must be found.

Repeatedly, Havens counsels against premature conclusions. He cites Emerson's dictum that the largest part of man is that which is not inventoried:

We are all now and then guilty of the folly of judging others at a glance, across a crowded room. It is the nature of first opinions to classify: in or out, strong or weak, dumb or smart, shrewd or naive. . . . At root the judgments are tribal: does the observed belong, or can I defeat him? This is not folly at the city gates in a time of siege. But it is if we mean to understand human nature and not be admissions officers to our little aristocracies.

There are two modes of perception, one adequate for emergencies, one for the sort of serious apprehension of the other that should govern intimacy. Havens would agree with Lou's concern, that advice makes too many presumptions about unknowable others. But I am reassured by Havens's easy awareness of what he does know. He does not feign ignorance of Jeanne's wealth and beauty and their allure to predatory men—those are evident across a crowded room. Havens oscillates between a Sullivanian adeptness with the facts of daily life and an existentialist's insistence on his ignorance of the goals and values of the unformed person before him. Though he is careful not to trespass upon territory he aims to liberate, Havens seems from the outset to have his own wish, for Jeanne to escape the undue influence of those who would possess her. I take Havens's act of sitting, metaphorically, beside the patient to be a form of advice. It says, there are alternatives to relationships in which others impose their will on you. It says, take the time and space to develop your own identity, goals, and values; they are worth waiting for.

Lesser degrees of trespass and possession can be seen as the root of much ordinary trouble in relationships. Bowen's position can be restated in these terms: What bears fixing is the tendency to cede self to others, the phenomenon Bowen calls low self-differentiation. Certainly Havens finds that people regularly trespass on one another's minds. The demanding impose expectations. The loyal are exploited for their loyalty. Havens's view of flawed marriages is a nightmare of projective identification: One partner "may want to please the other, and therefore empowers him or her. People go for years doing things that neither wants but each has imagined." So possession is a metaphor for trouble of more subtle sorts.

In a particularly pessimistic passage, Havens suggests:

> Set yourself not to possess or abuse or escape another human being, and you see quickly the thin curtain separating our hope of civilization from the savage practices of slavery and cannibalism. Most loving couples begin their relationship with a stern resolution to honor and respect. And yet they have hardly left the church before the slowness of one or the haste of the other, the disappointment of one expectation or the unwanted fulfillment of another, reveals the snarling beast.

I once skied with Eric Nesterenko. Now a ski instructor, Nesterenko survived twenty-one years in the National Hockey League, sixteen as right wing for the great Chicago Blackhawks teams that included Stan Mikita and Bobby Hull. Nesterenko characterizes hockey as a game of possession. Through intimidation, one player gains space at the expense of another. The game consists in finding an opponent's weakness and exploiting it relentlessly. One player "owns" another. If the dominated player wants to repossess himself, he will need to face fear and bear pain. Nesterenko has applied his hockey philosophy to his new sport—the self-possessed skier is one who continually challenges what frightens him. Other professions, and certain sorts of upbringing, can provide this possess-or-be-possessed perspective, one that is then applied in all arenas, including love and marriage. The well-lived life entails repeated confrontation of one's fears, and constant vigilance against encroachments.

When I first met Havens, I experienced him as a man intent on blocking all possibility of possession. It was Havens, among others, whom I had in mind when I said that in my medical school psychiatrists treated students like analytic patients. Havens held himself apart in an almost provocative way, declining to act the role of the teacher who responds to the eager-beaver student. At first I thought he wanted to possess me, by showing what I would now call the "still face." In time I understood that what he wanted was the opposite: not to possess me, and not to make me assume a false persona. His quizzical stance blocked my offering myself up for possession, as zealous students do. Nor would he be trespassed upon, in the way that teachers are by ambitious trainees. Havens's air of apartness said that people are not known readily and that what they offer of themselves (what I was offering of myself) must be taken fictively.

Havens, as much as Bowen, shaped my appreciation of differentiation. By holding himself aloof, Havens forced me back on my own resources. His caution was a form of advice, to develop and consult my own values and passions. When I got to know Havens better, he seemed tender, kind, and generous. I wondered whether he had changed or whether the posture he first assumed, that insistent countering of projection, was a form of generosity.

I recognize in Havens a passion for protecting the possessed, especially those unaware of their enslavement; this passion parallels my own for protecting against insidious depression. In the dialectic between autonomy and intimacy, Havens values intimacy, but like Bowen, he finds autonomy prerequisite. Too many are eaten alive in the name of relationship. Much of life entails the securing of safe space.

Caution was also an element in Lou's perspective, and my training took place in its shadow. But I also have concerns in the opposite direction. Awareness of trespass can be overlearned. A person can be excessively self-possessed, unnecessarily concerned about incursions, and unable to draw as much strength as he safely might from relationships. I do encounter the possessed; but more often I see in people the quality I initially ascribed to you, a reasonable degree of self-sufficiency, enough to hear advice without its constituting a threat to autonomy, enough to risk the rotation method. Though I understand the applicability of the metaphor of trespass, I find enslavement to be not a universal but a special circumstance—or only one aspect of the universal.

As a therapist, I am constantly moving in and out of patients' force fields. To do any good at all, to know you, I must allow myself to be possessed for a time, to subject myself to your projective identification and other influences you exert. This experience of being distorted or stretched is both a technical tool—a means of finding you—and a privilege of psychotherapy as a profession, a means through which I discover and develop aspects of self. That repeated and intermittent experience, made safe by the therapist's return to a position of relative autonomy, mirrors the more profound self-discovery and self-creation that is the upside of the permitted incursions that characterize most intimate relationships.

I have wanted to locate myself for you, and the consideration of possession may be a touchstone in that process. In the broad sweep of society, I would be seen as a sober pessimist. Even within the range of psychotherapists—considering Carl Rogers, say, or some of the self psychologists—I am dour. But compared to the therapists I most admire, traditionalists such as Lou or existentialists such as Leston Havens, I appear a lightweight optimist. I recognize pathological possession, and I worry over it as I worry over totalitarianism in the political arena—as a constant threat but not a universal condition.

People captivate one another, and impress them, and hold them in thrall. We may be programmed with a certain inertia, a tendency to bond for a time (seven years, it was once said, before we get a distracting itch, and I vaguely remember some supportive research), just as we seem to be programmed, in terms of our moods, to be a trifle unrealistically optimistic. Though dangerous, this naive giving over of self has it uses. It supplies space for the working through of minor incompatibilities.

Sometimes one person's tendency to bond is taken advantage of by another who would possess. But there is this to be said against possession, in evolutionary terms: It diminishes the total of a couple's resources, just as totalitarianism, for all its other logic as a form of organization, diminishes the sum of societal resources. I have a weak but persistent doubt that possession is likely to be the predominant form of organization in couples. I suspect we want to be married to a whole person—one who is well differentiated or skilled at connection—and to be a whole person ourselves, because that is what works. Since (reversible) possession is a form of communication, of cross-pollination, of sharing of perspectives, to possess and be possessed intermittently—as occurs in psychotherapy and in relationships where intimacy is intense—adds a degree of coordination that should only increase a couple's capacity to face challenges.

This sense of possession as an ordinary and, in moderation, helpful aspect of relationship allows me to consider advising to be a reasonable undertaking, even though it entails the momentary assumption of authority. And the instances of destructive possession in relationships serve only to underscore the importance of a distinct, external, expert perspective in the psychotherapist.

I have referred repeatedly but in passing to the philosophy of Stanley Cavell. I first encountered Cavell in a course in which he presented a novel reading of *King Lear*. In the opening of Shakespeare's tragedy, Lear offers to divide his kingdom among his daughters if they will declare their love for him; the devoted daughter, Cordelia, is silent and gets nothing, leaving Lear at the mercy of the unloving Regan and Goneril. This establishment of the plot's premise is traditionally understood as a formality, perhaps an incorporated fragment of an older drama, mere fairy-tale prelude to the real play. In a lecture that later formed part of a broader essay with a different focus, Cavell asked what might follow from our taking the opening seriously. He understands

Cordelia's declination of a ceremonial relation to her father to be a request for authentic intimacy and mutuality. Cavell further understands Lear to be aware of that request and to deny it, because he is not ready to bear the force of his faithful daughter's love.

More recently, Cavell has suggested a similar approach to the biblical story of Isaac's blessing: How would it read if we assume that the blind father is able to distinguish his sons' voices, Jacob's from Esau's; and if we then assume that Isaac is quietly complicit with Rebecca's ruse with the goat kid stew and pelts? Perhaps Isaac is grasping a means to create an exception—to circumvent tradition, reward his true inheritor, and honor his wife's wish; and perhaps Rebecca knew that Isaac would know. In Cavell's view, what appears to be miscommunication is most often communication of the fullest sort.

I attended Cavell's *Lear* lecture my freshman year of college, and it resonated with my sense of how we know one another ordinarily—apparent misunderstanding often masks accurate apprehension. At least this viewpoint is one pole of the truth: We know one another well, despite the confusions of speech or silence.

A scene in my favorite of Havens's books, *Coming to Life,* reminds me of Lear and Cordelia. Havens writes admiringly of a devoted young woman who repeatedly declines gifts. "Twice at deathbeds she had refused to accept rings from significant people." At first, Havens sees these refusals as masochistic self-abnegation. Then he realizes that the devoted young woman wants to come and be with the dying person, as she wanted to come and be with her mother, who had to leave her years before. The devoted young woman is unpossessive because she understands what constitutes relationship. She wants not less than what is offered but more.

I must not accept the permission you offer, for me to advise, if to do so represents a denial of what constitutes relationship. If you have filled your life with authoritative others who tell you what to do, I will not want to validate that model. One must not accede to the sacrifice of self. But what if the self has already been sacrificed and needs now to be redeemed? Then it might be necessary to accept your giving of self, as it were, in escrow. Or to lend substance to what fragments of self you still possess.

That is why I take that other gift, the one your possessor offers by being shockingly unreasonable, to be so important a part of our transaction. Because it is yours, in the sense that your response to it is your own. In highlighting the gift, I hope to validate what remains of your perspective, saying, Yes, you have judged well. The advice follows the self-help admonition to listen to your own voice, with this difference: I point to one of your voices and say this one, and not the others. The voice that says: No human being should be asked to give what that man demands nor to accept what he imposes.

MERIT

20
What Means Should

WHY IS IT obvious that Nora should leave? Because she suffers while Philip thrives. Because the relationship is inequitable, and it shows no promise of changing. Because Philip has lost all claim to Nora's loyalty or trust. But then, who says relationships must be fair?

Well, everyone does. When you ask whether you should leave, what is at issue includes fairness. Is it disloyal for you to bow out? Is the commitment made to you being honored? Are you being taken advantage of? Is an isolated instance of betrayal a sign of abuse, or is there a level at which your partner remains trustworthy? Is your implicit bargain corrupt or honest?

Equity plays no role in most psychotherapies. Psychotherapy is grounded in psychological theories that concern themselves with what does happen, not what should. The closest that psychology comes to dealing with justice is a consideration of guilt, and often it is the victimized who feel guiltiest. Yet thinking in everyday terms about our question, should you leave, ethics is a prime consideration—a way of understanding "should."

Part of what sustains Ann Landers's revised advice to the Iowa housewife, to be herself rather than adjust her interests to those of her husband, is a concept of fairness. Why does he get to be himself and she not? How can the wife be fulfilled if she subordinates herself to her husband? She could in a culture where deference to husbands is an ideal; but not in the advanced societies, where that demand is unfair.

Thinking back to Iris, what is worrisome about her decision to stay with Randall is that she may be investing in a relationship in which there is no payback. Her staying would be easier to encourage if it were clearer that Randall had earned credit in the relationship through prior acts, credit that might justify Iris's residual trust even after Randall's misstep with Bunny.

Calculations regarding equity, trust, loyalty, and entitlement are likely to color assessment of any relationship. When Adam disappoints her over the beach club membership, Jonnie can stay with him because he seems trustworthy and has taken risks on her behalf. The discord between Francis and Frances will puzzle an outsider who judges their trade-offs to be equitable. The decision of Howard's somewhat manic wife to leave him for her photographer-friend Bart is dubious in part because her conniving seems disloyal and underhanded. If Mark and Sandy's relationship has anything going for it, in the face of her affairs and his new platonic romance, it is the way husband and wife have extended themselves for one another over many years. Questions of trust and exploitation are what determine our responses to Jeanne and Prince Charming, Rose and Abie, or Philip and Nora.

Couple therapy rarely attends to issues of fairness. As a result, it is vulnerable to the same critique that was once made of psychoanalysis: In easing the discomfort of those who should be uncomfortable, it sustains an inequitable status quo. It patches up relationships that should be dissolved because one member gives too much and gets too little. From a feminist perspective that sees most marriages as unbalanced in terms of power and benefit, couple therapy buttresses a pervasively unjust society.

As a culture we are fascinated by demographic claims—for example, that marriage holds health benefits for men but health risks for women—in part because they are markers of fairness. Such findings are Sullivanian facts, facts an advisor ought perhaps to take into account, but they are also more than facts, they are indicators of a distribution of burdens. If you object to the notion of women in ailing marriages staying to work things out, it might be on the basis of inequity. Murray Bowen's solution to marital conflict—further investment in the self—is attractive because it does not demand additional accommodation from those who have accommodated too much already.

It might seem that any evaluation of couples would begin with attention to fairness. But to my knowledge, among contemporary secular psychotherapies, only "contextual therapy," the work of Ivan Boszormenyi-Nagy, recognizes any prominent role for ethics.

Nagy (the name rhymes with Taj, in Taj Mahal) was born in Hungary in 1920, the son of a supreme court justice whose father and father's father were also supreme court justices. Nagy emigrated to the United States just after the Second World War. Like Bowen, Nagy began by studying schizophrenia and then, in response to the difficulties in applying the analytic model to psychosis, turned his attention to family functioning. Bowen considered Nagy the scholar most likely to bridge the gap between psychoanalysis and the family viewpoint.

Nagy's talent is for what he calls "multidirected partiality," the ability in a discussion to take each party's perspective in turn, so that each feels fully understood in the presence of the others and each hears the others' case presented in a favorable light. (I think of multidirected partiality as a systemized variant of the fictive attitude: The therapist continually retells the family's story in the imagined voice of each member.) As a psychiatric theorizer, Nagy aims for a comprehensive perspective, one that integrates as many viewpoints as possible, a combination capped off with his own unique contribution.

Nagy's theory recognizes four dimensions to a person's relational reality. The first covers objective "facts," such as genetic makeup and physical health (elements of what I have called the essentialist view), and social pressures and constraints, such as the unemployment or divorce rates (the sorts of facts important to Sullivan and Dicks). The second dimension is "psychology," the mental inner world, including defenses, such as projective identification and selective inattention. The third dimension is "transactions," characteristic patterns of interaction in relationships, on the basis of such factors as communication and power.

These domains are familiar. What distinguishes Nagy's theory is his insistence on a fourth dimension, the realm of "relational ethics," which Nagy also calls the ethics of "due consideration" or "merited trust."

In this regard, Nagy draws on Martin Buber's philosophy. Buber attends to the "reality between man and man," which includes justice. In 1957, when Buber gave his series of addresses to an American psychiatric audience, he told the story of Melanie, a patient "of more intellectual than spiritual gifts . . . [and a] more impetuous than passionate need for love." Melanie has wronged another woman by stealing her fiancé and then, when the rival attempts suicide, unjustly accusing her of feigning. When Melanie is supplanted in turn, she develops a hysterical disturbance of vision. Melanie's symptoms are cured by a psychoanalyst who relieves her of her feelings of guilt by convincing her that she is a "genius of friendship," thus fostering her vigorous reentry into social activity. Buber comments, not without scorn, "The price paid for the annihilation of the sting was the final annihilation of the chance to become the being that this created person was destined to become through her highest disposition." Even though Melanie seems to function well, she remains incomplete as a person. She behaved unjustly to her rival, and comprehensive treatment would require that Melanie address the sphere of human justice. Nagy brings that dimension into psychiatry.

Invisible Loyalties, Nagy's revolutionary contribution to family therapy, appeared in 1973. When Lou introduced me to the work, I took to Nagy's concept of dimensions, but I have wondered ever since what to make of this odd duck "relational ethics." Nagy insists that by ethics he is referring not to values but to an aspect of reality. The relationship is real—this is Buber's claim, the substantiality of "the Between"—and its supply of merited trust is one of its qualities, as much as neurochemistry and personal history are qualities of its participants. This is a tough idea to get one's arms around. What draws me to it is that many patients treat this dimension as if it were not only substantial but primary.

Loyalty and disloyalty are big issues in the multiethnic city where I practice. The word "loyalty" is a portmanteau, containing the many old-fashioned virtues of cultures under stress. Let us suppose that you are a recent immigrant from the Azores or Sicily or rural Ireland or Southeast Asia or the Middle East. Or your roots in America go back generations but you are the scion of a family with a long military tradition and highly formal rules and standards. You have married a young woman from your own ethnic background who is a bit more "modern" or acculturated than you. Things go well until they stop going well, at which point you start to have grave doubts about one another.

Your wife does not suffer with her problems, she talks about them, not only with her mother but also at work and to complete strangers, which is what you consider her friends. She discusses your job demotion, your temper, even your sexual shortcomings. Her behavior is intolerable to you because it is disloyal, and in your book loyalty is the hallmark of trustworthiness.

Recently you suffered a series of panic attacks, and your internist suggested you see a psychiatrist. You declined, but when you ran into one at a party, you asked whether the profession does not have some provision for the giving of discreet advice. You have a problem and nowhere to air your views. When you arrive at my office, you say that the problem is the marriage, which you now know you must leave. You would love your wife dearly if only you could trust her. Without privacy there is no trust; without trust there is no sense of home. What is marriage but the creation of a home?

To respond, I must show partiality to your viewpoint, that you are entitled to loyalty. Your wife owes you respect for the marriage's privacy. A more comprehensive examination of your situation will ask how much of your discomfort is attributable to other dimensions: facts (for example, your demotion), psychology (your anxiety), and transactions (the distribution of power in the marriage). But the injury that troubles you, injustice, cannot be reduced to any of these.

I might be tempted to view your problem as purely psychological. Fear of inadequacy has made you rigidly self-righteous. Structurally, your position resembles that of Guy toward Lena, an inferiority complex masquerading as cultural superiority. There may be truth in this formulation, certainly it is one that therapists or even your neighbors might make. But there are dangers in dismissively translating ethical complaints into feelings, the same dangers that early in the century attended on labeling frustrated women as hysterical. Perhaps, as you indicate, an injustice has been done.

Your wife considers herself the injured party: You fail to provide the security or companionship implicit in the marriage contract. Given her isolation, how can she not look outside the relationship for sympathy? She no longer trusts you to be emotionally generous or even reasonable. She will not allow the marriage to pull her back into a culture where wives are readily dominated by their husbands, especially since she does not have the traditional supports such a culture provides women. The issue here is not primarily unhappiness; like you, she could bear some unhappiness in a fair relationship with a trustworthy spouse. You and your wife agree on one point: Emotion and circumstance aside, the relationship is disturbed because of a conflict in the realm of relational ethics.

How does a person whose faith has been breached decide whether to stay? Nagy refers to what he calls residual trust. Loss of trustworthiness or merit is rarely absolute. Nagy says that each relationship contains an invisible slate or ledger of give-and-take, what I might call a "trust fund." Partners deposit trustworthy acts, earn merited entitlement, and owe due obligations. For Nagy, earned entitlement is the coin of the realm.

I once asked Nagy if he could make the dimension of ethics, and the concept of earned entitlement, more real to me. He replied by describing storks he saw caring for their young in a village where he vacationed as a child in Hungary. The storks sought food and tended the nest, risky and exhausting tasks. Once the young were fledged, the parents stayed on and seemed to enjoy themselves together. Nagy takes due consideration and loyalty to be something like animal parenting functions, which, if attended to, bring mental and physiological rewards. So essential are caregiving and fair dealing that merely providing the opportunity to care, as an infant does, might also earn entitlement.

Nagy attributes to earned entitlement the same benefits that Jean Baker Miller says connectedness brings to women: increased capacities for zest, creativity, trust, risk-taking, and generativity toward others, as well as what Nagy calls "A growing freedom to claim one's own side in relationships, including a person's independence from parents." That is to say, earned entitlement brings differentiation. And as Bowen claims with differentiation, Nagy asserts that level of earned entitlement is a strong factor in determining the choice of a partner.

Within a relationship or family, entitlement is credit on the ledger. Strong balance sheets make stable marriages. But if one partner continually overdraws the account, the other will feel justified in retaliating or leaving—though factors from other dimensions, such as good sex (fact) or excessive guilt (psychology) or power arrangements (transactions), might complicate the decision.

An additional complication is that people are poor bookkeepers. They attribute credits and debits to the wrong accounts. In Nagy's view, ethical relations are intergenerational. A child is due reliable care by his parents. If he does not get that care, a child is owed restitution; but once in adult life, there is no one appropriate from whom to seek it. The deprived child will enter adulthood with destructive entitlement, which is as debilitating as earned entitlement is salubrious. Looking at his own ledger, the destructively entitled person is owed and should be allowed to take without giving recompense. In marriage, destructive entitlement creates further injustice, since it is not the spouse who has created the imbalance in the books. Perhaps you demand excessive loyalty because you have been treated disloyally elsewhere, just as your wife demands support that she has been denied elsewhere. If you each treat the other unjustly, the relationship will be further depleted of resources of trust.

Buber writes, "All real living is meeting." For Nagy, meeting begins with dialogue, verbal or gestural. Perhaps a solution between you and your wife will arise from wordless dialogue. A kindly touch from you may bespeak support. A kindly touch from her may waken you to your unacknowledged attraction to acculturation of her modern sort, to your covert awareness that her gossiped intimacies have their equivalents in the behavior of women back home or in past generations. You may each alter your assessment of how the ledger balances. Perhaps the trustworthiness cupboard is not altogether bare.

Like Bowen, Nagy turns to intergenerational solutions in therapy. You may want to work matters out with your parents, in hopes that a negotiated settlement with that generation will free you to deal equitably in the marriage. Exoneration of others for past debts can erase destructive entitlement and enrich the current relationship. The extent to which solutions of this sort are possible will shape my opinion about whether you can come to terms with your too-modern wife.

When I first read Nagy's work, I asked Lou how justice can be a distinct dimension of relationships, separate from psychology. As a medical student, I was evaluating a mentally fragile young woman whose employer had taken her on as a lover and then dropped her abruptly. He was a business leader with a public reputation for boundless narcissism. The patient depicted him as sauntering through life taking from everyone, giving nothing, and believing that he dealt equitably. His success was in part attributable to his sincere conviction that he treated others fairly—an enormous intrapsychic and interpersonal asset. Every story the young woman told about this man ended the same way, with him smiling beneficently on the human wreckage around him. If he owed others entitlement, the burden was somehow invisible to him. How, I asked Lou, do contextual therapists respond to the contentment of those who have no conscience, or who happily balance every ethical transaction in their own favor?

Lou's only immediate reply was an admonition to listen to my patients. But a year later Lou published a short story, "Pinkerton Sings," that I believe was inspired by our conversation. In "Pinkerton," the otherwise unnamed narrator, whom we soon recognize as the *Madame Butterfly* villain, sits on a tropical verandah and reviews his life. With the charm of a Somerset Maugham storyteller enjoying a tumbler of whiskey at a seaside bar, the retired naval officer recounts his colorful successes on voyages the world over. The irony derives from what we already know of this character from outside the story—our awareness that his well-being arises from his capacity to forget the havoc he wreaks in others' lives, from his mastery of selective inattention. He is a happy man, admired head of a thriving family.

Lou seemed to be saying that as regards relational ethics someone with low standards for himself and high standards for others has an advantage in arriving at a sense of earned entitlement. Is there really a difference between the satisfaction an altruist feels on giving and that an egotist feels on taking? If there is a difference, in whose favor is it?

I have since read more extensively in contextual therapy without finding an answer to the objection that selfish behavior often leads to contentment. For me, entitlement is a function of the individual's value system or psychology. Nagy argues to the contrary: An obligation can be "ontological," a necessary part of any conceivable ethics or set of human relationships. For example, a child is due care; if she is not given care, the resulting debt of entitlement will unbalance the family ledger, with prices to be paid by all concerned. But few obligations are as clear as the duty to care for a dependent child. And breach of this obligation affects people differently: Jean-Jacques Rousseau seems to have neglected his children without scruple.

Nor is it clear that neglecting relational ethics always does patients a disservice. Buber criticizes the therapist who ignored Melanie's moral obligations. But by highlighting Melanie's social strengths, the therapist helped Melanie to rejoin her friends and colleagues; the approach sounds like a precursor of Jean Baker Miller's attention to skill at connection. Reintegration into a social group may have been an ideal treatment for Melanie, one that gave her the context she needed to resume her development according to her own lights. When he proposes that Melanie has a best self she is meant to become, Buber reveals a strain of rigid idealism. In taking the position that entitlements are objective, the therapist risks finding himself—like Buber when he insists that Melanie must acknowledge her guilt—in a superior and judgmental position.

Even the posture that Nagy recommends, multidirected partiality, may not protect a therapist from acting arbitrarily. Multidirected partiality demands examining each point of friction from the perspective of every person involved. But to what part of a person must one be partial—the surface, which may represent defensive self-justification, or a deeper and even unconscious level, which may be more self-critical? You say your intent is to deal justly, even generously, with your wife. How is anyone to take this claim? Surely with a mixture of credulity and skepticism; in the era of authenticity, conscious intention is suspect.

And yet, for all its difficulties, I find myself attending to Nagy's dimension of ethics, because the opposite choice, to ignore the balance of obligations in a relationship, seems entirely unreasonable.

The notion of entitlement helps pinpoint what is so troubling about certain impasses within couples. Consider a contretemps that is not at all rare: In the course of a brief dalliance, a married man impregnates an unmarried acquaintance, and she chooses to bring the pregnancy to term. Relational ethics makes quick sense of what is impossible here. The extent of the married man's obligation to the pregnant lover is debatable; in some subcultures she might have been expected to abort. But (outside theologies in which the sins of the parents are transmitted across generations) the child's entitlement is clear; the child is due as much care as any child, which in this culture includes the attentions of a father. At the same time the man's wife is fully entitled to the loyal attentions of a husband. These simultaneous debts are irresolvable. Harm has been done and prices will be paid. To be sure, relationships are resilient, and there are ways for the man to work toward entitlement. He may "make it up" to the wife psychologically and at the same time support the child financially. But whatever the facts, emotions, and transactions, these four lives are burdened by a difficult reality in the arena of obligation.

The notion of entitlement also helps in approaching marriages that are not quite entered into freely. Often a first marriage will be a response to subtle duress. In order to extricate herself from a threatening or abusive family of origin, a young woman will accept a proposal from a much older man. The considerations that ordinarily govern choice, such as matched differentiation of self, will not enter into such arrangements, or they will enter in an odd fashion, the man being as mature as the woman only in ways that are not adjusted for age. He may, in fact, be little better than the woman's overcontrolling father. The woman may soon want to leave the marriage but feel bound by duty. The most direct way to help her is through addressing duty directly.

Just what is the young wife's obligation? Since the bargain was corrupt to begin with—since the husband has earned only slight entitlement—the obligation is limited. Such, I believe, is the social consensus, and the contextual therapist can make this claim for the culture and perhaps also for the wife in her own voice. Following multidirected partiality, the therapist will want to make the husband's claim and the parents' as well. It is useful to separate the voices, not to require the wife to speak for her husband or parents. With the various claims made explicit, the wife may find a way to respond to them in a just, proportional manner, which may include ending the marriage. Therapy of this sort has a good deal in common with straightforward advice. This version of multidirected partiality contains the message that no one has an absolute right to ruin a young life.

In more balanced relationships, what is just? This is the great marital question of our time. A major reason women give for marital tensions, thoughts of divorce, and actual application for divorce is a husband's failure to share household chores equitably. If husbands do any work at all, then to leave—to divorce—may entail more total work for the woman, as well, often, as a financial loss. Presumably the wife's calculation is something like this: She is willing to forgo benefits in the domain of facts to obtain benefits in the domain of relational ethics. More than occasional help, she wants fairness.

But what is fair? If the husband and the wife both have careers, is it fair that he do almost as much housework as she? What if he does more child care than his or her father ever did, but not nearly so much as she does? Does it make it equitable if his job pays more than hers? Can he argue that he is already giving more than he ever expected to give, and perhaps more than she once expected him to give? Why must he do things now that were not in the deal when they married?

Anyway she is too demanding about what the house looks like. When he was a bachelor, he tolerated dishes in the sink for days and was no worse off for it. It is unfair for her to ask that he do the work but not let him set the standards. Yes, he is willing to move in her direction, but he has done that already, and by the way, while he is being an ideal husband from the woman's standpoint, where is the real equity, where does he see her trying to be the ideal wife from the man's standpoint?

This chain of argument is most readily addressed by an inquiry into each side's assertions about entitlement, via multidirected partiality.

* * *

Contextual therapy addresses an issue that otherwise seems to have no home in psychology: the meaning of the marriage contract or of the implicit compact in any relationship. To commit is to establish a moral standard for change, the one alluded to in some wedding ceremonies by "for better or for worse," and thus to set a cost, in terms of entitlement, for abandonment. Commitment sets the threshold for leaving—not for light or transient causes, not merely to trade up to a more desirable partner. I have referred to the distaste for entropy, the penchant for continuity and complexity. These preferences are aspects not only of psychology but also of ethics.

Attention to ethics seems necessary. But whose ethics? In times of social change, there will be disagreement about what is equitable. How is a therapist to catalyze justice, or an advisor to access the possibility of fairness, without a common standard? One cannot rely on the couple's standards. Psychology and power affect judgment. The injured are often unjust to themselves. When Philip takes credit for Nora's ideas, steals her business, cripples her psychologically, and betrays her with other women, she explains that she has disappointed him and should give more. Nora is an unreliable narrator because she is an unreliable judge. What is it to be partial to a person who is not partial to herself?

Contextual therapy has answers to such objections. Nagy speaks about "overgiving" as depriving the other of the opportunity to earn entitlement. Nora's version, that she has not given enough, might change in the course of a series of supportive discussions; or what I have called a "gift" might cause her to reexamine the ledger, make accounting changes, discover dividends of entitlement. But what happens if Nora remains convinced that she is giving too little? Must I join her in this belief? Where fairness is at issue, the therapist or advisor is often thrown back on his own values; relativism might be outright dangerous, as in cases of abuse.

And then there is the problem that relational ethics exists in a world dominated by facts, psychology, and transactions. Perhaps, on the levels of facts and transactions, Philip is happy in his prosperity and power. Perhaps he will be happier yet if, after sucking Nora dry, he hides his assets and divorces her in favor of a trophy wife. He loses sacksful of earned merit but gains in the dimension of facts. Why not sacrifice merit in exchange for good sex, constant admiration, and money? A therapist or advisor who had Philip's well-being in mind might have to agree, go ahead. (Though I should say: That is not what my advice is likely to be about; I am not out to help you with that sort of contentment.) Sometimes, as Jeremiah complains, the ways of the wicked prosper, and they are happy who deal very treacherously.

Having given two cheers for contextual therapy, I should add that I am surprised that it has not been more popular in recent years. The idea that relationships' success depends on their fairness would seem in tune with the upsurge of sentiment for psychotherapy to incorporate spiritual and religious codes. And relational ethics ought to have drawn support from a quarter century of interest in the biology of altruism.

Animal ethologists, notably Frans de Waal, a senior zoologist at the Yerkes Primate Research Center in Atlanta, now describe an innate "moral ability," akin to the innate grammatical structures posited by linguists. Behaviors entailing loyalty, trust, and fairness have been observed in apes and monkeys, with fragments of the same tendencies evident in whales, elephants, dogs, and bats. Mammals seem to be internally rewarded, or preprogrammed, for helping behaviors, and they apply those behaviors creatively in situations that call for complex judgment. Females will protest if a dominant male monkey is too vigorous in his pursuit of a wayward subordinate male; and in many species a troop will care for a handicapped member, even at a cost to the community. In humans, so the theory goes, while any preprogramming doubtless allows for differing ethical codes, not any arbitrary code will do; the range of what will feel "right" has its limits.

Of course, animal altruism constitutes a low-end sort of morality. Much of it occurs within a hierarchical troop in which equity is absent. In *The Moral Sense,* James Q. Wilson comments that whatever innate sympathy we have is "easily aroused but quickly forgotten; when remembered but not acted upon, its failure to produce action is easily rationalized." And immorality, from selfishness to a penchant for deception, may also be rooted in our animal heritage.

Still, the belief that relational ethics is an inborn aspect of human psychology is much more popular today than it was when Nagy proposed his therapy. In 1994, *The Moral Animal*, Robert Wright's brief that moral sentiments are often biological imperatives, became a best-seller (although Wright also makes the case that aggression and deception should feel "right" in certain circumstances). Walter Burkert, in *Creation of the Sacred*, now locates a basis for religion in Darwinian ethology, including, to cite a chapter title that would please Nagy, "The Reciprocity of Giving." The times would seem ripe for a perspective that attends to the internal price a person pays for misusing or leaving a committed relationship.

Regardless of whether there is a natural standard for bookkeeping in the realm of ethics, people do live with a sense of having been treated well or ill, and most carry a sense of obligation within a relationship. In time, partners use those sensibilities to create a joint story about entitlement, although often each reserves the right to read the story differently. That story will come to seem objective or substantial. Success at meeting one's obligations within the parameters of that story brings self-esteem; failure to give or receive fairly entails a cost. No alternate approach is an adequate substitute for addressing this dimension of entitlement head-on.

Whether you should leave is in part a function of whether it is right to leave—how you value the marriage contract, if you are married, or what loyalty you owe in return for your partner's sacrifices, or what it means that your partner is gravely ill. As a psychiatrist I have seen people faced with deciding whether to leave a relationship when their partner is in a mental hospital. Considerations of happiness compete with those of obligation, and the prospect of failing in an important obligation casts its shadow over future happiness, in the form of the threat of loss of entitlement, perhaps expressed as loss of self-respect.

It seems inevitable that when we meet we should address issues of fairness. Perhaps you feel ill-treated. The relationship always had its limitations, but until you came to feel taken advantage of, you never contemplated leaving. When you ask whether you should leave, you begin on the level of relational ethics: Is the partnership equitable? This concern often turns on the nature of contracting. When you and your partner made a commitment, what is it you committed to?

21
The Art of the Deal

YOU ARE A sober businessman, a man of your word and successful because of this quality, in a firm and in an industry where many are too clever by half. Ethnically Jewish, you have been married for ten years to a lapsed Catholic with whom you have one daughter, who has just turned nine. By external standards, you are the more desirable and attractive member of the couple, but you have never been confident about others' sentiments for you. You feel unlovable. You would never admit as much, and few would imagine it of you. You used to say that you were lucky in your marriage. You bolstered this luck with presents and concessions, trying to make the home and the relationship just as your wife wanted. You catered especially to her family—more than she would have—taking their schedules into account in planning celebrations, lending a generous hand when they got themselves into trouble, favoring her parents over your own.

Your wife has nonetheless been unhappy. Amidst the plenty you provide, she has felt uneasy, out of place, useless, deracinated. She has undergone psychotherapy. You have, too, but you sense that therapists don't know what to do with you, you are so accommodating and so uninterested in the dark aspects of life. You accept a degree of dissatisfaction as the best that can be expected. You strive for what others fear, the "marriage without weather." What you hope to avert, through your constancy and your extra efforts in times of crisis, is the outright despair that periodically breaks through in your wife's emotional life.

This instance, however, is different. Your wife has transgressed an absolute boundary. She has decided, through psychotherapy, that her feeling of anomie can be addressed only by a dramatic return to her roots. She has let you know that she intends to enroll your daughter in catechism class—that she must if she is to feel right within herself—and that she will want the daughter to attend mass regularly, a habit your wife has recently resumed herself. Your daughter is neutral on the subject. You sense that she cares little about religion—leans, if anything, because of her familiarity with Old Testament stories, toward a sort of God-fearing, nonliturgical Judaism. But you know that she feels closer to her many Catholic relatives than her few Jewish ones, and like you, she is constitutionally eager to please.

Before you married, you and your wife discussed religious differences at length. You were both aware that mixed marriages often fall apart when children are born and questions of religious education or affiliation arise. The conversations began lightheartedly. Neither you nor your wife could lay claim to a belief in God. Common leanings—a love of books and quiet evenings—seemed more important than differences of faith. Nevertheless, you began to find yourself anxious when the topic of religion arose, as if some powerful, hidden force could snatch your family from you. You and your wife agreed that any children would be brought up neither Catholic nor Jewish. You came easily to a consensus about holidays, cultural enrichment, and the age at which a child could decide for him- or herself.

But the hammering out of this simple agreement was so onerous to you that you exacted a single promise from your wife, that the topic would never be opened for discussion again. The negotiation made you unhappy to a degree you could not account for. You knew only that anyone who cared for you would leave this issue alone. Over the years, when anything like a discussion of formal religious training for your daughter arose, you left the room or brooded or angrily reminded your wife that you were a flexible man, giving in every arena, but that you considered her silence on this topic a point of honor.

You come to the office and say you are not interested in psychotherapy. You have had quite enough of that, and your wife a bit too much. You want a simple piece of advice. Your wife has proven herself untrustworthy, insensitive, ungrateful, and more attached to her blood relatives, including your daughter, than to you. That betrayal is not the only problem. In the last few weeks you took a look at yourself in a way that you never did in psychotherapy. You found yourself lonely. After years of doing everything for this family, who is for you? A man should not give so much and get so little. You decided to leave your wife. And then, at a party, you found yourself speaking to someone you had never met before, a psychiatrist, and in the midst of small talk you were overcome with confusion. Like a schoolboy stammering out a foolish question, you asked if it was possible to get advice for an important choice you are facing.

Perhaps it is best to begin where you begin, with this matter of the broken pact. I gather you are comfortable with contracts; you are a businessman, you see how deals pan out. I see deals, too. Sometimes I wonder, as you are wondering now, what makes an agreement succeed or fail—what makes a good bargain. Early in my career I saw an unlikely contract succeed. I was treating a chronically depressed woman when her fiancé proposed a deal that took my breath away: He would marry her on the condition that she not commit suicide for the first year of the marriage.

You are annoyed that I should mention this odd proposal. Your objection is that I am interrupting our consideration of your ordinary marital arrangements to discuss an agreement that is on its face absurd.

But why is one deal more absurd than the other?

You say, because of what it means to be suicidal. When people are depressed and suicidal, they are also irrational and impulsive. Suicide is less an option than an imperative. The woman can hardly contract to keep herself alive. What is the man's recourse if she defaults?

It does seem like a joke: What's he going to do, kill her? But psychotherapists sometimes demand such a contract of suicidal patients, get them to sign a sheet of paper that says they will phone if they are about to kill themselves. Human ties—obligations, trust, commitments—are powerful. It is not just threatened punishments that give contracts force. Especially in intimate relationships, you honor promises because you care about the other and about your own integrity. Your own disagreement with your wife concerns integrity as much as consequences.

Even so, you don't see how it makes sense to marry a woman who is suicidally depressed. And to ask for a one-year commitment misunderstands the concept of marriage.

But that's the beauty of the proposal. The man's good sense is in that request for a single year. Who, in despair, can see beyond a year? The fiancé is saying, I ask only for what you can imagine. For the woman, a year is an eternity; more is being required of her than of most brides, not less. At the same moment, the man puts his optimism on the table: Vouchsafe me a year of your love, and I will show you reason to live. There is appealing nerve in the offer. And perhaps there is in this explicit codicil a useful unspoken demand on the fiancée: Since they are looking only to one year, he can expect extra effort on her part—the intensity of a sprint, where most brides foresee a marathon. Though I agree with you, the proposal sounds absurd, where absurd also means blackly humorous. Perhaps its potential to coax a timid and bitter woman forward lies in its ridiculousness. Humor has the power to evade defenses, obviate objections.

I answer you from the vantage of hindsight. Had I ventured advice, I would have gotten this one wrong. To either party I would have said what you say—it's impractical. To the man: Why bind yourself to someone so weakly committed to life? To the woman: Will this obligation panic you, push you over the edge? I feared for both of them as the day approached. My unspoken thoughts before that wedding stand in memory as a warning against the delusion that I can predict the course of relationships.

My concerns overlooked what Henry and Mona each saw in the other: her tenacity, his talent for denial. We think of denial as blindness, but it is a form of vision—obliterating the world as others see it in favor of a kinder reality. Henry was a virtuoso of denial, a visionary. Denial had preserved his spirits as a child, allowed him to grow up cheerful in objectively hopeless circumstances. I have sometimes wished for the capacity to deny at this level. I have often wished it for badly injured patients.

Mona was a woman of principle. She kept her word precisely because the world had never kept its to her. When she agreed to the marital bargain, she kicked herself for playing the fool one more time. She knew she would do her damnedest to hold up her end, even if it meant a year of fruitless suffering. In her talks with me, she expressed only mistrust, of institutions and life. But in the binding of the illusionless maid to the visionary man, vision must have the edge, else why wed?

Against all odds, these two psychologically battered people began a marriage that would last (to date) sixteen years. Mona kept herself alive twelve months, then renewed the pact. In time, the arrangement became less formal, though suicide remained an issue, as a yearned-for relief from the pain of facing each new day.

Mona groused that Henry's deal forced suffering on her, but she found herself entangled in so many obligations that her conscience would not let her take the easy way out. What sustained her life was the helplessness of Henry's family. (A contextual therapist would say that she was sustained by earned entitlement—she made up, in the domain of relational ethics, for what she could not change in the domain of psychology.) Not a week passed but Mona had to rescue in-laws. They were all marks in the world's crooked game, battered Candides whose sole protection was Mona's cynical practicality.

Henry's genius lay in the sphere of matched differentiation of self. He came from a chaotic family, and beyond denial, optimism, and good judgment, he had few tools for dealing with emotional dangers. But among the siblings, he was the one with the most successful marriage. His brothers and sisters chose people as globally disorganized and needy as they. Henry had found a woman whose weakness was concentrated in one arena. If he could keep her alive, she would be otherwise competent. He had known from the start—this is what makes the deal rational— that Mona, herself so often disappointed, was a woman who could not bear to disappoint, who would find in duty a pretext for living.

Mona and the marriage survived a host of misfortunes—chronic illnesses, career disappointments, money troubles. Henry and Mona beat the odds; or rather, they calculated the odds better than anyone around them.

So many agreements fail, the ones that demand a promise not to drink, gamble, womanize, turn violent again. Henry's is indistinguishable in form from these unpromising compacts, and yet it succeeds, as Mona's constant giving succeeds where yours fails. But how?

One answer concerns "meeting," as when Buber says, "All real living is meeting," or when he says that what the I knows of the Thou is "Just everything." (Ivan Nagy uses the word "dialogue," an undefensive mutual revelation of self.) I take Henry's handcrafted proposal to be a meeting. Henry indicates that he appreciates Mona's perspective. He will take her as she is, if she will take him as he is. The offer recognizes that the basis for this marriage is Mona's decision to live, a decision that must ultimately be private. Henry can expect Mona to commit to him only if she is also free to reevaluate at reasonable intervals. This respect for her inwardness must be reassuring to Mona. Henry's odd proposal suits her in a way that the mass-produced wedding vow cannot.

Implicitly, Henry is saying: I know you are flawed, and I have no concern for how that flaw reflects on either of us. Henry does not ignore Mona's struggle but neither does he hold himself to be better than Mona at her worst. If Henry's proposal bespeaks humility—his open-eyed awareness that by some standards he is not a catch himself—there is also pride and confidence in his offer, more than in many muscular assertions of self-worth. The proposal indicates a tacit understanding that Mona will often be depressed and irritable, that she may even deem Henry a fool for his optimism. While its form is constraining—thou shalt not—the content of Henry's offer is permissive. The proposal declares comfort with matched differentiation of self, and at the same time it is a differentiating act, a declaration of comfort with what sets Mona apart. And it is an entitling act, an act of generosity both in its acceptance of Mona and its offer to her of a chance to give in return.

• • •

I hope that in referring to "meeting" and "dialogue" I have not made you think of "communication." I suspect, from what you say of having enough of therapy, that you have been advised to communicate better. "Communication" is the word that patients in psychotherapy hate most.

I am ambivalent about the value of communication as it is commonly understood. On one hand, I respect the research that says communication style is a fair indicator of a marriage's potential for survival. There are interpersonal stalemates that are essentially communicative—patterns of interaction that are so harmful and so firmly established that they require external interruption. Teaching troubled couples how to listen and how to express dissatisfaction constructively probably improves marital satisfaction. Indeed, the efficacy of this sort of simple intervention is one reason couple therapists lean on the side of your staying—it doesn't take much to save many marriages that come to clinical attention.

On the other hand, the patients I see tend to know this material already. Everyone is aware of the societal consensus about communication. My own sense—the sense that Stanley Cavell's account of Lear and Cordelia addresses—is that human communication is remarkably efficient. People know each other well enough to make matches based on refined calculations of differentiation of self or earned entitlement. In order to enact mutual projective identification, partners must even understand which behaviors have the power to elicit specific elements in each other's personality. The premise of many psychotherapeutic perspectives is that we know one another well at the level that communication theory addresses—but that there remain problems of deception and selective inattention. Those problems will not be solved by "communication"; they demand the fictive attitude.

If we avoid "dialogue" or "meeting," often it is in order to preserve the right to selective inattention, or to avoid the compromise inherent in making deals. But humans communicate with exquisite precision. We read signals too subtle to be captured in language. To lack these skills is to be different—handicapped. In large part, we are transparent to one another.

*   *   *

The assertion that as distinct "cultures" men and women do not understand each other has given rise to a small publishing industry. This claim is unlikely on its face. Men and women are raised in the same families, share conversations, observe the consequences of behavior. As the lucid feminist Katha Pollitt puts it, "men are from Illinois and women are from Indiana"; they are different, but not in especially confusing ways. To the extent that men and women are dissimilar, they are adapted to cope with one another (such adaptation, in species from the fruit fly on up, is the subject of any amount of research by students of behavioral evolution), and human coping tends to be built around communication, especially the decoding of intentions.

At the heart of the alleged intergender misunderstanding is a single observation: Women want their feelings validated, men want to solve problems. Many books and TV sitcoms are built on this simple premise. Whether this difference is real and, if real, how it arises seem to me very much up in the air, along with many other ideas about how men and women "just are." The modern presumption of difference is preferable to the premise that prevailed for centuries, that women are irrational or incomprehensible; but even if difference exists, the corollary might be less that men don't understand women's feelings than that they don't always want to respond to them.

What is called miscommunication may more often be discomfort. Men and women alike resist offering levels of intimacy they find intrusive; when pressed to offer more intimacy, they may avoid discussion because so often the function of discussion is to increase closeness. Men and women alike want to share their discomfort actively—make their partner uncomfortable—and when asked to rationalize their communication they may refuse because rational communication is not sufficiently entangling. People in relationships do leave many matters unaddressed or unresolved—they attend selectively—but it must be rare that they have no concept of each other's starting point.

What may make you leery of "communication" is that, despite a pretense of evenhandedness, pressure flows in one direction, toward explicit discussion. Few are the communication specialists who argue that the emotionally fluent should be quiet and demonstrate their love through fixing up the house. You may have been advised to share your feelings with your wife about your daughter's religious education; but that advice takes your wife's side against yours—the agreement was that you would never again be required to discuss the issue. Even without that discussion, your wife can hardly fail to be aware of your wishes.

Or perhaps there is a problem in communication after all. You have become less certain about how to read your wife's unspoken messages; a subtle element of dyssemia has complicated the "communication" picture. There is evidence that responses that look like dyssemia can be contextual. In studies going back to the early 1980s, John Mordechai Gottman, a careful quantitative student of marital interaction, found that men in troubled marriages are selectively impervious to messages from their wives. As a test condition, wives were asked to deliver an ambiguous request such as "I'm cold, aren't you?" conveyed so as to mean "I would like to snuggle" (as opposed to "Please adjust the thermostat"). Happily married men could decode the signal. Unhappily married men could decode the signal if it was delivered by the wife of someone else in the study, but not if delivered by their own wife. The unhappy men had developed a "decoding deficit" specific to their wives' nonverbal cues.

The men Gottman studied proved to be emotionally and even physiologically vulnerable—in terms of cardiovascular and hormonal responses—to strong negative emotions directed at them by their wives. Their method of protecting themselves and deescalating conflict was to withdraw. The result was an apparent loss of social skill within the marriage. This line of thought adds a useful complexity to the assertion that men "just don't understand" women. While it is common to claim that emotional difficulties in relationships stem from flawed communication, behavior that looks and functions like a communication problem may have its roots in preexisting emotional conflict. Men are more likely to "get it" when they do not feel threatened.

You might deny that your communication skills are at issue. You do get it. It is your wife who is missing nonverbal cues. By doing so much for your wife and her family, you have conveyed your commitment through actions. To misinterpret your message, your wife would have to be either dense or incapable of gratitude. Where is the recommendation, from therapists, that your generosity should be acknowledged as valid, fully expressive communication? Where is the acknowledgment that registering your daughter for religious school is aggressive communication that requires much more justification than your wife has been willing to provide?

If you and your wife are communicating, it might make sense to ask what is being said. I want you for the moment to act as a contextual therapist and assume an attitude of partiality toward your wife. She might say that you are giving what you want her to want—not what she does want—and then claiming entitlement.

Barbara Krasner, Ivan Nagy's student and colleague, says that people are often more wedded to the marriage context than to their partner. You love the marriage and the family, but do you love your wife? She believes that you care more about her parents and her daughter than you do about her. You have been crowding your wife into a conventional family, when she wanted her marrying you to be a rebellious act. Your niceness, which is hard to say no to, has stifled her rebellion, and therefore her individuation. She is saying, If you love my parents so damned much, let's go whole hog and give them what they really want, a Catholic granddaughter. Since you have not allowed your wife to form a family of a new sort, she has reconsidered her relationship to her roots.

Or perhaps your wife thinks you have tried to buy her affection by appealing to her parents where the task is to court her directly: to let her love you for who you are. You have acted as if she would not value your affection. Your wife, who has needed support, has now turned to the church for that function, freeing you to give less; but do you want to be free in that fashion?

Your wife might ask why you are so dutiful to her family of origin and so neglectful of your own. This asymmetry makes your giving untrustworthy. It has a defensive quality, as if it were a pretext for avoiding what would really make you entitled, namely to engage your parents—and to engage your wife. Perhaps you have been more confident about your tie to your daughter than the one to your wife, and your wife is redressing a balance and making you face her. You say you have given too much, but there is a sense in which you have not asked enough of the marriage. You have not trusted your wife to make a marriage with you alone, have not trusted her to know your worth independent of what you do for her family.

This fictive reworking of your wife's behavior casts the issue of betrayal in a different light. Many betrayals, including sexual affairs, are requests for a meeting or announcements that a meeting has not taken place. In a sense, marriage has not occurred, or remarriage is called for, in which case the contract is up for grabs, subject to renegotiation. In Buber's language, you are being challenged to move from "seeming" to "dialogical" speech, "speech with meaning."

Already you are more emotionally aroused than you have been in years. What your wife is giving you, in perverse fashion, is the courage to have needs, the courage to be loved. Perhaps your wife is like Cordelia, and what looks like an insult is better seen as an opening to mutuality and directness. In that case, her transgression is not so great as you have made it out to be. You might want to stay and fight out this issue of religious training for your daughter. What is the worst that you will learn? That you are valued as a source of financial security, and that your feelings and beliefs are of no importance? Well, for years you have been acting as if that were the case.

* * *

The make-or-break issue is not unusual in quiet marriages, those characterized by conflict avoidance. Researchers who study marital typology say that conflict avoidance often produces stability, but it has attendant risks: that you will live with unsolved solvable problems, that you will be unduly frightened by negative emotions, and that when unavoidable conflict does arise you will lack the skills needed to resolve it. People in marriages characterized by conflict avoidance are often those who have trouble emerging from "absorbing states," negative postures that, once assumed, are difficult to drop. You may become absorbed by a grievance. You decide you partner is untrustworthy. A line has been crossed and the contract is nullified.

What makes a contract viable? I think of a codicil that sometimes motivates visits to the couple counselor's office. A couple marries with the explicit agreement not to have children. Usually the decision is made during courtship. If one partner has a deep emotional need for children and the other a deep need not to be a parent, then perhaps there should be no marriage. But what if the partner who wants children accepts the codicil and later changes his or her mind?

Let us say that a couple injured in their own childhoods have vowed never to become parents themselves. Now the wife is pregnant, through a flaw in contraception, and she has decided not to abort. The husband feels betrayed. He has made only one firm demand, that she not turn him into a father; and it was not even a demand but a mutual agreement, freely entered into.

The wife acknowledges the justice of the husband's claim. But she has changed. She has come to terms with her family and her childhood memories, she feels capable of motherhood, and she believes her husband would make a good father. She did not choose this pregnancy, but now that it has happened, it seems heaven-sent. She made the contract, but to enforce it against her will would display an ignorance of human psychology. She would believe the same if she wanted to abort and it was he who wanted to continue. Indeed, she believes he has a moral obligation to stay married to her—for better or for worse—and to help care for the child.

He says that the word "father" is like a curse to him. He has avoided church for all of his adult life because of what he feels when he hears the words "God the Father." And yet if he is to be a father he cannot bear the thought that he would be a bad one.

Extensive discussion reveals no workable ambivalence on either side. The obvious feelings are too strong, the time pressures on decision-making too urgent. The husband knows how abandoned he will feel if the pregnancy proceeds. The wife has discovered an almost visceral need to be a mother. Realistically, she is too old to count on divorce and a second marriage and another pregnancy. If she is to have a child, it will be this one.

There is some analogy between the grounds of this marriage and certain written contracts that courts have looked at in surrogate parenting. Whichever way the decision goes, the courts give weight to the immediate feelings of the birth mother. How a surrogate mother will feel about giving up a baby is not something she can be expected to know until after the child is born. In cases of adoption, generally an interval is required before the contract becomes final, because society understands feelings about decisions of this sort to be unknowable in advance.

Marriage is a poor arena for restrictive fixed agreements. After a time, the marriage must be sustained by whatever assets—call them trust or entitlement or even inertia—have accrued. The contract never to have a child, while common and on its face reasonable, misunderstands what marriage is. People change, and the overall marriage agreement is for husband and wife to work together as they change. The unwilling father and the pregnant wife must meet here and now to the best of their abilities.

In contrast, awareness—and even hope—of change is built into Mona and Henry's contract. For all its grimness, the codicil is good-humored. It promises a marriage tolerant of further absurdity, and of further self-differentiation. Theirs is a contract for dialogue. When you are so reasonable in the form of the bargain—when you are so appreciative of the other—you can ask the impossible and get it.

More restrictive prohibitions commonly attract trouble. The fruit of the tree of knowledge will be eaten, Pandora's box will be opened. Often we choose partners who will reproduce the very problems we have vowed to avoid, and then we are on the lookout for the least sign of transgression—Francis worrying over hysteria and Frances over machismo. Prohibitions outline the stories couples are working on.

Psychotherapists often refer to "boundaries." These include the simplest of rules regarding issues outside the main work: The patient will arrive at a certain hour, pay a certain fee, and so on. But patients arrive late and forget to pay and phone between sessions precisely because there is a sense in which the boundaries provide a realm for intense expression, for the testing and redefining of the relationship. I tell residents that to attend to the talk in the session and ignore the boundaries will do less good than to do the reverse.

Many sorts of prohibitions create a tension with the idea of marriage, or even of relationship. Relationship implies a sphere of comfort in which growth can take place. Within a relationship, very decided self-expression and experimentation are expected. Whole books have been written about how relationships are settings for aggression or rebellion—how, if a relationship ceases to resist the incursions of culture or parents, it becomes moribund. To forbid change creates a codicil that contradicts the contract, a codicil that threatens to overwhelm the contract, especially since all the energy for change is bound to gather around the terms of the codicil.

Perhaps most people take marriage vows the way popes are permitted to make contracts, with unspoken reservations in the heart. So long as you do not begin drinking the way my father did. So long as you do not force me to face the inadequacy I feel. So long as you do not make me move more than two blocks from my parents' home. So long as you stay beautiful. So long as you do not get a horrible disease that reminds me of the one my mother had. These tacit reservations serve mostly to outline areas where negotiation has been postponed and will need to be taken up when the relationship is more solid.

A flawed contract is preventing a meeting between you and your wife over the question of your daughter's religious education. One thing is certain: You are not bound by any codicil. You are not bound to leave just because you have always told yourself you would. Yes, you admire people who resign on principle; but the principle here is murky. Nor is it clear how your marriage will progress if you stay. Your apprehension is that you will be further marginalized by your wife. But perhaps you are at a turning point that will move matters in the opposite direction. Nor can we know how things will go between you and your daughter or between your daughter and God. By your account, your daughter has little talent for religion. Perhaps she will be possessed of as much autonomy as you and your wife.

It does not seem that you are about to leave. Your initial certainty about leaving was a postponement of despair and an expression of your apprehension over the social skills at your disposal. But you do have an aptitude for negotiation; perhaps you will choose to use it at home. When you ask whether you should leave, I hear you asking a more urgent question: whether you can finally enter the marriage.

You have relatives in Israel and have wanted to visit them with your daughter, but your wife has always said it is too dangerous. You have acceded to her because you have not wanted to rock the boat and because you have wanted to avoid raising any issue remotely involving religion. Now your wife has put religion at issue. And to you, Israel feels less dangerous than catechism class.

I see that you have been preparing for negotiation. Though a trifle aggressive, your bargaining position has optimistic overtones—overtones of multidirected partiality. By evoking your wife's fear, you help her appreciate your own; although if I am right about communication, your wife is already aware of your fear and is addressing you through it. Perhaps your daughter will visit both catechism class and the Wailing Wall. Perhaps your wife will accompany you to Israel. In favor of staying and renegotiating the marriage is the hope that you will come to feel fairly treated or that, if you decide in time to leave, you will do so with a solid sense that you are lovable and deserve better.

The breaching of a restrictive codicil overwhelms selective inattention and brings the partners face-to-face. If Cavell is right, that the only genuine marriage is remarriage, then the only valid marriage contract is one that anticipates its own revision, through meeting.

■　　■　　■

It is the eve of your visit. I have mixed feelings. I am grateful to you for having made yourself available as my "second person"; I wonder whether I will feel a sense of loss when you appear in the flesh and close off a universe of alternate possibilities. At the same time, I await your arrival keenly. Sometimes I think human beings are purposely constructed with inadequate imaginations lest we choose fantasy over reality. That's what's wrong with the old joke about the man who prefers masturbation—"You meet a better class of women"; it overlooks the quality of the encounter, the neurological response to presence. When we stand before a particular other, we see how pale imagination is. I look forward to meeting you.

How shall we proceed? You will tell your story, and if I have an opinion I will offer it. Can I be said to have prepared myself or—if you have looked over my shoulder—you? If theory is veiled autobiography, perhaps all I have done is to introduce myself, as an inheritor of an eclectic American tradition that tolerates diversity, admires and mistrusts ideology, settles for pragmatism.

Are opinions, finally, based on theory? As you speak to me, I will or will not rely on my assessment of your duplicity, inattention, differentiation, connectedness, commitment, dysthymia, hypomania, dyssemia, projection, enslavement, and entitlement. These concepts and the others that characterize ways of looking—the fictive attitude, the essentialist perspective, multidirected partiality—are clumsy approximations of ways in which one person apprehends another. Listening, I will likely lose track of theory. The way out of your impasse will seem obvious. I will say: Separate. Or: Recommit. Or I will fashion a nugget of advice meant to allow you to see your relationship afresh. I will offer a perspective, you will add it to those you already entertain, and you will stay or leave or continue to vacillate.

MEETING

22
Wednesday at Ten

T HE BELL RINGS, and I walk through the waiting room to open the outer door. You are someone I know too much about already. You are Lou.

I am confused, like the guest of honor, coaxed by a ruse to the surprise party, who on arriving sees friends through the window but does not yet get it. Noticing my dislocation, you take me by the elbow and walk me into my own office. You find your place. I find mine.

You apologize. You have taken advantage of my trust. What happened was this: You were thinking of ways to help me focus my advice project, perhaps by encouraging me to imagine a particular person seeking guidance. And then you found yourself at Jonnie and Adam's party, and something strange happened. It was like a waking dream: People began to give hints of the troubles in their relationships. An impressive, big-boned woman, a publisher, confided in you about a somewhat violent attack she had made on a faithless lover. Other guests addressed you or talked nearby. A hirsute, Woody Allenish fellow could not decide whether to accompany his sleek-looking girlfriend on a job move; an ad executive spoke with intensity about her plan to dump her husband for a photographer she works with; a couple joked uneasily about misplaced theater tickets; a woman described to a friend how her husband's midlife crisis had been alleviated by medication; another woman asked Jonnie how she and Adam had handled their differences over the children's religious education. And then you witnessed a distressing interchange: A man berated his wife so severely that Jonnie had to take the woman aside and comfort her. Wherever you looked, people were discussing the dailiness of life and how hard it is for two people to sustain intimacy.

Those around you seemed—so much that you felt paranoid—to be alluding to aspects of your own marriage with Terry: misunderstandings, distorting mood states, the constant sense of having chosen poorly. And you thought it was you who could use a word of advice. You had considered referring the impressive publisher, but the thought of subjecting an unknown soul to a chancy experiment made you uneasy. How much better to refer yourself. If I would not, in the end, encounter a stranger looking for advice, I would nonetheless have profited from the intervening days of imagining one.

You and Terry? I ask. Although I would rather not sound shocked, I do. It was you who taught me how hidden are the workings of couples. You used to quote Jane Austen: "Nobody, who has not been in the interior of a family, can say what the difficulties of any individual of that family may be." Still, I carry idealized pictures of certain marriages, yours among them.

I half-think that you will begin another of our discussions of psychiatry, that you intend to tell me how misguided you consider the whole business of advice. At the same time, I see it is true that you are here for yourself. The prospect of advising you makes me lose heart. You may be right that the undertaking is impossible. You and Terry are people of such complexity and substance. But then I take all people to be complex and substantial, at least I tell myself I do; perhaps advice must by nature overreach.

You pause and ask whether I would like you to proceed. Have I the courage of my convictions? I nod.

It is not any one thing, you say, but everything. You married Terry on the rebound, when you were not quite yourself. For a while, it went well in the way that the extended honeymoon of second marriages can: the relief that it is not the first marriage with its particular indignities; the pleasure at one's ability once more to take pleasure with another; the openness to the remarkable potential of the everyday; the substitution of light opera for grand. Your honeymoon was better than most, because of Terry's cheerful ability to organize life. Terry's liveliness played off your tendency to understatement. There was constant teasing, the air of a long sleep-over party.

I interrupt and ask what you have asked me: Do you want to go through with this?

Absolutely, you say. You have the still face, your stock-in-trade: no grim determination, no self-belittling humor. You are putting me to the test, and yet I see that it is not only a test. You want a piece of advice.

Why shouldn't you? I understand you well enough to parse subtext. You are saying it is time for us to drop the student-teacher routine, or to reverse it. I am not all that much younger than you. Why must you carry the burden of playing the sage? If I am qualified and ready to advise an adult, why not you? Why should you not say what is on your mind, and expect a helpful response?

The problem is, I feel stripped of tools. Bowen, Whitaker, Sullivan, Miller, Kaiser, Nagy, Horney, Dicks, Rogers, Havens, and the medical psychiatric diagnosticians—who are they? Yes, they are bright people, but no brighter than you. They are simply men and women with their own histories, their own perspectives, expressed in theory. I think of Havens's reminder that we each stare forth from a unique nervous system onto a changing universe. The theorists are no more useful than Tolstoy, Dickens, Balzac, Thomas Hardy, George Eliot. Feeling alone and stripped of expertise, I settle myself by remembering Hellmuth Kaiser's admonition to listen simply, as one might to a neighbor when he asks whether your electricity has been cut off, too.

At first you take up the narrative dutifully. The gist of your account is that there was no single date or event—no beribboned e-mail, no betrayal of a promise from courtship days, just a sense of growing disconnection, of individual problems not solved by the marriage, of happiness lying elsewhere. The honeymoon days did not produce a sufficient bond. Odd that no theory in our profession explains what really matters, how some relationships create the illusion of necessity while others, equally reasonable, feel forever contingent.

Without transition and in the same steady tone you begin speaking of death. You are constantly aware of your mortality. Isn't that the issue in marriage? Sometimes you think, Since it is all over so soon, why strive, make waves, cause unhappiness? And then you answer, But if I have only one life, should it be spent with this limited other? How can anyone settle for less than full measure?

Full measure? I ask.

You say that you do not know what would suffice. You disagree with the contextualists who say that what gives relationships value is radically honest dialogue. You had plenty of that in your first marriage, to Leslie, and it led straight to divorce. It can be nasty stuff, don't I agree, Speech with Meaning? But in reading the material I sent you this week, you were reminded of how often your old friend Ivan Nagy is on target—how much fairness matters. You know that you could not be happy leaving Terry in the lurch; you owe too much. But as the years pass, Terry's "merited entitlement" will only grow, which is one reason you want to leave now, before you owe more and before anything really bad happens to either of you. When the chronic illnesses of age set in, you will not be able to bring yourself to desert (or liberate) Terry. Morality is a funny business. It's okay to leave in anticipation of bad news, exhilarating to get out just under the wire; but once misfortune strikes, you're in for the duration.

You like the remark I quoted, about more people being wedded to context than to spouse. Terry gives good context. So do you. You each get to do your work, the children are free to visit or not, everything runs smoothly. You provide ballast, gravitas, a useful second income. Terry is an organizer, full of energy, plans, good intentions. But good context is not enough to hold you in the marriage.

Nagy is right when he says that a person can earn entitlement by providing another the opportunity to contribute. I feel the generosity in your taking on the part of advisee, though I am not sure you fully inhabit the role. When you raise serious issues, you approach them like a psychotherapy patient instructed to free-associate. You speak before me and not to me. Even to yourself, you frame your choice oversimply: Desert Terry now or suffer forever—as if there were not infinite alternatives, the variety of arrangements people accept in their private lives. Your speech has the quality Kaiser called duplicity: It lacks immediacy. Kaiser depicts a patient caught between two obsessional thoughts: "The one runs: '. . . and so it will go on forever and ever! How awful!' And the other goes: 'Somewhere, at some time it will stop and it will be as if there never was anything, as if nothing had ever happened.' And that is just as terrible!" Kaiser presents that dichotomous rumination as the voice of a person avoiding self-awareness.

Hearing duplicity in your voice allows me to feel in role—at home again here in my office. Immediately I wonder, as you have trained me to, what expectations you are projecting. Am I to act the guru? You ask what, in the shadow of our mortality, is the function of relationship. I cannot answer that question. If you want more from marriage, you just do; and if you will settle for less, well, most will. It is not my role to define your values and desires, only to say something about the odds, how this marriage looks from the outside.

That's it? I ask. No concrete problems, just a relationship on the wane? I don't buy it, this story of random drift and quiet deterioration—just as I don't believe in "philosophical suicide"; I understand that on a considered, existential basis a person might decide that life is not worth living, but in every alleged instance of philosophical suicide I expect further inquiry to reveal mood disorder, drug abuse, brain tumor, embezzlement, data falsification on the verge of public discovery. Your story does not yet have the sort of detail that I can respond to. Bowen used to say "You could live with the devil if you had to." Certainly with a minimum of effort you could live well with a person who shares your interests and history as Terry does and who gives good context. You have not allowed me to understand the dilemma. Rubbing my thumb against the fingers, I say: I need more texture.

You plunge in: If I am asking discreetly about your sex life, you can assure me the problem is not there. You desire Terry readily enough. Since the kids have grown and gone, you and Terry have experienced a rekindling of physical passion. It's remarkable how a full family dampens ardor. You notice that your most intense sessions tend to occur just after the children end a visit, especially if Terry has managed to make a fool of you in some trivial way. Never mind, you are grateful for ardor at your age, will accept a dose of humiliation if it does the trick. You even enjoy Terry's new heft. And you like the effect of long familiarity, the combination of comfort and occasional surprise. But lately it has seemed that sex is merely part of the good context. It does not deepen the relationship; it is one of the conveniences the relationship brings.

Convenience? Really? I find it unusual that good sex within a marriage should matter so little. And what does it mean simultaneously to mistrust dialogue and devalue context? Your goal is neither intimacy nor comfort? I find your speech duplicitous in this sense: You ignore that the whole does not add up. Your willingness to jump to a discussion of the most private matters I take only as a marker of selective inattention, an attempt to make me complicit with you in avoiding some painful perspective on the self. I ask: If the problem is not physical desire, what then? And finally you do supply something like texture.

Many months ago, Terry suffered a tennis injury—an ankle, nothing serious, but it required the usual rigmarole, bandaging, ice pack, foot elevation, aspirin, even Darvon. So there was Terry installed on the settee in the sitting room next to the kitchen as you were preparing dinner. Terry could barely see what you were doing, but from that settee came an uninterruptible stream of advice. Let the oil surprise the onions, devein the shrimp, don't crush the garlic, salt the water for the pasta, don't drown the zucchini, bring the pot to the water not the water to the pot. This barrage of advice caught your attention for a simple reason: Terry cooks once in a blue moon, and then reluctantly.

People in pain or on opiates do jabber away. What bothered you was your response: You were damned if you would do a thing that Terry told you. You resist advice. All you could be in that kitchen was an annoyed automaton who performed the opposite of each of Terry's commands. You turned out an inedible dinner, rubber shrimp in bitter garlic sauce on a starchy clump of spaghetti, accompanied by waterlogged vegetables and weak tea.

The worst of it was, you knew Terry didn't mean to be overbearing. Terry gives advice, always has, always will. Terry's last words will be advice to the mortician. You don't think it's a matter of control or competitiveness. Terry rarely takes offense—hardly noticed the botched dinner. You don't begrudge Terry the right to express an opinion on every subject; but you can't stand how those opinions control you, how they force you to do the opposite. They make you aware of a hard kernel of undifferentiation in your character.

Since that evening, Terry's chatter has driven you wild. A student of Bowen and of psychoanalysis, you have worked all your adult life to achieve differentiation. Why should you be so affected by Terry's suggestions? Were your parents intrusive? Not that you remember. You think this is just how Terry and you are, the unselfconscious advisor and the unwilling advisee. Now that you are prone to listen for it, in everything Terry says you hear "intentionality": attempts to lean on you, correct you, adjust your views and your feelings. You wish for a marriage less dense with communication, a marriage in which people can be together and let one another alone.

The week after Terry's tennis injury, you went to a conference on the West Coast, and you realized how much you liked the silence. You spent some time with an attractive colleague. It went only so far. What you liked was the way the encounter lacked intentionality. Oh, there may have been hidden intentions to become more deeply involved, but there was no intent to change one another, to send tacit messages, to mold through praise or criticism. You liked the silence. You know what I will say, that this attractive colleague had no stake in you yet, that there was no advice because there was no relationship.

What is relationship? you ask aloud. It is not, as Nagy and Buber would have it, a concrete entity; it is an illusion in the individual mind. Once the hypnotic spell is broken, everything looks bare. You have sympathy for Frink exclaiming in his misery "Like a pig!" With the magic faded, there is nothing special about Terry; and you doubt you would trust the magic if it returned. Perhaps the capacity for relationship—Dicks's "fitness for marriage"—is biological and you never had your full quota. You lack the natural talent for attending selectively and fictively in a generous manner, the talent for deceiving the self.

With awareness of Terry's intrusiveness came disturbing insights. Terry's lightness, the quality that attracted you as you were trying to get over Leslie, is really something like disengagement. Every marriage requires work, but here you are expending effort on behalf of someone who cannot resonate with the disturbing themes that move you. Terry's sociability keeps you at a distance. It amazes you that someone so vivacious can be so underinvolved. It is as if you were not married at all, except for context.

Though no lies have been told, you have suffered a loss of trust. You no longer believe what Terry says. As you enjoy the modest successes of the older psychiatrist, Terry celebrates with you. But the praise always sounds false. You are—unless you are paranoid, which would not be good either—secretly derided in your own home.

There is the gist of it: You are secretly derided and openly advised. The relationship is too far gone for repair. On and off you have broached your concerns in discussions with friends. They find your dissatisfaction unsettling, but the mere statement of the possibility that you might leave fills you with hope. At the same time, you know that your friends are right when they say that grown people do not have epiphanies of this sort—or if they do, they view them with suspicion.

I am shaken by the intensity of your distress, by your certainty about the failure of this second marriage. It is one thing to know that important aspects of self remain hidden in the people to whom one is close—and quite another to have you here saying your life is a shambles. I want to tell you how sorry I am and thank you for letting me know that you have private reasons for disliking advice, reasons unrelated to your sense that people are understandable only after the most delicate of inquiries. But I am disturbed by the way you tell your story. Your account is studded with claims that Terry "just is" certain ways— pragmatic, intrusive, controlling, undifferentiated, voluble, light, derisive. Mustn't each of these traits have an explanation, in Terry's history or your own projected onto Terry? And how is it that you "just are" unfit for marriage? Betray Terry if you must, but don't betray your vision of how people function.

You say you are less Freudian than I imagine. You have been trying to make me understand how vulnerable Terry makes you feel—how lost, how immature. You are equally lost in your profession; the material

I have been forwarding you, about Bowen and Miller and the rest, has made you aware of that. The problem Bowen poses, whether a person can hold on to self, is the one you face in all aspects of your life. In your work, you have the same overresponsiveness as at home. When the world attacks Freud, you adopt an orthodoxy that is out of proportion to your actual beliefs.

You do genuinely respond to Freud's darkness, to his constant awareness of deep flaws in humans, the marks of fear and longing that bleed through to the surface. But the specifics of Freud's thought now seem indefensible, and it was the specifics that made psychoanalysis special: the shameful drives, the telltale defenses, the tracing of symptoms to a particular moment in the patient's history—when the pudding was burnt and the Herr Direktor showed his intolerance for unworthy subordinates. No, left on your own, you might well have edged away from classical psychoanalysis.

But as Terry took an interest in your interests—adopted the causes of the mid-century thinkers whose works you once studied—those theorists, whose originality once charmed you, came to seem naively optimistic. Their simple forms of faith—Miller's in connectedness, Kaiser's in plain speech, Nagy's in justice, Bowen's in mischief—came to seem inadequate to the conundrum of how we choose and why we leave. However much they intend to help us face it, these single-minded psychiatrists deny our existential aloneness. The essentialist perspective is the most preposterous: that the complexity of human choice can be explained by the mix of humors that bathe the neurons. Faced with these inadequate alternatives, and with Terry's bouncy enthusiasm, you found yourself casting your lot with unconscious drives toward rapine and murder—a retreat to Freudianism. Now that you have more distance from Terry, you question your reconversion. All the years that you championed psychoanalysis, were you just giving voice to despair and isolation? You no longer know your own mind.

You used to be able to express yourself. You believe you will again, once you are on your own. Terry is too powerful a force, too enveloping and too intrusive. The mere thought of ending the relationship makes you bolder. And yet you hesitate. At your age, heaven knows, you don't want more psychotherapy. Years of psychoanalysis have taught you what

Freud told Ferenczi: In the end a person must act. So you are prepared to hear a word of advice.

*   *   *

It is obvious to me that you should stay—a bit longer at least.

But how is it obvious? Only by way of proposing an alternative perspective to your own, as an element in a conversation? Or do I mean that you should act on what I say? You have taught me that the obvious is often the result of self-deception and flawed theory. Perhaps I am especially likely to be wrong when it comes to advising you. I had no idea you were unhappy in the marriage, and my misperception pains and worries me. Is it a matter of selective inattention—the two of us complicitly unaware of your despair?

I was aware of your withdrawal into the life of the professional administrator, and perhaps that change should have given me pause. As they age, people do leave the academic battlefield for deanships; I have treated brilliant professors who told me that they could live comfortably with the knowledge that they would never make another intellectual contribution, and I have had the impression that they understood what mattered to them. I treated you as if you were like those deans. I did not recognize that the recent years of your life, the years since *Pieces of Resistance*, constitute what Tillie Olsen calls a silence—an unnatural alienation from your calling. I fear I avoided important truths and failed you as a friend. I would like to succeed this time.

In one regard, I am comfortable advising you: I have no concern that you will be overwhelmed by my authority. I would more likely accede to yours. That balance of power—the advisor humble before the advisee—avoids the sort of trouble Freud got into. I see advice as a good way to reach you, because it is so ordinary a form of communication between friends.

You are, I might add, not so different from the "you" I had imagined. You value perspective, continuity, and obligation. You believe that people should exercise control in matters of the heart. You are in a substantial relationship, one it feels painful to stick with or to leave. You are self-sufficient and resourceful. Surely you know the rules—and you wish to be an exception. I feel free to advise.

* * *

I will begin by discarding bits of your story. I do not buy your expression of urgency, the need to leave before the disasters of old age strike and your obligation multiplies. Almost always, urgency is projective identification, an attempt to induce in the listener a shared feeling of the magnitude of distress. Age is no reason for haste.

Nor do I believe that your choice of Terry was inexact. The length of your marriage is one measure of the aptness of your choice. Another is the distress of your friends when you contemplate leaving. My own sense has always been that Terry suits you well. I take your claims—of urgency and poorness of fit—as attempts to avoid clarity of thought and speech.

How am I to see through to the relationship? I might begin by asking what it is you want, since your complaint (that good context and an energetic, funny, sexually exciting spouse do not suffice) requires understanding. You have never struck me as the sort that wants solitude. Even today—when you speak of the attractive colleague who did not try to mold you, and when you complain that Terry is not believably admiring—you imply that you want a fulfilling relationship.

The easy guess is that you want happiness. This answer is both inadequate—you will also want justice, true self, space, recognition, zest, and other benefits of relationship—and complicated. I take you to be saying that you have enjoyed only superficial happiness. You have taught me to value superficial happiness as a strength, that capacity to get along in life and enjoy certain of its details even over an underlying feeling of emptiness or dread. You do find enjoyment in pleasurable context. You are often in a good humor, which is one reason I have been able to ignore your discomfort. You imply that but for Terry's injury, you might have remained unaware of your own disaffection. You feel desperate, but only occasionally, which is why you were slow to blame the marriage. Our recent conversation about advice and your strange experience at the party—where relationship seemed the sole topic of conversation—have made the matter seem more pressing.

What reason have we to expect that relationships that bring superficial happiness will also bring deep happiness? That is the dilemma with which the successful confront psychotherapists. You stand amidst plenty, but what's for you?

Freud understood the great contradiction to be between devotion and passion: "Where they love they do not desire and where they desire they cannot love." Modern marriage bears the burden of desire, which for much of history was assumed to occur elsewhere, so that the husband or wife who gave good context had done the whole job. This is the observation of Germaine Greer—that through the Middle Ages romantic love was adulterous and rebellious, and that strains emerge when a single relationship must serve both romance and Establishment.

Since the sexual revolution of mid-century, we have introduced solutions to the part of this problem that is framed strictly in terms of the opposition between love and sexual arousal: sex therapy, "sex aids," "open marriages," bedroom role-playing in which partners act perverse or rebellious. If those solutions do not work (if they are overobvious in the way that Freud found the suggestions of the young nerve-specialist to be), there is psychoanalysis, one of whose goals is to reunite love and sexual desire.

Perhaps the contradiction between affection and passion obsesses us less than it once did. Sometimes you have to choose, and each choice has its virtues. Either way, a person can probably have good-enough sex. Neither Freud nor George Orwell anticipated the extent to which sex could be extracted from what they took to be its natural setting—the rebellious, primitive self. As you put it, good sex is sometimes just context, a routine aspect of a conformist society.

Within your marriage you enjoy both sexual passion and Establishment context, and yet you want more. Given both sex and affection, your question is whether you love at all—or whether you can be said to exist at all within your superficially ideal marriage. Relationships should enhance self, and you fear that yours has diminished you. This is a common complaint not only about marriage but also about our culture. It is comfortable but it swallows passions beyond the merely sexual and acquisitive; and it swallows self. We are all in the belly of the whale—at least it sometimes feels that way to you.

*   *

As I look for something to grasp, I find I am curious about your complaint that Terry's malign effect extends to your career. I remember your therapeutic recommendation: When the love life is paralyzed, turn the discussion toward work. You say that your professional achievement feels tainted and alien. You have lost your voice. I remember years ago our discussing Cavell's reading of *Lear* and your saying that Cordelia's silence—"What shall Cordelia speak? Love, and be silent"—was her perfect voice. You are a lover of silence, which is why Terry's banter irks you and perhaps why you are drawn to the more passive modes of psychoanalysis. But silence is not your perfect voice; nor is the voice of the administrator or the defender of the faith truly yours.

When I was a student, you tried to teach me your own goals: to hear with full attention, to exercise a generous fictive attitude, to speak without duplicity while taking into account the expectations of the person before you. I wonder whether you abandoned those goals after the divorce from Leslie. Often in difficult times we do abandon difficult goals and settle for conventional ones. Perhaps the analyst who said you would be fine once you remarried did you a disservice; you were fine superficially, but not deeply.

I, too, overlooked your silence—your abandonment of the inspired and absurd calling of illuminating our profession through quirky fables built on critiques of obscure theorists. You continued to write, as a preserver of psychoanalysis, and I found your perspective, in that role, to be reasonable. You are with Lionel Trilling in believing that, however gravely flawed, "Freudian psychology is the only systematic account of the human mind which, in point of subtlety and complexity, of interest and tragic power, deserves to stand beside the chaotic mass of psychological insights which literature has accumulated through the centuries." You defend Freudianism as a bulwark against Darwinism and self psychology and the many schools of family therapy that ignore our willful self-blindness. In the era of managed care, simplistic political correctness, lightweight therapeutic theories, and the psychobiology that has interested me, you speak for mystery.

But you no longer speak with mystery. In the old days, you would have done the field the favor of distilling what is dark in Freud and then playfully undermined that enterprise. This is the injury that you attribute to the marriage: loss of self, expressed as loss of ambiguity.

Subtle erosion of self is hard for others to assess. There is nothing wrong with settling for context—accepting the role of the elder statesman who is publicly praised and privately dismissed. It is fine to be Lear and give over your scepter to colleagues who love you only superficially, if that is what you want. But you cannot hand over the scepter and then want power and (more to our point) true love. Regarding your work, I suggest the possibility that Terry is your Cordelia—someone who has preferred to be silent about your loss of voice rather than praise what you do not yourself respect. The sound of Terry's silence is endless advice on trivial matters.

I am trying to make sense of that other bit of texture you have provided me, Terry's nattering, though I do not entirely buy your report on that issue either. Having seen the two of you interact, I doubt that Terry's advising is as incessant as you make it out to be. If it is, I would want to know why. Perhaps Terry is asking you to speak, as I would in Terry's place, as I do now.

For years, your short stories have been with me, in the way that other distinctive perspectives are: Murray Bowen's account of his trip home to Waverly, Harry Stack Sullivan's curiosity over the ethnicity of nannies, Henry Dicks's eye for romance in the cat-and-dog marriage, Hellmuth Kaiser's ear for duplicity, Leston Havens's solicitousness for possessed and prepossessing patients, Ivan Nagy's auditing of the trust funds of storks and humans, Jean Baker Miller's celebration of connectedness in underappreciated homemakers, Carl Whitaker's faith in greataunts and cosset lambs, Karen Horney's concern for an overgenerous eight-year-old. Every great therapist contributes a voice, a perspective, and a characteristic story. Your fables, taken together, are such a contribution. They offer the voice of the generous skeptic, the perspective of agnostic eclecticism, the story of stating and undermining. For you, as for me, much in psychotherapy is flawed and admirable.

In recent years, when we discussed what I am now calling your silence, you would speak of the vulnerability of the field. Under attack, psychotherapy needs simple vindication, not ambiguity. But back when you wrote your short stories, you prefaced them with a joking reference to *The Book of Adler*, Kierkegaard's prophetic denunciation of the Danish church; you believed then, with Kierkegaard, that reformation protects, that criticism sustains. I trust that there is a private reason for your years of silence. An unresolved aspect of your first marriage, perhaps. Or the onset of a mild and chronic depression dating to the separation from Leslie and giving rise to the thought that the world is not so much paradoxical as painful. Or some extreme attachment to loyalty—since Leslie was disloyal to you, you will be loyal to your profession. Your silence expresses deep unhappiness.

Here is one way I construct your story: You recovered poorly and slowly from the breakup with Leslie. The torture of ending the first marriage made you reluctant to connect. What you required of Terry was respite from intensity. Terry complied with your wishes—as have we all. We have respected your relinquishing the goal of your early years, to broach serious issues playfully. Your withdrawal—to orthodoxy, to context—has had complex effects. It has made you feel unworthy and at the same time it has brought you honor and plenty, so that the gulf between the way you experience yourself and the way the world treats you has grown impossibly wide. Under the circumstances, who would know how to address you in a marriage? Perhaps you have used the forces that arise in relationship—projective identification, selective inattention—to shape Terry into a horrific mirror, one that reflects and mocks your emptiness. Or perhaps you are just reading unpleasant messages into Terry's naturally buoyant behavior.

A moment in your account that had texture for me was Terry's humiliating you before the children and then rewarding you with sex—or your rewarding Terry. I take your meeting of bodies to be what you say you mistrust inside the home, communication. You feel most susceptible to passion when you have been understood, through humiliation.

Relationships are odd entities. They exist, as you say, only in imagination, and yet they bring into play forces that are utterly compelling. Relationships are at once optional and necessary, arbitrary and inescapable. They express self and demand relinquishment of self. They provide space for growth and space for regression—for giving oneself over to blind and deep forces. Civil engineers speak of "insubstantial barriers": stop signs and red lights that restrain drivers only through symbolism. Relationships are hedged about with insubstantial barriers. You can pass through at any moment, though at some risk and some cost. For much of your marriage you have been aware of this insubstantiality and treasured it. You have told yourself that your bags were packed, you could leave at any moment. Perhaps your urgency today results from your growing realization that it is this insubstantiality that is illusory.

You are not someone who can leave. For you, Carl Whitaker's dictum holds: Marriages never end. You have not quite managed to leave Leslie, and surely Terry will stay with you. Whenever you see the children, you will think of Terry. The old friends with whom you might enjoy dallying will exist in contrast to Terry. You are connected, you are married for better or for worse. The illusory prospect of leaving has sustained you in the marriage but also allowed you to postpone full engagement. Since you will never realize your fantasy of leaving, perhaps it is time to drop it. Now is the moment for remarriage.

It may be time to remarry your calling as well. Here is a possible route into the marriage: Stay with Terry and write as you once did, mischievously and without excessive regard for your reputation. You may want to give up an organization presidency or two—to be crazy, small, only yourself. In advising you to transform your needs in this fashion, I profess no disinterest. I miss your voice. I hope that you have consulted me because you want an answer grounded in prejudice. I would love to hear you speak. I envisage you producing work with the form of late maturity, like Beethoven's chamber pieces, spare and allusive.

I have declared my own fantasy. I hope I am sufficiently attentive to yours—I mean, finally, yours about the marriage. I suspect you have made the same choice in love as in work. You have retired prematurely, opted for context and then decided, in a panic, that you do not have love. The two spheres overlap: Devaluing your work, you fear that Terry will express a disrespect that echoes your own.

Are you depressed? There are "soft signs": your mild paranoia (I mean, beyond your mistrusting Terry's praise, your impression that the talk at the party was directed at you and your sense that Terry constantly intends something—mild "delusions of reference"), your cynicism, your pattern of retreat in work and home life, your focus on death and darkness, your alienation from Terry's good humor. At one level, these are aspects of your seriousness, though I might consider your seriousness to be a soft sign as well. While we are entertaining the thought that people "just are" a certain way, I will want to raise the possibility that you just are depressed—that the magic of the marriage will return when your depression responds to treatment. At the very least, you seem to be in a self-critical state that has its own inertia. Feeling unworthy, you forbid Terry to address you directly.

Thinking of Cavell's reading of *Lear*, I want to ask of your marriage: What happens if we assume that everyone knows everything? This is a question I tend to ask when evaluating couples. Mortals (you have often reminded me) can keep no secret. Certainly not you and Terry. You have eyes to see and ears to hear, and a special sensitivity to the revelation of self that forces its way through every pore.

You have suffered a crisis of confidence, perhaps in a way that is related to your professional writing, perhaps just to depression, perhaps to a stressor I know nothing about. In your shame, you have asked Terry to speak duplicitously. Terry has complied. The result is a flood of trivial advice, in place of the deeper advice you have enjoined. Like Cordelia, the seemingly loquacious Terry is loyally silent on the main point. You and Terry have what amounts to an agreement to attend selectively, to ignore your self-doubt. This sort of corrupt bargain or pessimistic deal is frequent, and hard on marriages. In asking not to be heard or addressed, you are requiring that Terry take a vow of dyssemia.

My fiction gives a basis for an opinion, namely my usual one, that before thinking further about leaving, it would not hurt to push the current difficulty to its limits. (It might even be useful to converse. Just as differentiation makes a marriage safe for childish behavior, a period of open conversation might "clear the field" for silence.) You want existential freedom; there is a chance that you will find it at home—as much as anyone ever does find it.

How crucial is autonomy? I want to remind you of Jean Baker Miller's case for connection; and of Carl Whitaker's belief that it is all right to be coddled. I am not swayed by your claim that the relationship distorts your identity: The point of relationship is to be (modestly) possessed. Or if coddling has begun to feel like smothering, you may want to free Terry to see and speak clearly—and to reexamine the way you see Terry.

Perhaps you are in love after all. Often I think it is our own desire and devotion that we are most prone to ignore. As important as his blindness to Cordelia's constancy is Lear's disregard of his own love for his silent daughter. Since the breakup with Leslie, you have been afraid of connection, afraid of loss of self. And so you have attended selectively to what you feel for Terry, or what you know you could feel. I wonder whether you can regain the freedom to connect, and to taste passion, through exercising your powers of differentiation, through seeing Terry anew.

Cavell writes, "The attestation of one's autonomous power of perception may come in recognizing the autonomy or splendid separateness of another, the sheer wonder in recognizing the reality of the presence of someone whose existence you perhaps thought you had already granted." Cavell is referring to Emerson's outlook, but the theme is Murray Bowen's as well, a theme you taught me. We gain self through admiring those we are close to. If you can permit yourself to wonder at the reality of Terry's presence, perhaps the trance will reassert itself.

Here is my fiction: that Terry's nattering is a form of respectful silence, one that deserves a respectful response. In medical school days, when I was working with my first psychiatric outpatient, I mentioned to you something I had felt compelled to say in the course of a clinical hour. You smiled and quoted Leston Havens to the effect that when trainees feel compelled to say something, they should remain silent, because psychotherapy must always arise from free, not compelled, acts. You were teasing me about the limitation of my perspective; it is a joke I took to heart. Regarding your crisis today, I would say nothing if I could not entertain alternative fictions—for instance that you married Terry for a limited reason, to deal with the pain of betrayal of intimacy by Leslie. In that version, there is no reason to believe that this ersatz marriage should last and every reason for you to pursue what you are now clear you want, true marriage.

After quoting Havens and seeing me nod in acknowledgment, you said the opposite: that if a therapist feels compelled to say something, he or she should say it, because speech in therapy must be spontaneous. And that juxtaposition of imperatives—not to speak when compelled, to speak when compelled—made me think about the varieties of compulsion. The interpretation that compels me today is the one that concerns your loss of voice and Terry's busy silence. I am inclined to find a way to give expression to that story.

I will say: You are right. No outsider can advise. You remember what Freud wrote Ferenczi about choice in relationships: "One certainly can't judge these matters, not on behalf of another, either. In nothing is another so different."

My hope is that you will smile, recognizing that the quotation comes from a letter Freud wrote in the midst of his protracted campaign to convince Ferenczi to marry Frau Gizella Pálos. And if you do smile, I will continue. Hoping to capture some of your former mischievous voice, I will say, Shouldn't you turn to Terry? Perhaps the problem is that Terry is giving too little advice. And then I will trail off, looking beyond you and speaking to myself: I have often wished you would write more stories about the paradoxes of marriage.

Or perhaps I will just face you and give a piece of advice: Stay.

■ ■ ■

Or you are not Lou. You are someone I have never met before, a stranger seeking advice in a matter of the heart. As you speak, who you are will become apparent. What you must do will seem obvious.

And yet a thousand obstacles will stand between us: the unreliability of the obvious; my idiosyncrasy as an observer; your wish to be treated as exceptional. Are the odds against you? Are you just depressed? Are you possessed, or self-possessed? Your troubles will be greater than those I have imagined. Relationships do not stand free but are hedged by illness, money troubles, power inequities, religious constraints, stigma, complex living and working arrangements, the needs of children. Desires compete with obligations. Race, class, ethnicity, and sexual preference will play prominent roles in your story, and my consultation will need to take these specifics into account, since advice must arise from attention to social norms and probabilities.

No amount of preparation can be adequate to my task—and at the same time, preparation has its disadvantages. Though it may arise from a tradition, the best advice, like the best jazz, is improvised on the spot. Finally there is no substitute for finding you, a task that will not end when you appear. You will be simultaneously frank and duplicitous, open and defended, differentiated and shaped by context. Even as you sit before me I will need to imagine you.

Like everyone else you live a life, in Cavell's words, of "absolute separateness and endless commonness, of banality and sublimity"—words that to my ear resonate with Havens's description of his father's mistakenly finding "the ordinary boring, when in fact it is often extraordinary." Your complaints may sound insubstantial; often it is the fate of relationships to founder on pebbles. The insubstantial merits attention because we are creatures who elaborate, who give meaning. It is the sublimity of your life—your extraordinariness—that I would do well to keep in mind.

You will take a seat and tell a story. We will stare forth at each other from our individually shaped and genetically different nervous systems in this time and place, and we will discover whether we can meet in any useful way.

The bell rings, and rather than buzz you in I walk through the waiting room to the outer door. It is you. Simultaneously quoting the immortal words of *Portnoy's Complaint,* we greet each other: "Now vee may perhaps to begin. Yes?"

NOTES

CHAPTER I: *A Piece of Advice*

15 The whole of this book flows from the first sentence, which rattled around my mind for some years. The potential of the second person in descriptive narrative was brought to my attention by W. P. Kinsella in a summer writing course at the University of Iowa. Jay McInerney, whose *Bright Lights, Big City* has a second-person protagonist, helped me expand my list of examples. As much to glean encouragement as techniques, before and during my own writing I read *If on a Winter's Night a Traveler . . .* by Italo Calvino, *Aura* by Carlos Fuentes, *Cowboys Are My Weakness* by Pam Houston, *Self-Help* by Lorrie Moore, *Buffalo Soldiers* by Robert O'Connor, *A Model Childhood* by Christa Wolf, any number of uncollected short stories, and *Written on the Body* by Jeanette Winterson. In Winterson's book, the more striking technique is the author's leaving the gender of the protagonist-narrator unspecified; the voice is almost certainly that of a lesbian woman, but by keeping open the possibility that the character is an atypical heterosexual man, the author emphasizes how much can be hidden even about someone whose inner life is an open book. That theme, the otherness of the familiar other, is common to many of these works. It is enhanced by the claim that the protagonist is to be "you," an act of presumption that invites an oscillation between empathy with and distance from a particular imagined life.

15 when a psychiatrist writes: P. D. Kramer, *Listening to Prozac* (New York: Viking, 1993/Penguin, 1994).

17 Either will be wrong.: Like much other wisdom, this sentiment is recycled. It was shared with me many years ago by Naomi Rothwell, author, with

Joan Doniger, of *The Psychiatric Halfway House* (Springfield, IL: Charles C. Thomas, 1966). For a current view of bereaved children, see E. B. Weller, R. A. Weller et al., "Should Children Attend Their Parents' Funeral?" *Journal of the American Academy of Child and Adolescent Psychiatry* 27:559–62, 1988, and M. A. Fristad, R. Jedel et al., "Psychosocial Functioning in Children After the Death of a Parent," *American Journal of Psychiatry,* 150:511–13, 1993.

18 "There are few things that I think are so harrowing . . ." is from a 1944 lecture by Sullivan, cited at length in one of my favorite footnotes in the psychiatric literature, on pages 201–3 of H. S. Sullivan, *The Psychiatric Interview* (New York: W. W. Norton, 1954).

19 "He who has eyes to see . . .": S. Freud, "Fragment of an Analysis of a Case of Hysteria" [1905], *The Standard Edition of the Complete Psychological Works of Sigmund Freud,* vol. 7 (London: Hogarth Press, 1953), 1–122. Freud is echoing Ezekiel.

CHAPTER 2: *Al Fresco*

23 Harry Stack Sullivan . . . how we appear to others: Sullivan, *The Psychiatric Interview.*

CHAPTER 3: *Finding You*

34 The "fictive attitude" in the work of Sullivan is discussed in L. Havens, *Participant Observation* (New York: Jason Aronson, 1976, 1983).

34 The Ann Landers column was syndicated for January 30, 1995. Regarding the changing content of advice to women, see A. R. Hochschild, "The Commercial Spirit of Intimate Life and the Abduction of Feminism: Signs from Women's Advice Books," *Theory, Culture and Society* 11:1–24, 1994.

37 "the achievement of human happiness . . .": S. Cavell, *Pursuits of Happiness* (Cambridge, MA: Harvard University Press, 1981).

40 Kaiser's play, *Emergency: Seven Dialogues Reflecting the Essence of Psychotherapy in an Extreme Adventure;* Kaiser's Kierkegaard-like musings, "The Universal Symptom of the Psychoneuroses"; and a brief biography of Hellmuth Kaiser are collected in *Effective Psychotherapy: The Contribution of Hellmuth Kaiser,* L. B. Fierman, ed. (New York: Free Press, 1965). *Emergency* was first published in 1962; "The Universal Symptom" appeared posthumously. One brief essay by Kaiser (referenced below) appeared in 1955 and is reprinted in the anthology. Like Sullivan, in his lifetime Kaiser was known primarily through his teaching.

42 "counterprojection": Havens, *Participant Observation.* See also L. Havens, *Making Contact: Uses of Language in Psychotherapy* (Cambridge, MA: Harvard University Press, 1986).

43 The analogy of the child learning to skate: M. Tolpin, "Corrective Emo-

tional Experience: A Self Psychological Evaluation," in *The Future of Psycho-analysis*, A. Goldberg, ed. (New York: International Universities Press, 1980), 56.

44 not operatic passion: The theory of psychotherapy has surprisingly little to contribute in the way of systematic thought about passion, except via such concepts as obsession and addiction. This absence of framework is, in effect, the theme of books on the subject, such as E. S. Person, *Dreams of Love and Fateful Encounters: The Power of Romantic Passion* (New York: W. W. Norton, 1988).

CHAPTER 4: *Welcome to the Club*

49 "Why pick on me?": Sullivan, *The Psychiatric Interview.*

51 "only those can genuinely marry . . .": Cavell, *Pursuits of Happiness.*

54 "applies only in contexts . . .": Ibid.

CHAPTER 5: *Obvious Pitfalls*

58 S. Freud, " 'Wild' Psycho-Analysis" [1910], *The Standard Edition of the Complete Psychological Works of Sigmund Freud,* vol. 11 (London: Hogarth Press, 1957), 219–27.

59 Horace Frink: L. Edmunds, "His Master's Choice," *Johns Hopkins Magazine,* April 1988, 40–49.

59 Sándor Ferenczi: *The Correspondence of Sigmund Freud and Sándor Ferenczi,* vol. 2, 1914–1919, E. F. and E. Brabant, eds. (Cambridge, MA: Harvard University Press, 1996).

62 Leo Szilard . . . Allen Wheelis: L. Szilard, *The Voice of the Dolphins and Other Stories* (New York: Simon and Schuster, 1961); A. Wheelis, *The Illusionless Man* (New York: W. W. Norton, 1966).

62 slim volume: L. J. Adler, *Pieces of Resistance* (New York: Scribners, 1983).

63 "Miss Lucy R.": Sigmund Freud, "Miss Lucy R.," in J. Breuer and S. Freud, *Studies on Hysteria, The Standard Edition of the Complete Psychological Works of Sigmund Freud,* vol. 2 (London: Hogarth Press, 1955), 106–24. Regarding governesses, see M. J. Peterson, "The Victorian Governess: Status Incongruence in Family and Society," in *Suffer and Be Still: Women in the Victorian Age,* M. Vivinus, ed. (Bloomington: Indiana University Press, 1972), 3–19.

65 selective inattention: See H. S. Sullivan, *Clinical Studies in Psychiatry* (New York: W. W. Norton, 1956); Sullivan, *The Psychiatric Interview;* Havens, *Participant Observation;* and L. J. Adler, "Selective Inattention: Overlooked Concepts in the Metapsychology of Harry Stack Sullivan," *American Psychiatrist* 65:1356–63, 1969.

66 "My God, yes! . . ." and "you practically have to arrange": Sullivan, *Clinical Studies in Psychiatry.*

66 Regarding Sullivan's personal history, see H. S. Perry, *Psychiatrist of*

America: The Life of Harry Stack Sullivan (Cambridge, MA: Harvard University Press, 1982).

67 1940s case seminar: *A Harry Stack Sullivan Case Seminar*, R. G. Kvarnes, ed. (New York: W. W. Norton, 1976).

69 "Nonsense, you were happy . . .": Sullivan, *Clinical Studies in Psychiatry.*

69 " 'Why, how did you ever decide . . .' ": Sullivan, *The Psychiatric Interview.*

70 "If psychoanalysis does not also facilitate . . .": A. Phillips, *Terrors and Experts* (Cambridge, MA: Harvard University Press, 1996).

71 Dorothy Schiff: J. Potter, *Men, Money and Magic: The Story of Dorothy Schiff* (New York: Coward, McCann & Geoghegan, 1976).

CHAPTER 6: *Guy Talk*

76 "rotation method": S. Kierkegaard, "The Rotation Method: An Essay in the Theory of Social Prudence," *Either/Or*, vol. 1 (Princeton: Princeton University Press, 1959), 279–96.

CHAPTER 7: *Biancas*

85 "Why are you so angry . . . ?": W. Bion, cited by G. Gabbard and O. Kernberg in "My Hardest Case," Clinical Case Conference: American Psychiatric Association Annual Meeting, Miami, FL, May 1995.

86 Murray Bowen: M. Bowen, *Family Therapy in Clinical Practice* (New York: Jason Aronson, 1978); M. Bowen, "Theory in the Practice of Psychotherapy" and "Family Reaction to Death," in *Family Therapy: Theory and Practice*, P. J. Guerin, ed. (New York: Gardner Press, 1976), 42–89, 335–48; M. E. Kerr and M. Bowen, *Family Evaluation* (New York: W. W. Norton, 1988); M. Bowen and M. E. Kerr, "Background Aspects of Differentiation" (audiotape), Bowen-Kerr Interview series No. 20, Georgetown Family Center; with additional material from *The AFTA (American Family Therapy Association) Newsletter*, No. 44, Summer 1991, and *The Family Therapy Networker*, March/April 1991, and interview with LeRoy (Mrs. Murray) Bowen, July 1996.

CHAPTER 8: *Homecoming*

94 The depiction of Bowen's development is based on the sources cited just above.

95 "universal psychopathology" . . . "fusion": The Kaiser quotations here are from his essay "The Problem of Responsibility in Psychotherapy" (1955) in Kaiser, *Effective Psychotherapy*, 1–13; Bowen knew Kaiser socially and as a colleague, but there is no way of knowing how well acquainted he was with Kaiser's theories; none of Kaiser's writings in English appeared until after his resignation from the Menninger Clinic in 1954.

97 February 10, 1967: "On the Differentiation of Self," in Bowen, *Family Therapy in Clinical Practice*, 467–528. Regarding February 1967, in my interview with her, LeRoy Bowen, Murray Bowen's widow, did not recall having been on that dramatic trip to Waverly; she saw her husband's work with his family as gradual and repeated—raising the possibility that Bowen's account of the weekend is itself a narrative dramatization.

CHAPTER 9: *Allegiance*

103 Carl Rogers: See P. D. Kramer, "Introduction" in C. R. Rogers, *On Becoming a Person* (Boston: Houghton Mifflin, 1965), ix–xv, and B. Thorne, *Carl Rogers* (London: Sage Publications, 1992).

103 attributed to Kierkegaard: Much American therapy is simplified Kierkegaard, often as imported by maverick European-born analysts like Kaiser and Horney. The simplification misses the ways in which Kierkegaard, with his multiply-layered pseudonyms, stands for the elusive, fluctuant, multiple self; what American therapy has adopted from him is the notion of a locatable or developable "true self." Of course, this existentialist individualism can also be traced to Emerson and Thoreau.

104 Emerson: The quotations and history are taken from *Selections from Ralph Waldo Emerson*, S. E. Whicher, ed. (Boston: Houghton Mifflin, 1960), and the Library of America (1983) edition of R. W. Emerson, *Essays and Lectures*. My sense of what to attend to in Emerson and Thoreau has been influenced by three books by Stanley Cavell: *The Senses of Walden*, expanded edition (Chicago: University of Chicago Press, 1972, 1981); *This New Yet Unapproachable America* (Albuquerque: Living Batch Press, 1989); and *A Pitch of Philosophy* (Cambridge, MA: Harvard University Press, 1994).

CHAPTER 10: *Also Connect*

106 Emerson has been faulted: See Q. Anderson, *The Imperial Self* (New York: Knopf, 1971) and *Making Americans* (New York: Harcourt Brace Jovanovich, 1992). Regarding Emerson citations, see note just above.

107 ancient Greeks valued *ataraxia* . . . : See M. Nussbaum, *Therapy of Desire* (Princeton, NJ: Princeton University Press, 1994).

108 *"that inner certainty . . ."*: K. Horney, *Neurosis and Human Growth: The Struggle Toward Self-Realization* (New York: W. W. Norton, 1950).

108 a compliant eight-year-old . . . : Horney, *Neurosis and Human Growth*; but see the more culturally relativistic thrust of K. Horney, *The Neurotic Personality of Our Time* (New York: W. W. Norton, 1937).

109 Jean Baker Miller: J. B. Miller, *Toward a New Psychology of Women* (Boston: Beacon Press, 1976). Other material on Jean Baker Miller is from J. V. Jordan, A. G. Kaplan et al., *Women's Growth in Connection* (New York: Guil-

ford Press, 1991); J. B. Miller, "Women's Psychological Development: Connections, Disconnections, and Violations," American Psychiatric Association Annual Meeting, New York, NY, May 1996; and interview with J. B. Miller, May 1996.

109 "It is mature . . ." and subsequent quotations: H. M. Lynd, *On Shame and the Search for Identity* (New York: Harcourt, Brace, 1958). In adopting the surname Erikson (he had been named Erik Homburger), as if he were self-made, the psychoanalyst had made a striking claim regarding the value and possibility of autonomy.

110 Buber had lectured: The William Alanson White Memorial Lectures, at the Washington School of Psychiatry. M. Buber, "Distance and Relation," "Elements of the Interhuman," and "Guilt and Guilt Feelings," *Psychiatry* 20: 97–129, 1957, reprinted in M. Buber, *The Knowledge of Man* (London: George Allen & Unwin, 1965).

110 "the basic pronouns . . .": M. Buber, *I and Thou,* 2nd ed. (New York: Charles Scribner's Sons, 1958), paraphrased in I. Boszormenyi-Nagy and G. M. Spark, *Invisible Loyalties* (New York: Harper & Row, 1973).

110 Baudelaire: Lynd, *On Shame and the Search for Identity.*

111 "makes no sense . . .": H. S. Sullivan, *The Fusion of Psychiatry and Social Science* (New York: W. W. Norton, 1964).

113 the "relational" approach: S. J. Bergman and J. L. Surrey, "Couples Therapy: A Relational Approach," Works in Progress, No. 66, Wellesley, MA: Stone Center Working Paper Series, 1994.

115 "By differentiation, I do not mean . . .": J. L. Surrey, "The Relational Self in Women: Clinical Implications," in Jordan, Kaplan et al., *Women's Growth in Connection,* 35–43.

116 "You Will Be Fine . . .": Adler, *Pieces of Resistance.* The story can also be seen as a commentary on the case of Melanie, in Buber, *The Knowledge of Man,* in which a psychoanalyst cures a woman by convincing her that she is skilled at socializing. See below, Chapter 20.

119 Phyllis Rose: P. Rose, *Parallel Lives* (New York: Knopf, 1983).

121 Carl Whitaker: See C. Whitaker, *Midnight Musings of a Family Therapist,* M. O. Ryan, ed. (New York: W. W. Norton, 1989), and C. Whitaker, "The Hindrance of Theory in Clinical Work," in *Family Therapy: Theory and Practice,* P. J. Guerin, ed, 154–64.

CHAPTER 11: *Imperatives*

126 An accomplished editor: Peter Davison, the poet.

127 The advice was delphic: Parenthetically, Thomas De Quincey in his essay "The Pagan Oracles" concludes that they were not especially delphic: "The great error is, to suppose the majority of cases laid before the Delphic Oracle strictly questions for *prophetic* functions. Ninety-nine in a hundred

respected marriages, state-treaties, sales, purchases, founding of towns or colonies, &c., which demanded no faculty whatever of divination, but the nobler faculty (though unpresumptuous) of sagacity, that calculates the natural consequences of human acts, coöperating with elaborate investigations of the local circumstances." In other words, the Delphic Oracle dealt primarily in Sullivanian facts and likelihoods.

132 Erica Jong: E. Jong, *Fear of Fifty* (New York: HarperCollins, 1994).

133 "If you are way in the back seat . . .": W. Witherell and D. Evrard, *The Athletic Skier* (Salt Lake City: The Athletic Skier, 1993); the eighty-twenty rule is also from this book.

CHAPTER 12: *Like As*

143 Vicki Hearne: V. Hearne, *Adam's Task: Calling Animals by Name* (New York: Knopf, 1986).

144 Stop wearing your partner's clothes: Compare an op-ed piece by a woman emerging from a failed lesbian marriage: "From the start, people often got us confused. We chalked it up to being the same height and having similar coloring, but the truth is our identities were slowly merging into one." K. Duggan, "I Earned This Divorce," *New York Times,* July 25, 1996, A23.

147 A psychologist friend: J. Blum, *Living with Spirit in a Material World* (New York: Fawcett Columbine, 1988).

147 "Courage *is* luck, sweetheart.": J. C. Oates, *What I Lived For* (New York: Dutton, 1994).

CHAPTER 13: Force Majeure

155 Research studies: Summarized in M. Karpel, *Evaluating Couples* (New York: W. W. Norton, 1994). See especially M. Weissman, "Advances in Psychiatric Epidemiology: Rates and Risks for Major Depression," *American Journal of Public Health* 77:445–51, 1987.

CHAPTER 14: Enfant de Bohème

165 "cerebral joy-juice": See P. E. Meehl, "Hedonic Capacity: Some Conjectures" and " 'Hedonic Capacity' Ten Years Later: Some Clarifications," in *Anhedonia and Affect Deficit States,* D. C. Clark and J. Fawcett, eds. (New York: PMA Publishing, 1987), 33–50.

CHAPTER 15: *Howard's End*

173 "Lux et Veritas": Adler, *Pieces of Resistance.*

175 "does not open himself . . .": "Martin Buber," in *Carl Rogers Dialogues,*

H. Kirschenbaum and V. L. Henderson, eds. (Boston: Houghton Mifflin, 1989); and Buber, *The Knowledge of Man.*

CHAPTER 16: *Unequivocal Eye*

177 unequivocal eye: the phrase is from Jane Kenyon's poem "Having It Out with Melancholy," in J. Kenyon, *Constance* (St. Paul, MN: Graywolf Press, 1993), and J. Kenyon, *Otherwise* (St. Paul, MN: Graywolf Press, 1996).

CHAPTER 17: *Mixed Signals*

191 Stephen Nowicki, Jr., and Marshall Duke: S. Nowicki, Jr., and M. P. Duke, *Helping the Child Who Doesn't Fit In* (Atlanta: Peachtree, 1992).

194 psychologists looked at the difficulties: R. Rosenthal, J. A. Hall et al., *Sensitivity to Nonverbal Communication* (Baltimore: Johns Hopkins University Press, 1979).

195 Asperger's disorder . . . pedantic speech: M. Ghaziuddin and L. Gerstein, "Pedantic Speaking Style Differentiates Asperger Syndrome from High-Functioning Autism," *Journal of Autism and Developmental Disorders* 26:585–95, 1996.

196 Monkeys isolated: See, for example, C. O. Anderson and W. A. Mason, "Competitive Social Strategies in Groups of Deprived and Experienced Rhesus Monkeys," *Developmental Psychobiology* 11:289–99, 1978; and M. A. Novak, "Social Recovery of Monkeys Isolated for the First Year of Life: Long-term Assessment," *Developmental Psychology* 15:50–61, 1979.

200 In his autobiography, Miller writes: A. Miller, *Timebends: A Life* (New York: Grove Press, 1987).

CHAPTER 18: *Abie's Irish Rose*

205 his earliest theorizing: S. Freud, "Extracts from the Fliess Papers: Draft H: Paranoia," in *The Standard Edition of the Complete Psychological Works of Sigmund Freud,* vol. 1 (London: Hogarth Press, 1966), 206–12. The vignette of the younger sister and the boarder is from this draft. I have chosen this example (of the difficulties inherent in Freud's use of projection as an analytic tool) because it is brief and because it shows how problems are apparent "from the start"; in Freud's mature work the concept of projection, especially as it relates to paranoia, is fraught in similar ways.

207 "We all stare forth . . .": L. Havens, "What Is Psychiatry All About?" Benjamin Rush Award Lecture, American Psychiatric Association Annual Meeting, Miami, FL, May 1995.

207 Psychoanalysis no longer trusts: See S. A. Mitchell, *Hope and Dread in Psychoanalysis* (New York: Basic Books, 1993).

208 "still face": E. Z. Tronick, "Emotions and Emotional Communication in Infants," *American Psychologist* 44:59–66, 1989.

211 Henry Dicks: H. Dicks, *Marital Tensions* (London: Routledge & Kegan Paul, 1967).

217 Reiss's work: See, for example, D. Reiss, "Genetic Influence on Family Systems: Implications for Development," *Journal of Marriage and the Family* 57:543–60, 1995; S. McGuire, J. M. Neiderhiser, D. Reiss, E. M. Hetherington, and R. Plomin, "Genetic and Environmental Influences on Self-Worth and Competence in Adolescence: A Study of Twins, Full Siblings, and Step-Siblings," *Child Development* 65:785–99, 1994; and R. Plomin, D. Reiss, E. M. Hetherington, G. W. Howe, "Nature and Nurture: Genetic Contributions to Measures of the Family Environment," *Developmental Psychology* 30:32–43, 1994.

220 "fitness for marriage": H. V. Dicks, "Fitness for Marriage," in *Psychosomatic Disorders in Adolescents and Young Adults*, J. Hambling and P. Hopkins, eds. (Oxford: Pergamon Press, 1965).

CHAPTER 19: *Simple Gifts*

224 even purists will often advise: Perhaps the most abstract form of contemporary psychoanalysis is the "intersubjective" variant of self psychology, which demands that the analyst rely exclusively on empathy as a tool; but even here instances of possession become the occasion for interventions that look a good deal like advice. See P. D. Kramer, "Empathic Immersion," in *Empathy in Medical Practice: Beyond Pills and Scalpel*, H. Spiro, M. G. M. Curnen et al., eds. (New Haven: Yale University Press, 1993), 174–89.

224 mental trespass and psychological possession: L. Havens, *Coming to Life* (Cambridge, MA: Harvard University Press, 1993), and L. Havens, *Learning to Be Human* (Reading, MA: Addison-Wesley, 1994).

224 Judith Lewis Herman: J. L. Herman, *Trauma and Recovery* (New York: Basic Books, 1992).

225 domestic violence by men: J. C. Babcock, J. Waltz et al., "Power and Violence: The Relation Between Communication Patterns, Power Discrepancies, and Domestic Violence," *Journal of Consulting and Clinical Psychiatry* 61:40–50, 1993.

226 the belly of the whale: Havens, *Learning to Be Human*.

231 Havens's specialty: Havens, *Making Contact*. Havens, like Stanley Cavell, is an admirer of the "ordinary language" philosopher J. L. Austin, from whom Havens takes the concept of performative language.

232 children who are abused: B. A. van der Kolk, "The Compulsion to Repeat the Trauma," *Psychiatric Clinics of North America* 12:389–441, 1989.

233 baby monkeys will prefer: H. F. Harlow and R. R. Zimmerman, "Affectional Responses in the Infant Monkey," *Science* 130:421–32, 1959. Attachment

theory, largely an elaboration of the research of John Bowlby, has become an important strain in contemporary psychotherapy.

234 "found the ordinary boring . . ." and subsequent quotations: Havens, *Coming to Life*.

235 "she was not in possession . . ." and Jeanne's story: Havens, *Making Contact*.

236 "We are all now . . .": Havens, *Learning to Be Human*.

237 "may want to please . . .": Ibid.

237 "Set yourself not to possess . . .": Ibid. I hear echoes of Thoreau in this passage and others in Havens's writing.

239 the securing of safe space: L. Havens, *A Safe Place: Laying the Groundwork for Psychotherapy* (Cambridge, MA: Harvard University Press, 1989).

240 a novel reading of *King Lear*: "The Avoidance of Love: A Reading of *King Lear*," in S. Cavell, *Must We Mean What We Say?* (New York: Scribner, 1969). The reading of the Isaac story, which bears a resemblance to Thomas Mann's version, is from Cavell, *A Pitch of Philosophy*.

241 "Twice at deathbeds . . .": Havens, *Coming to Life*.

CHAPTER 20: *What Means Should*

247 "contextual therapy": See I. Boszormenyi-Nagy and G. M. Spark, *Invisible Loyalties;* I. Boszormenyi-Nagy and B. R. Krasner, *Between Give and Take* (New York: Brunner/Mazel, 1986); I. Boszormenyi-Nagy, *Foundations of Contextual Therapy: Collected Papers of Ivan Boszormenyi-Nagy* (New York: Brunner/Mazel, 1987); A. van Heusden and E. van den Eerenbeemt, *Balance in Motion* (New York: Brunner/Mazel, 1987); B. R. Krasner and A. J. Joyce, *Truth, Trust, and Relationships* (New York: Brunner/Mazel, 1995). In June 1996, Ivan Boszormenyi-Nagy and Barbara Krasner kindly granted me interviews that also inform this chapter.

248 Melanie: Buber, "Guilt and Guilt Feelings" and *The Knowledge of Man*.

250 "A growing freedom . . .": Boszormenyi-Nagy and Krasner, *Between Give and Take*.

251 "All real living is meeting.": Buber, *I and Thou*.

252 "Pinkerton Sings": Adler, *Pieces of Resistance*.

255 A major reason women give: A. Hochschild, *The Second Shift* (New York: Viking, 1989).

257 a quarter century of interest: counting from the publication of R. L. Trivers, "The Evolution of Reciprocal Altruism," *Quarterly Review of Biology* 46:35–57, 1971, followed shortly by E. O. Wilson, *Sociobiology: A New Synthesis* (Cambridge, MA: Harvard University Press, 1975).

257 Frans de Waal: F. de Waal, *Good Natured* (Cambridge, MA: Harvard University Press, 1996); the James Q. Wilson quotation is via de Waal.

258 Robert Wright: R. Wright, *The Moral Animal* (New York: Pantheon, 1994).

258 Walter Burkert: W. Burkert, *Creation of the Sacred: Tracks of Biology in Early Religions* (Cambridge, MA: Harvard University Press, 1996).

CHAPTER 21: *The Art of the Deal*

260 "marriage without weather": Carol Anderson and Diane Holder, cited in Karpel, *Evaluating Couples.*

264 "Just everything.": Buber, *I and Thou.*

266 "men are from Illinois . . .": "Marooned on Gilligan's Island," in K. Pollitt, *Reasonable Creatures* (New York: Knopf, 1994).

267 John Mordechai Gottman: J. M. Gottman, *What Predicts Divorce? The Relationship Between Marital Processes and Marital Outcomes* (Hillsdale, NJ: Lawrence Erlbaum Associates, 1994).

268 Barbara Krasner: Interview, June 1996.

269 "dialogical" . . . "speech with meaning": Buber, *The Knowledge of Man.*

269 Researchers who study marital typology: Gottman, *What Predicts Divorce?*

272 relationships are settings for aggression: See, for example, O. F. Kernberg, *Love Relations* (New Haven: Yale University Press, 1995).

CHAPTER 22: *Wednesday at Ten*

281 "The one runs . . .": Kaiser, "Emergency," in *Effective Psychotherapy.*

286 Tillie Olsen: T. Olsen, *Silences* (New York: Delacorte, 1978).

288 what's for you?: "What's for me?" is Havens's question in L. Havens, "What Is Psychiatry All About?"

288 "Where they love they do not desire . . ." is Freud's summary of an essential problem, in S. Freud, "On the Universal Tendency to Debasement in Love" [1912], *The Standard Edition of the Complete Psychological Works of Sigmund Freud,* vol. 11 (London: Hogarth Press, 1957); this and the Germaine Greer passage, from G. Greer, *The Female Eunuch* (New York: McGraw-Hill, 1971), are cited in S. Cavell, "Two Cheers for Romance," in *Passionate Attachments: Thinking About Love,* W. Gaylin and E. S. Person, eds. (New York: Free Press, 1988).

289 "Freudian psychology is the only . . .": L. Trilling, *The Liberal Imagination* (New York: Viking, 1950/1951).

294 "The attestation of one's autonomous power . . .": Cavell, *A Pitch of Philosophy.*

295 "One certainly can't judge these matters . . .": Freud to Ferenczi, 27 November 1918, in *The Correspondence of Sigmund Freud and Sándor Ferenczi.* Freud is discussing Otto Rank's marriage.

296 "absolute separateness . . .": Cavell, *A Pitch of Philosophy.*

ACKNOWLEDGMENTS

This book celebrates a legacy in psychotherapy. The character Lou is fictional, but elements of Lou's mentoring are drawn directly from contacts with dedicated psychiatrist-teachers: Leston Havens walked the fens with me discussing the independent study topic "How People Change"; Theodore Nadelson supervised elective clinical work I did with psychiatric patients in the first years of medical school; Behnaz Jalali supported my curiosity about Murray Bowen and other family theorists; and Donald Cohen provoked me to write by agreeing I would be crazy to do so.

I mean this book also to be a tribute to patients; the lessons patients have taught me inform the whole. I trust that there are enough hints, in my use of the second person and in the tone of the remainder, that the advisees and patients in *Should You Leave?* (other than the patients of Freud, Sullivan, and other historical figures) are imagined. The stories, whether presented in the second or third person, generally incorporate fragments of episodes from my work with patients, but only in rare cases is a substantial segment of a vignette taken directly from life; and here the stripping or addition of detail and simplification or alteration of personality traits are so extensive as to create a fiction. Freud wrote "that it is far easier to divulge the patient's most intimate secrets than the most innocent and trivial facts about him"; in a book concerned with the significance of externals, I have reversed the customary pattern and borrowed everyday details while fabricating whole people. I hope that this preference for imagining over reporting accords with a theme of the book, that the generation of stories is a useful and even inevitable approach for apprehending those we care about and our relationship to them.

The portraits of psychologists and psychiatrists other than Lou are fictional only in the sense that all attempts at biography must be. Jean Baker Miller and Ivan Boszormenyi-Nagy kindly agreed to sit for interviews. I am especially grateful to LeRoy Bowen for consenting to speak with me about her late husband.

George Fishman was generous in directing me to works in the psychoanalytic literature. Barbara Krasner walked me through difficult issues in contextual therapy. Michael Kerr provided a brief experience of Bowen-style therapy as well as access to Bowen audiotapes; Andrea "Punkin" Maloney-Schara tracked down Bowen videotapes and obituaries. Robert Rosenthal introduced me to early writings on sensitivity to nonverbal cues. John Kerr led me to the work of John M. Gottman; Peter Gay responded to a question about advice in Freud's career; Frederick Goodwin helped with the literature on assortive mating and mood disorder; and David Scharff supplied details about Henry Dicks's character.

Jeffrey Blum, Leston Havens, Mark Karpel, Diana Lidofsky, and Michael Stein read drafts of the manuscript and provided invaluable critiques. As a literary agent, Chuck Verrill encouraged me to write the book I wanted to write—this odd hybrid of fiction, nonfiction, and self-help—rather than a medication-centered sequel to *Listening to Prozac*. Nan Graham stole time from her duties as Editor-in-Chief at Scribner to shepherd the book along and to line-edit every draft. She is extraordinary for her enthusiasm and her unequivocal eye.

My deepest thanks are to Rachel Schwartz. Most of what I know about relationships comes from ours together. I hope neither of us is going anywhere.

INDEX

Plato, 37
pleasure:
    inability to experience, 163–67
    as motivation, 232
Pollitt, Katha, 266
possession, psychological, 226–32, 232, 240
    advising in cases of, 224–25, 231–32,
        240, 241–42, 305n
    childhood abuse and, 232
    differentiation of self and, 234, 235, 238
    ending, 222–25
    gifts for ending, 223–26, 231, 242
    Havens and, 238–39
    hockey metaphor, 237–38
    intermittent reinforcement schedule
        and, 234
    as point of relationship, 293–94
    power relations and, 225–26, 234–35,
        237–38
    projective identification and, 237
    reversible, 240
    self-possession and, 235–39, 241–42
    submissiveness and, 233
    vulnerability to, 232–34, 239–40
post-traumatic stress disorder, 196, 207
power:
    abuse and, 225–26
    enslavement and, 234–35, 237–38
    practical, in psychotherapy, 61–62, 64–65,
        66, 68–72, 218–20
pragmatism, 107
precepts:
    on change, 129
    on differentiation of self, 128–30
    self-help, 127, 128
pregnancies, resulting from affairs, 254
    see also abortion; family formation
presentation of self, 75, 86, 228
probabilities, social, 70–72
projection, 205–9, 216–17, 281, 304n
    of idealization, 215, 220
    therapist-patient interaction and,
        207–9
    see also counterprojection
projective identification, 208, 239, 287, 291
    abuse and, 213–14, 219, 221
    coining of term, 211
    destructive, 221
    differentiation of self and, 216, 220
    external stressors and, 218–20
    limitations of concept, 216–18, 220
    mutual, 209–11, 212–17, 218–21, 227, 265
    object relations and, 211–12

paranoia and, 208–9
    positive side of, 220
    psychological possession and, 237
psychiatric attitude, see fictive attitude
psychiatry:
    essentialist perspective in, 165, 195, 196,
        202, 217–18, 232, 285
    expression of opinion in, 18–19, 49,
        51–52
    feminist, 108–14, 115, 119–20
    naming of ailment in, 194
psychoanalysis, 206–7, 285, 288
    Bowen-style therapy, 100, 101–4
    comparison to surgery, 57–58
    critiques of, 173, 206–7, 285
    neutral stance in, 208
    object relations theory, 211–12
    projection problem in, 205–9
    social difficulties as viewed in, 202
    therapist-patient interaction in, 102–3,
        207–9, 239
psychopharmacology, 38, 105–6, 165, 167,
    183, 233
psychotherapeutic attitude, 33–34
psychotherapy:
    advising proscribed in, 18, 57–61, 69–72
    boundaries, 271
    commonly held rules drawn from,
        38–39
    equity considerations absent in, 245
    expertise in, 70–71
    motives for seeking, 170
    passion not explored in, 299n
    performative language in, 231
    relating friend's troubles in, 188, 201
    role of practical in, 61–62, 64–65, 66,
        68–72, 218–20
    search for reliable method in, 69–70
    societal factors considered in, 68, 69,
        70, 247
    speech in, 294–95
    task of finding patient in, 32–34, 239;
        see also construction, mental
    theorists' backgrounds, 103–4

reconciliation, bias toward, 55
    see also remarriage
Reiss, David, 217
rejection sensitivity, 156, 183
relational approach, to couple therapy, 113
relational ethics, 248–58
    biology of altruism and, 257–58
    commitment, 256

A PENGUIN READERS GUIDE TO

SHOULD
YOU LEAVE?

Peter D. Kramer, M.D.

INTRODUCTION TO *Should You Leave?*

"When a psychiatrist writes a bestseller, he is then urged to write a book of advice. But I think our culture's awash in advice. The problem is we don't know whether it applies to us or whether we're an exception."
—Peter D. Kramer, from an interview with the *Detroit News*

In *Should You Leave?* Dr. Peter Kramer explains why therapists often refuse to give patients answers to questions. In contrast to the self-help books that crowd the shelves, *Should You Leave?* questions the very existence of objective advice—for giver and receiver. What masquerades as advice, he argues, is often little more than a general transmission of values. Real advice can begin only with a thorough understanding of the individual advice seeker, who may or may not share the same values or belief system as the adviser.

In what he describes as "a hybrid of fiction, non-fiction, and self-help," he spotlights a wide range of fictional patients—all close to breaking up with their partners—from a kaleidoscopic series of viewpoints, speaking simply to "you," the composite patient. Whether any of these individuals should leave is no easy question.

First, the variables of personality and the dynamics of relationships and circumstances invite an endless array of interpretations, scenarios, and solutions (just as in the best of fiction, which Kramer calls "the most serious attempt to understand the human condition").

Second, the entire concept of relationships is rooted in an interplay between values of self and other. To this debate, filtered through his fictional mentor, "Lou," Dr. Kramer introduces major perspectives from philosophy and clinical psychiatric thought. They range from Freud's theories of the early family to Murray Bowen's championship of individualism in context; and from Leston Havens's pathology of possessor and possessed to Martin Buber's view of personhood as indivisible from relationship. Each patient in *Should You Leave?* can be viewed through the lens of one or more of these theories.

Iris, a self-made and flamboyant editor, is confronted with a cruel betrayal by Randall, whom she feels to be her ideal partner. To stay would be, according to Ivan Boszormenyi-Nagy's "relational ethics," investing in a love with no payback. Murray Bowen would want Iris to assert her autonomy. Jean Baker Miller, with her stress on "relational awareness," might see the strength of Iris's attachment as a greater personal and social good. Whereas Kramer wonders if she might translate her autonomy skills in business into a relationship with Randall that could foster similar growth in him.

Rose, a feisty but nurturing Irishwoman, and Abie, a Jew of Mediterranean heritage, have fed into their ethnic stereotypes of each other. To Melanie Klein or Henry Dicks, the pioneer of couple therapy, their "mutual projective identification" is cause for a breakup. But Kramer speculates on a cluster of factors: on the real balance of power in the relationship; on whether Rose could leave if the courts denied her child custody; on whether she will settle for staying because Abie, though violent, is the best deal she's yet found in a man.

From these psychiatric masters, and writers from Shakespeare and Ralph Waldo Emerson to James Joyce and John Updike—even from a cultural about-face by Ann Landers—*Should You Leave?* draws lessons on the importance of everyday detail and "selective inattention," emotional maturity in the context of conflicting ideals, and how to distinguish a truly independent self from its manifestation in a relationship. Kramer moves us beyond a simplistic "Mars and Venus" image of men and women toward a more subtle review of the intricacies of communication in general. How do mood states—

including, so often, depression—affect our assessment of each other? What does "working on a relationship" entail? When should we work to improve a relationship, and when should we walk away?

Ultimately, this book places the personal balancing act of autonomy, connection, and community in a larger context. It also challenges conventional ideas of intimacy: Has our culture miscast marriage as an entitlement to happiness? Are gender differences an intrinsic roadblock toward intimacy? How far will personal growth go toward saving and transforming a relationship? Can our society, in fact, survive with autonomy as its ideal—or are we overripe for a return to connectedness and contractual responsibility?

Should you leave? In the end, concludes Dr. Kramer, the only valid advice will be found in a garment woven from threads explored in this book—tailored exclusively to each one of us.

A Talk with Peter D. Kramer, M.D.

Q: In *Should You Leave?*, you not only take a therapeutic "fictive attitude" to cases, but build them around entirely fictional protagonists. And you say the classic psychoanalytic theorists "are no more useful than Tolstoy, Dickens, Balzac, Thomas Hardy, George Eliot." What are some specific examples from those, or other writers?

A: *Should You Leave?* is, among other things, a tribute to the mid-century psychotherapists whose work is implicit in my own. They are men and women whose ideas, often in overly simple form, serve as the basis for much popular self-help—I mean Helmuth Kaiser, Henry Dicks, Murray Bowen, and other thinkers to whose writings I refer when imagining responses to someone who might come to me for counsel. These theorists are largely forgotten; my hope is to bring them back into our consciousness, so that we can consider their contribution in fuller form. But I do not want readers to face their work uncritically. These thinkers are brilliant but capable of foolishness or error. In the end, a therapy is a perspective on the human condition, often an autobiographical perspective, though the function of therapy, for patient and theoretician alike, is to transcend autobiography, to escape an overly limited viewpoint.

Seen in this way, psychotherapy is like fiction—an attempt to make sense of the social surround and the individual story in that surround. I doubt that therapists can make the claim to be wiser than novelists.

Certainly the self-help books that arise from therapy seem less wise. Consider this thought experiment. In the midst of a complex life, you face a dilemma. You have before you two piles of books, one of self-help and one of literary novels. In which stack is your story in all its painful detail more likely to be represented? The self-help books may have more direct advice, they may offer relief of that sort. But they are likely to frustrate you because they lack the subtlety and ambiguity of life as you experience it.

I am not thinking only of dusty classics. I happened just now to read an early Edna O'Brien novel, *Girl with Green Eyes*. The protagonist is a young woman, a self-educated and sexually naive working girl, who is eager for a liaison with a wealthy, cosmopolitan, older married man. The affair can only be disastrous—no book of advice would encourage it, and as readers we are continually made anxious over the girl's well-being. The affair does end, and the young woman suffers. But she has the resilience to make the experience the basis for her entry into adult intellectual life. Social experiences are like that. They are not lived by just anyone, but by individuals with particular strengths. And they do not have one outcome—success or failure— but multiple ramifications.

The function of the novel, in additon to amusement, is to remind us of ambiguity, ambivalence, variety of viewpoint. Facing the notion that I might write a self-help book, I decided that my way of making it correspond to a serious understanding of relationships would be to draw on techniques of contemporary fiction, in the belief that the fiction of our time represents the reality of our time as well as it can be represented in written narrative. I hope that these techniques draw the reader into imagined dilemmas and allow readers to pick up tools (such as the perspectives of Kaiser, Dicks, Bowen, and others) in a sufficiently complex context.

I also like the idea of stuffing this advice book with fictions, because I think we come to know others through the "fictive attitude," in the sense of doubting what others say to us and instead creating stories that may predict future behavior. Images of others are creative acts. Relationships are creative acts.

Q: What special value did a second-person narrative have for you, here, and what works by other authors drew you to this literary device?

A: I like second-person fiction—for example the short stories of Lorrie Moore in her collection *Self-Help*—because it is at once personal and strange. When a protagonist is "you" ("All you want is a simple piece of advice"), the reader is being addressed intimately. At the same time, the reader knows that he or she is not Iris, enmeshed with Randall, so that the narrative retains a constant element of oddness. The final effect, I hope, is one of inviting the reader to try each vignette on for size while causing the reader to maintain a critical distance—perhaps oscillating between merger and autonomy just as people do in relationships.

Altogether, I wanted the book to have a quality I call (using a psychiatric term) "enactment"—I wanted to have the reader in the course of reading feel, in relation to the narrative, something of what each partner feels in a relationship. At the heart of the book is the theme of transparency and opacity. We know others in an instant, and yet after years of marriage important aspects of our partner may remain hidden. My hope is that the use of the second person enacts that theme.

I liked the second person for other reasons: It reflects the experience of receiving advice, which is often given in the second person. The second person is often the language of self-help books. I wanted to use elements of that genre while at the same time suggesting the virtues of a quite different sort of writing, namely contemporary fiction—as if to say to the reader, we both know that this is what it is like to face an impasse in a relationship. It is complex in this way.

The second person is not the only technique of modern writing that shapes *Should You Leave?* Since my mentor, Lou, is a fictional character, the short stories attributed to Lou, in the collection "Pieces of Resistance," do not exist outside the text of *Should You Leave?* The précis of Connie's story ("You Will Be Fine . . .") is the story; Connie's is a story told in the form of a critique of a story. I want for this method, difficult as it may sound in this description, to be unobtrusive in the book. The narrative should make sense on its own terms even as it dawns on the reader that Lou must surely be fictional and that these mid-century short stories must be reevaluated as contemporary stories.

And then there is the matter of Lou's gender. I suppose that initially most readers will assume that Lou is male. But soon I make mention of Freud's female colleague, Lou Andreas-Salomé. And it becomes apparent that our Lou, Lou Adler, has some stereotypically female traits. Lou is flirtatious. Lou is not the primary breadwinner. Lou is the cook in the couple. There may even be the rare reader who, thinking back to my first book, *Moments of Engagement*, recalls that my most influential mentor-in-residence was a woman. And then there are the references throughout *Should You Leave?* to gender ambiguity, as in "You Will Be Fine . . ." and in the vignette of Francis and Frances, and in the discussion of Phyllis Rose's book, *Parallel Lives*. So who knows? Who knows whether Lou, Terry, and Leslie are men or women? And does it matter? In a time dominated by self-help based on an almost obsessive attention to gender role (Mars and Venus, etc.), I thought I might make a quiet contribution by crafting advice for fictional spouses—Lou and Terry—whose gender is never specified. Does it matter? Would we see the marriage differently depending on the assignment or mix of genders? Does the issue of leaving always turn on gender?

Q: Is there a type of patient you find particularly intriguing, one that drew you into the issues of both *Should You Leave?* and *Listening to Prozac?*

A: I think that this culture is particularly rough on people who are sensitive, loyal, perfectionistic, and unassertive. Such people—I might say that they have elements of the melancholic temperament—have (or end up with) minor mood disorders. They tend to be troubled by anxiety, depression, and obsessionality. And often they have troubles in relationships, because they value continuity and complexity so highly, in a nation that all but encourages divorce. By the standards of our society, they stay too long and give too much. My patients are often people of this sort, and I care about them. They want (like Iris, like so many of the characters in *Should You Leave?*) to be exceptions—to resist the appeal in a materialist country of the next best chance.

In some regards *Should You Leave?* and *Listening to Prozac* are about the same topic, happiness. Both books ask about alternatives to the standard approach to happiness in a culture where assertiveness and autonomy are rewarded, happiness in a culture in which pleasure has been commodified. Both Prozac and divorce have their role, either can be life-saving. But I want to ask also whether there is, or should be, a role for the slow and imperfect fix, a role for relationship as a value.

Q: How significant is interaction between mood disturbance, especially depression, and emotional intimacy?

8

A: Crucially significant. The middle chapters in *Should You Leave?* all concern this issue. When does a bad relationship cause depression, and when does depression cause a relationship to fail—or to appear failed in the eyes of the depressed partner? Epidemiological studies show that mood disorder is likely to be a factor in any troubled relationship. Though depression is rarely a topic in books about troubled couples, on a statistical basis, in failing relationships the odds are that one or both partners are depressed now or were depressed when they entered the relationship. Whether or not the relationship contributes to the mood disorder, I would like to see the affected partner treated before he or she makes a decision about leaving. Again, the issue is one of perspective. Depression entails a constrained perspective.

Q: One technique you suggest, as part of relationship change, is "rotating the self." Could you expand on this?

A: I am referring to a phrase of Kierkegaard's—the "rotation method"—that has been picked up by psychiatry. Therapists may accuse patients, and I think "accuse" is the word, of rotating partners, or using the "geographic cure," that is, of leaving, instead of staying and confronting problems. I try to make sense of what Kierkegaard recommended, treating oneself as a field in which the crop is rotated, that is, experimenting with staying put and changing the self. What constitutes change (in terms of a person's capacities in relationships) and how might you attempt to change? That question, the meaning of change, is another theme of the book.

Q: Almost all the couples in *Should You Leave?* are childless. When it comes to leaving, you remark that "I tend to worry that divorce and remarriage will provide a child with four undeveloped parents instead of two." How would your evaluation of these cases, or others, be modified by the existence of children?

A: The presence of children in the family usually creates a presumption in favor of trying to make the marriage work—often so strong a presumption as to overshadow the sorts of issues that otherwise dominate between partners: matching, projection, fairness, and the like. Those same tensions do play themselves out in couples with children—I hope parents contemplating divorce will find *Should You Leave?* useful—but paying attention to them becomes harder.

Most of the cases in *Should You Leave?* are "close calls," at least I meant for them to be, and taking children into account would tend to tip the scale strongly in one direction or another. I doubt I would be content to see Sandy leave Mark (in the chapter "Unequivocal Eye") if a marriage with children were at issue. In the cases of psychological abuse ("Simple Gifts"), I would be quick and direct in urging separation if I believed children were being harmed within the marriage.

In my vignettes, I imagined childless couples or couples with grown children—and couples where other factors, such as finances, do not affect the decision to stay or go—because I wanted to get to the heart of relationship as relationship. I hope that this intensity of focus finally makes the book a social commentary—a commentary on this culture's values, what we sustain. Can we care about such oddities as commitment, intimacy, complexity, time together? Can we grant reality to the space between people? Can we think of a relationship as an entity, with its own interests, as separate from the interests of each participant? Do we honor connection, or only autonomy?

QUESTIONS FOR DISCUSSION

1) "When I read a self-help precept," says Dr. Kramer, "invariably I think that the opposite advice might be equally apt, for someone." Has his concept of targeted advice, and multiple perspectives, made this book of value to you?

2) How have you found *Should You Leave?* different from typical self-help books on relationship problems? What insights have you gained from its unique approach?

3) Does its ambiguous use of second-person narrative clarify its message? How does that technique reflect the intimacy and tensions of relationships?

4) In illustrating some of his points, Dr. Kramer refers to *Anna Karenina*, *King Lear*, and the Bible. Do you agree that a response to fiction can be more useful than a list of precepts? What works of fiction have produced that sort of response in you?

5) Do you feel a clash between autonomy and connection? Are women really more connected than men? Was the psychiatrist Murray Bowen, as recounted in *Should You Leave?*, right to manipulate his family to achieve both?

6) Is connection just an avoidance of selfhood, as some say, or is America blinded by its ongoing romance with autonomy? How should we, in this day and age, rate the Emersonian ideal of autonomy and the self-reliant individual? Or the "me first" revolution of the past decades? How has feminism balanced the tension between independence and attachment? How do you, or others you know, manage it—or are the two mutually exclusive?

7) Is it possible to talk about things that are good for a relationship as opposed to what is good and bad for the people involved in it? Is a relationship an entity?

8) Dr. Kramer quotes the feminist Katha Pollitt's remark that "men are from Illinois and women are from Indiana," and adds: "They are different, but not in especially confusing ways . . . they are adapted to cope with one another." Do you agree? How much does gender matter; and what does the story of Connie in *Should You Leave?* tell us about it? Does "Lou" gain power and meaning from being genderless?

9) Which "patients" in the book do you identify with most? Why?

10) Dr. Kramer writes about the complexities, and different styles, of relationships between therapist and clients. What has been your experience of these?

11) In the story of Melanie, Dr. Kramer questions Martin Buber's position that "objective entitlement," or justice, exists within a relationship. What do you think?

12) Are you well-matched with your spouse? If not, why not? What is "matching"? What is growing together? Is either of you depressed; and how could this have a negative, or even a positive, effect on events?

13) Does Dr. Kramer's description of "re-entering the marriage" at a higher level of consciousness and detachment open the door to a spiritual evolution?

About Peter D. Kramer

Peter D. Kramer received his M.D. from Harvard. A clinical professor of psychiatry at Brown University, he has a private practice in Providence, Rhode Island. He is the author of *Moments of Engagement: Intimate Psychotherapy in a Technological Age* and the landmark bestseller *Listening to Prozac*. His writings have appeared in *The New York Times*, *The Washington Post*, and other national publications.

Also available from Penguin:

Listening to Prozac
ISBN 0-14-026671-2

Moments of Engagement
ISBN 0-14-023790-9

For more information about other Penguin Readers Guides, please call the Penguin Marketing Department at (800)778-6425, email at reading@penguin.com, or write to us at:

Penguin Marketing Department CC
Readers Guides
375 Hudson Street
New York, NY 10014-3657

For a complete list of Penguin Readers Guides that are available online, visit Club PPI on our Web site at:
www.penguinputnam.com

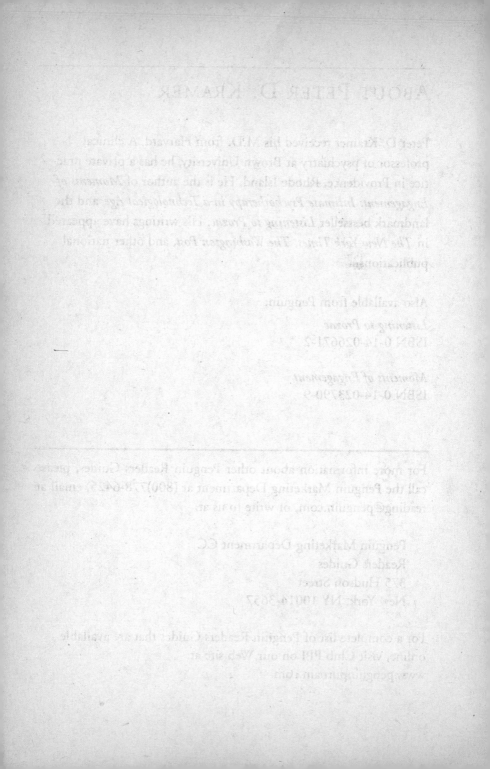

ABOUT PETER D. KRAMER

Peter D. Kramer received his M.D. from Harvard. A clinical professor of psychiatry at Brown University, he has a private practice in Providence, Rhode Island. He is the author of *Moments of Engagement, Intimate Psychotherapy in a Technological Age*, and the landmark bestseller *Listening to Prozac*. His writings have appeared in *The New York Times*, *The Washington Post*, and other national publications.

Also available from Penguin:

Listening to Prozac
ISBN 0-14-026671-2

Moments of Engagement
ISBN 0-14-023790-5

For more information about other Penguin Readers Guides, please call the Penguin Marketing Department at (800) 778-6425, email at reading@us.penguin.com, or write to us at:

Penguin Marketing Department CC
Reader's Guides
375 Hudson Street
New York, NY 10014-3657

For a complete list of Penguin Readers Guides that are available online, visit Club PPH on our Web site at:
www.penguinputnam.com